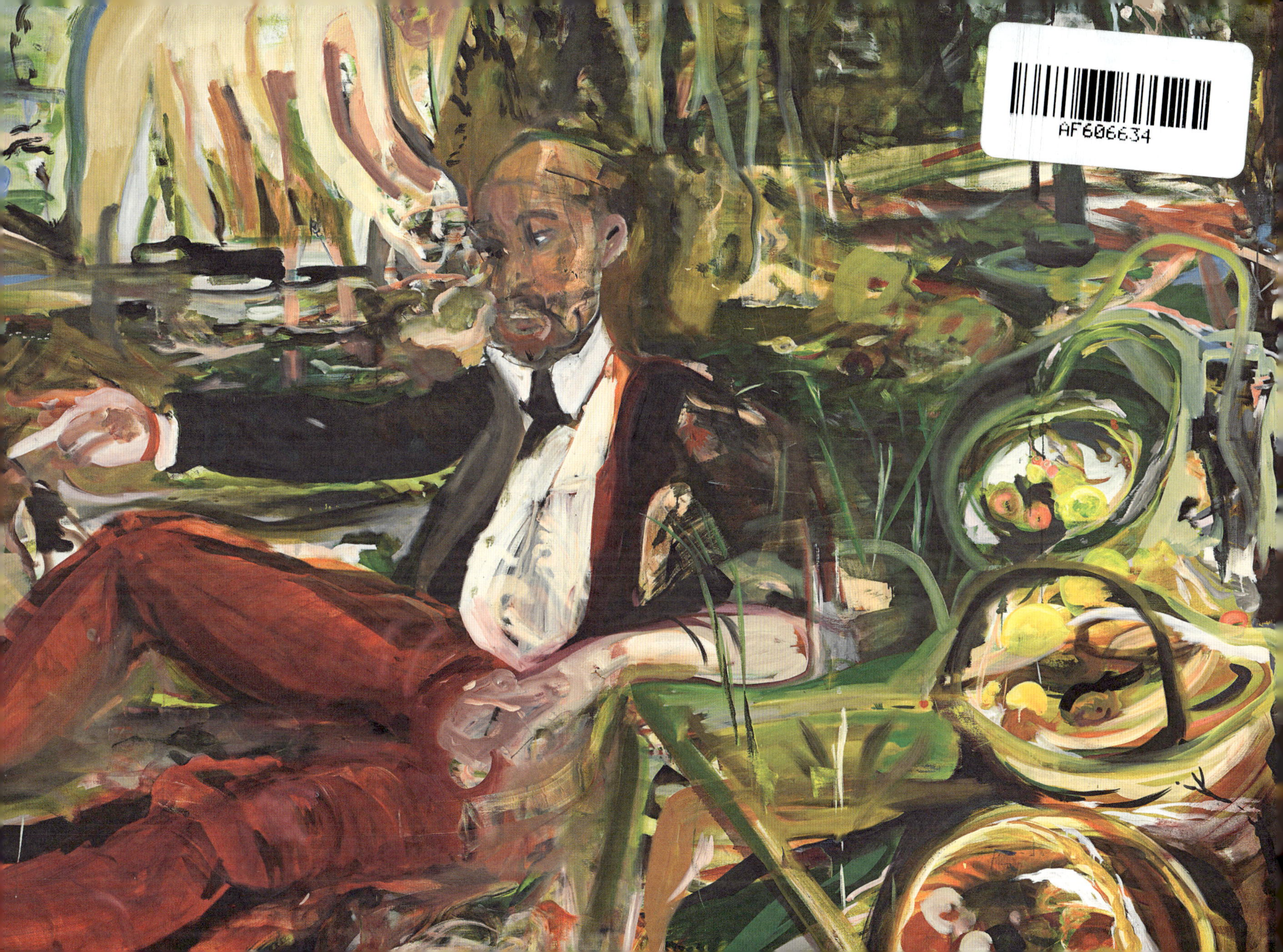

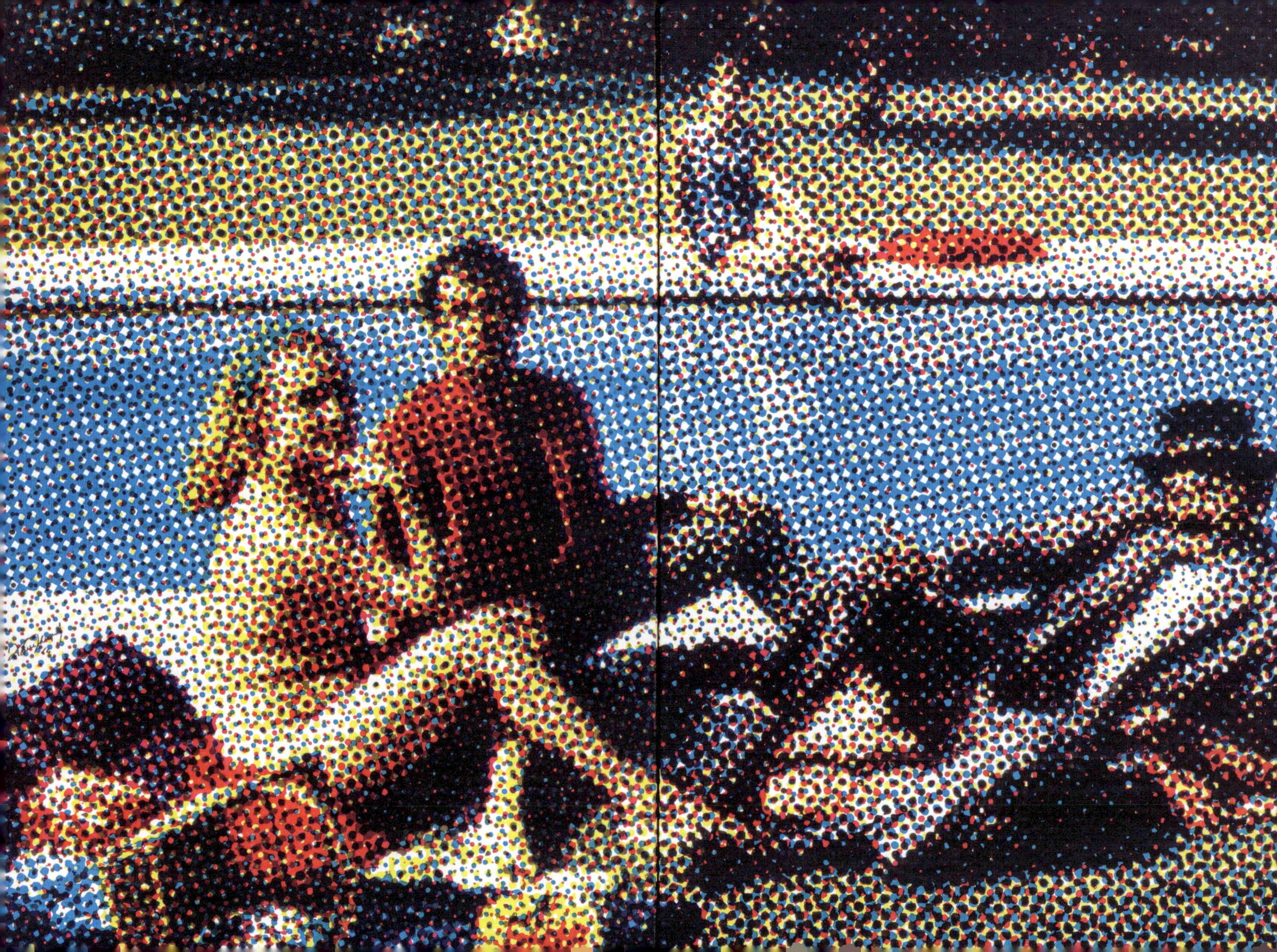

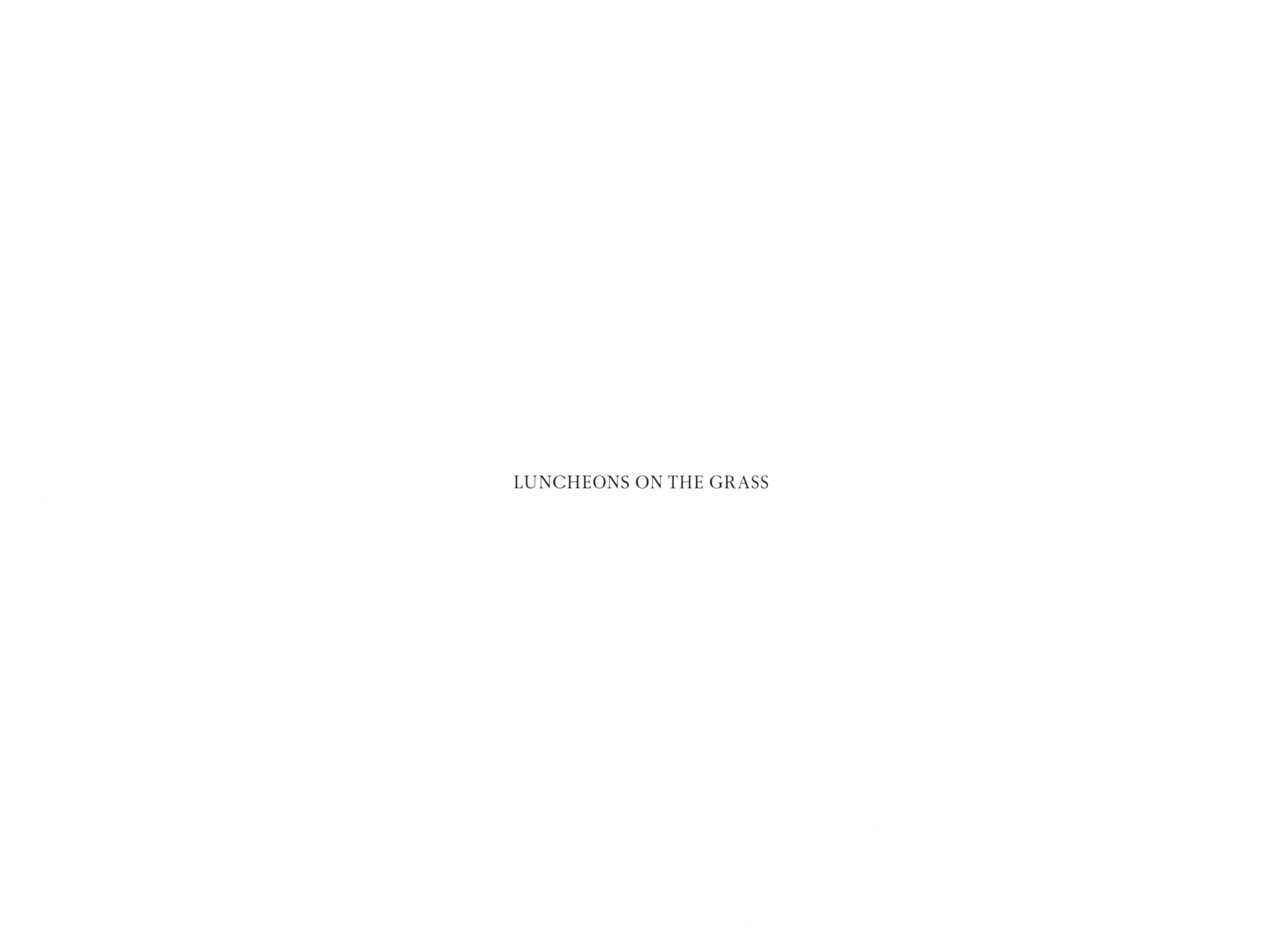

# LUNCHEONS ON THE GRASS

Reimagining Manet's *Le Déjeuner sur l'herbe*

# LUNCHEONS ON THE GRASS

Rizzoli Electa

## TABLE OF CONTENTS

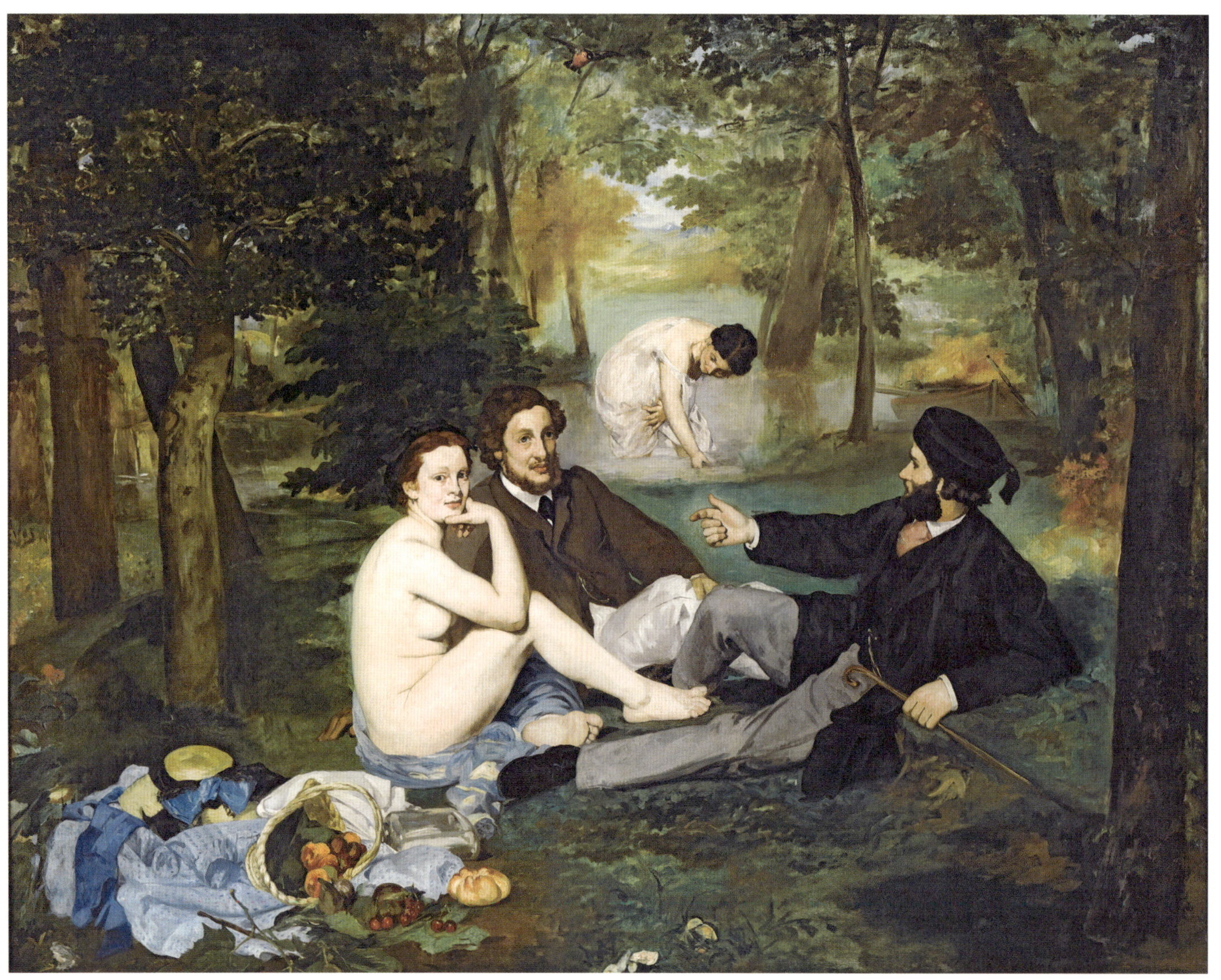

# LUNCHEONS ON THE GRASS
Jeffrey Deitch

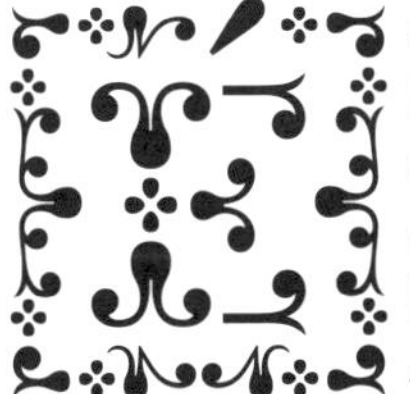
douard Manet's *Le Déjeuner sur l'herbe* (1863) [fig. 1] is regularly cited as the first modern painting. It is often featured as the first slide in art history lectures about the history of modernism. "The most audacious painting ever seen in France" is how Ross King described it in his book *The Judgement of Paris* (2006), the story of the development of modern painting in 1860s Paris. It is a "painting of modern life," as advocated by Édouard Manet's friend Charles Baudelaire, though the poet had used the phrase to describe the work of illustrator Constantin Guys, not Manet.

*Le Déjeuner sur l'herbe* astounded contemporary observers with its modernist innovations and, even today, retains the power to shock, especially when one experiences it in person at the Musée d'Orsay. The jolt of seeing two clothed men and two naked women assembled for a picnic still remains disconcerting. Manet adds absurdity to the scene by dressing his brothers Gustave and Eugène, who modeled for the painting, in frock coats and cravats more appropriate to the artists' gathering place Café Guerbois than to an outdoor luncheon. The most jarring aspect of the composition is the intense gaze of the female nude in the foreground, modeled by Victorine Meurent. She is rendered as a real person, not the allegorical nude of the typical academic painting.

The formal structure of the composition is also arresting, almost abstract. The positioning of the figures forms a dynamic geometry. The perspective is

Fig. 1 (left)—Édouard Manet, *Le Déjeuner sur l'herbe (Luncheon on the Grass)*, 1863, Oil on canvas, 81 ½ × 104 5⁄16 in. (207 × 265 cm), Musée d'Orsay, Paris

confounding, with the bather in the background too large for the illusion of receding space.

Contemporary viewers were upset by the deliberate lack of finish. An art critic reviewing the Salon des Refusés of 1863, where the painting was first exhibited, complained that the brushwork was so lacking in finesse that it could have been done with a floor mop. The perception of Manet's technique was very different when, one hundred years later, while immersed in the creation of his two hundred paintings, drawings, and sculptures inspired by *Le Déjeuner sur l'herbe* [fig. 2], Pablo Picasso observed that "one can see the intelligence in Manet's brushstrokes."

Visitors to the 1863 Salon des Refusés were also disconcerted by the absence of sculptural shading and the expected illusion of three-dimensionality. Manet uses contrasts of color rather than gradations of tone to give the figures their structure. At first glance, one might interpret the work as a plein air landscape, with the figures posing outdoors. As one studies the painting, however, it becomes evident that Manet is playing with illusion versus reality. He makes it clear that the painting has been created in a studio with the landscape functioning almost as a backdrop.

*Le Déjeuner sur l'herbe* is aggressively modern in its portrayal of real people, family members and an identifiable nude model, rather than idealized figures. Even today, the subject matter is transgressive. The work engages with contemporary culture, depicting the leisure activities of the new generation of

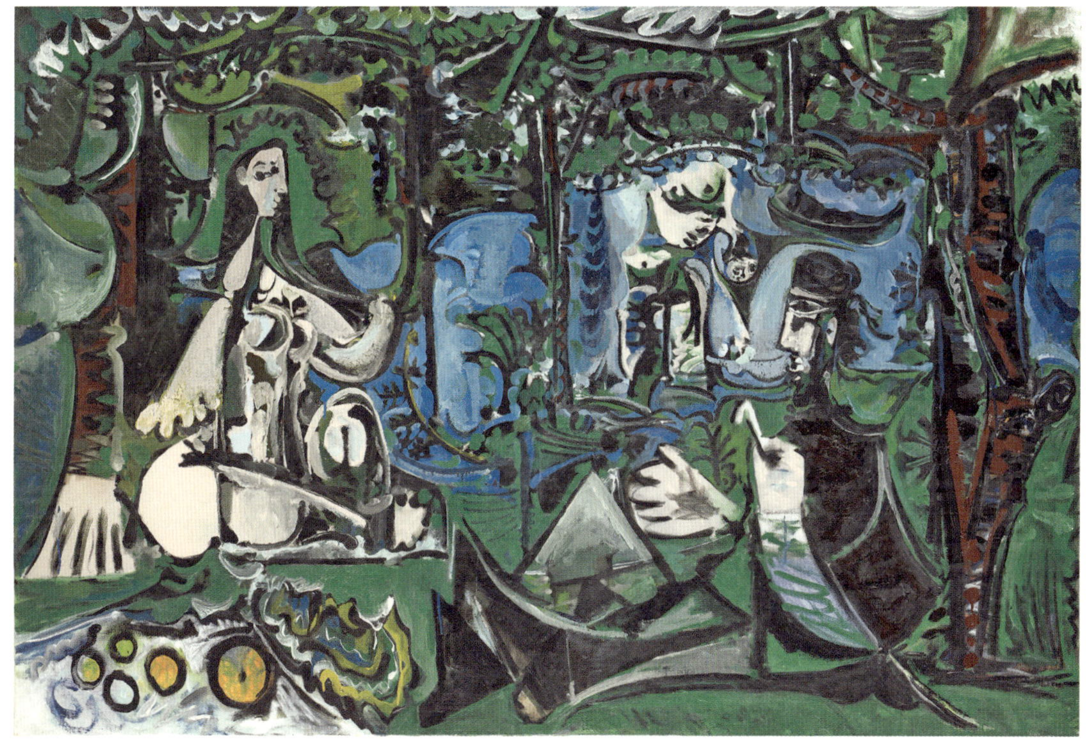

Fig. 2—Pablo Picasso, *Le Déjeuner sur l'herbe d'après Manet (Luncheon on the Grass, After Manet)*, 1960, Oil on canvas, 51 3⁄16 × 76 13⁄16 in. (130 × 195 cm), Musée Picasso, Paris

Parisians taking the train to picnic in the countryside outside the city. Manet sets up a modernist juxtaposition of opposites: clothed and unclothed, outdoors and indoors, reality and artifice. His visible brushwork, as opposed to the high finish of academic painting, reveals the painting process. *Le Déjeuner sur l'herbe* is fundamentally a painting about painting, one of the main reasons it is seen as key to the invention of modernism.

In the eyes of the Salon critics, perhaps the most unsettling element of the painting was its contradiction of what was accepted to be the most essential precept of academic painting: the teaching of moral lessons. *Le Déjeuner sur l'herbe* depicted what was interpreted as an immoral scenario. The first essay in this book, by Thomas E. Crow, returns to the infamous Salon des Refusés to examine the context of Manet's participation and reception. Crow addresses less-discussed stylistic influences, particularly the "*allures espagnoles*," lessons from travel, Velázquez, and the Louvre. Crow looks at Manet's life in Paris as both a "posh boulevardier" and a master who could surprise young painters with his "*strange* new manner." *Le Déjeuner*'s enduring shock, according to Crow, is not so much in subject matter or reference to contemporary life as in "so thorough[ly] unmooring...the cargo inherited from the past as to prepare a new aesthetic consciousness."

Like his art, Manet's life was replete with contradictions. He was arguably the most radical artist of his generation, but craved the recognition of the official Salon and the decorations bestowed on its honored artists. He coveted the Legion of Honor, which he was finally awarded in 1881 after his childhood friend Antonin Proust became minister of fine arts. He enjoyed a bohemian lifestyle, rendezvousing at a café every evening from 5:30 to 7:30 with his fellow artists in the working-class Batignolles district, while being supported by his landowning family of mayors and magistrates. He was a patriot, joining the National Guard to help defend Paris from the Prussian invaders in the Franco-Prussian War of 1870–71. He did not officially marry his companion, Suzanne Leenhoff, until after the death of his conservative father, who may not have approved of his son's liaison with his former piano teacher. Manet never confirmed the paternity of Suzanne's son Leon Koëlla, who was born out of wedlock prior to their marriage. While living in a modest apartment with Suzanne and his putative son, Manet and his mother hosted his friends every Thursday evening in his parents' well-appointed family home.

Manet was determined to show *Le Déjeuner sur l'herbe* in the Salon of 1863, but to his great disappointment, it was rejected. In response to the anger in the artist community about the unusually large number of rejections to the official Salon, Emperor Napoleon III decreed that there would be a Salon des Refusés. It is not where Manet had hoped to show his ambitious painting, but he wanted it to be seen, so it was entered into the Salon des Refusés. The reaction was extreme, both from the critics and from the mocking public. The admired critic Théophile Thoré (writing as "W. Bürger"), usually a supporter of Manet, wrote: "I can't imagine what can have made an intelligent and distinguished artist choose so absurd a composition." That was one of the more moderate critiques. A large part of the notoriety of the painting stems from its exceedingly negative reception. The hostility to the work eventually became a badge of honor to the modernist cause and an inspiration to succeeding generations of artists whose work was not appreciated at first because it was ahead of its time.

*Le Déjeuner sur l'herbe* may be esteemed as the first modern painting, but from today's perspective it might also be described as the first postmodern painting. Inside the provocative modernist composition, there is a deep foundation of art historical references and a painterly collage of styles and sources. It combines every genre of painting including landscape, portraiture, and still life. It transforms history painting, the most prestigious genre, from academic allegory into a social history of contemporary Paris.

For many years, *Le Déjeuner sur l'herbe* and other major paintings by Manet were interpreted by historians and critics of modern art as primarily formalist compositions, mostly devoid of emotion and humanistic content. The formal invention of the works was emphasized over their psychological resonance and their many art historical references. Later scholarship, such as Michael Fried's essay "Manet's Sources: Aspects of His Art, 1859–1865," which constituted the entire March 1969 issue of *Artforum*, explained how Manet constructed many of his compositions on art historical precedents. It presented Manet as an artist who immersed himself in the history of art as well as in the portrayal of modern life. Studying *Le Déjeuner sur l'herbe*, it is fascinating to discover the appropriation of compositions by Michelangelo, Raphael, and Titian. The art historian Robert Goldwater wrote, "No other painter of the century managed to get so much into a canvas."

The composition of *Le Déjeuner sur l'herbe* is animated by the curious pointing gesture of the male figure on the right. It is arresting, but somehow familiar. It may be inspired by one of the most resonant images in the history of art, Michelangelo's *The Creation of Adam* (ca. 1508–12) from the ceiling of the Sistine Chapel. Manet's adaptation of the image does not come directly from Michelangelo but is taken from an engraving by Marcantonio Raimondi based on a drawing by Raphael of the classical myth the Judgment of Paris [fig. 3]. The composition of the three foreground figures in *Le Déjeuner sur l'herbe* is appropriated from Raphael's portrayal of three river gods in the lower right corner of his drawing. Raphael has transposed Michelangelo's rendering of Adam onto the river god, with his arm pointing to the left rather than to the right. In Manet's painting, the figure modeled by his brother assumes the pose of Adam in Michelangelo's fresco, with the position of his legs as well as his extended arm reflecting Michelangelo's composition. The central gesture of *Le Déjeuner sur l'herbe* echoes Michelangelo's depiction of the creation of man. For Manet, it may also represent the creation of art.

The larger subject of Raphael's drawing *The Judgment of Paris* may also contribute to the meaning of Manet's painting. The classical myth about Paris

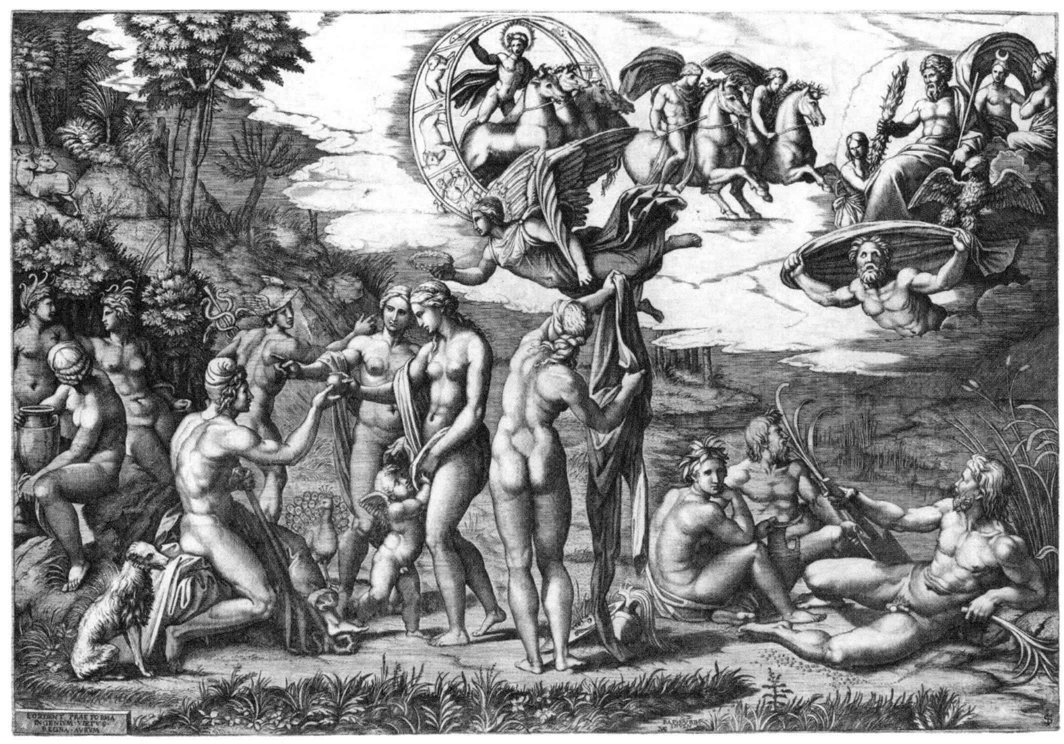

Fig. 3—Marcantonio Raimondi, After Raphael (Raffaello Sanzio or Santi), *The Judgment of Paris*, ca. 1510–20, Engraving, 11 7⁄16 × 17 3⁄16 in. (29.1 × 43.7 cm), The Metropolitan Museum of Art, New York

judging which of the three nude goddesses is the most beautiful is an allegory of aesthetic choice and an inspiration for many works of art. Is Manet setting up his own modern Judgment of Paris with the clothed men and the nude bathers? It is possible that Manet is also linking the name of the mythical figure of Paris with the city of Paris, inviting the contemporary Parisian audience to make their own judgments about the subject of the painting.

Titian's *Le Concert champêtre* (ca. 1500–25), which Manet would have seen in the Louvre, is probably the primary inspiration for the concept of *Le Déjeuner sur l'herbe*. Titian's mysterious painting, which during Manet's lifetime was attributed to Giorgione, is a poetic allegory depicting two clothed gentlemen and two idealized nude nymphs in a pastoral setting. The Louvre's catalogue description of the painting posits that the unreal nude figures exist only in the imagination of the men they inspire. Manet has transported this idealized allegory to the reality of modern Paris.

One of the most significant elements of *Le Déjeuner sur l'herbe* is the still life of the nude figure's discarded bonnet and clothing in the left foreground. The remnants of the picnic lunch spill out from the basket that has been thrown onto the crumpled dress. This is the most erotically charged section of the painting, more suggestive perhaps than Victorine Meurent's naked body. Manet had been looking carefully at Dutch seventeenth-century still life paintings, understanding how they can become abstractions of sensuality.

Manet drew on classical, Italian, and Dutch sources, with a deep reverence for Velázquez and his vigorous technique. His work builds on various national traditions, but he also determined to make his paintings fundamentally French. He fused his art historical foundations with a new modern sensibility, creating a universal concept of painting that embodies the rise of Paris as "the capital of the nineteenth century."

From today's perspective, *Le Déjeuner sur l'herbe* can be interpreted as blatantly sexist and exploitative in its subject. A contemporary viewer, however, might also see the two bathers as cool, liberated women, comfortable in their nudity. The figure modeled by Victorine Meurent is strong and confident, looking back at us without embarrassment. Aruna D'Souza's essay offers a number of convincing readings for the work: The painting may explore the privilege of the flaneur or the power and interruption of the male gaze, or it may be about *Le Déjeuner*'s relationship to other works. She also argues, uniquely in this volume, that this is a work about artistic rivalry, a "shot across the bow to Gustave Courbet." She explores artificiality, gender binaries, and, most interestingly, silence as possible themes.

Victorine Meurent, who also modeled for Manet's *Olympia* (1863), *The Railway* (1873), and other major paintings, was a fascinating individual: an artist herself and a personality in artistic circles. Her own painting was surprisingly academic considering her involvement with Manet and other radical artists. Ironically, her work was accepted in some of the Salons where Manet's work was rejected. She spent her later years living outside Paris with her longtime female partner.

*Le Déjeuner sur l'herbe* is a foundational work in the history of modernism but also an inspiration for a more contemporary approach to painting. Its fusion of historical, contemporary, and personal imagery and its references to traditional, vanguard, and popular culture connect with current artistic practice. As Manet did with *Le Déjeuner sur l'herbe,* some of the most provocative contemporary painting collapses the historical and the contemporary onto the same plane. Artists are now combining the real, the unreal, the personal, and the universal to create their own visions of artistic truth.

Marina Molarsky-Beck's writing in this book addresses how "a work of art can create a dialogue that unfolds over generations." Through her discussion of the works of Sam McKinniss, Cecily Brown, and Jill Mulleady, Molarsky-Beck traces contemporary interpretations of *Le Déjeuner sur l'herbe*. After touching on other adaptations, including the movie *Cruel Intentions* (1999) and Bow Wow Wow's album *The Last of the Mohicans*, Molarsky-Beck concludes that *Le Déjeuner* "remains such a crucial reference for today's contemporary artists in part because of this long arc of the painting's history, . . . and all the subsequent reinterpreters of the painting's theme."

Artists began creating works in response to Édouard Manet's *Le Déjeuner sur l'herbe* within two years of its exhibition in the 1863 Salon des Refusés. From Claude Monet to Man Ray, artists have turned to Manet's painting as a source of radical and contradictory possibilities for painting. The enduring radicality of *Le Déjeuner sur l'herbe* inspired me in 2021 to invite around thirty of today's most acclaimed painters to create their response to this painting. Their works were the subject of *Luncheon on the Grass*, an exhibition at my gallery in Los Angeles in 2022, curated with Viola Angiolini. The show also included a selection of existing works inspired by Manet's painting such as the ones by Diane Arbus, Robert Colescott, Alain Jacquet, Jeff Koons, Sophie Matisse, and Paul McCarthy, which together form the first plates section of this volume.

This book extends our exploration of Manet's influence through interviews with the artists, statements, and excerpts of previous publications that give more context on their responses to *Le Déjeuner sur l'herbe*. In addition to reproducing the works of the artists who participated in the exhibition, the volume also includes a sampling of the many other artists, ranging from Beauford Delaney, to Fernando Botero, to Kara Walker, who have been inspired to interpret *Le Déjeuner*'s themes, in a second plates section. Alongside the artists' contributions, the essays by Thomas E. Crow, Aruna D'Souza, and Marina Molarsky-Beck provide important context, new interpretations, and a sense of *Le Déjeuner sur l'herbe* as "a kind of art historical starting point, ripe for reinvention—as much today as it was already in 1865."

# THE "ALLURES ESPAGNOLES" IN MANET'S LE DÉJEUNER SUR L'HERBE

Thomas E. Crow

Few stories in the history of art are as familiar as the saga of Manet's *Le Déjeuner sur l'herbe* making its first public appearance at the watershed Salon des Refusés in 1863. Even as the episode has worn itself out from repetition, it is nonetheless remarkable what little curiosity has been extended to the striking details of its first presentation. Yes, the authors of works rejected by the jury for the official Salon exhibition were invited to send them along, to be to be displayed off to one side in the same setting, the Palais de l'Industrie. But seldom noted is the character of the venue, an immense edifice erected as the main exhibition space for the Exposition Universelle, the Paris world's fair of 1855. Meant to surpass the Crystal Palace in London by the scale and daring of its iron-and-glass armature, the hall boasted a classical envelope of imposing grandiosity, its cornice adorned with the names of history's greatest artists and architects. Both the accepted and the rejected shared this singularly honorific enclosure.

The autocrat of the Second Empire, Napoleon III, by this conspicuous indulgence toward the excluded and misunderstood, seems to have been aiming to expose his chief arts administrators and the artists they favored as out of touch with the times—one minister was forced to resign over the affair. Thus, the stubborn idea that the Refusés was a setup, intended to provoke a carnival of ridicule, stands in need of revision. Ridicule there certainly was, and it is a key part of the Manet legend that he was personally crushed by the vituperation to which *Le Déjeuner* in particular was subjected. But patient work by scholars, however, poring over the whole gamut of printed commentary, has brought to light a good deal of guarded praise for the fresh color and bold execution that distinguished Manet from the murky tonalities and hackneyed themes that surrounded him.[1]

Not that his canvases stood out as all bright bouquets, in that the most dominant of his colors was black, a quality underscored by the manner in which his submissions were hung. This crucial circumstance has likewise never been prominent in the retellings of the tale. It is rare enough to read that Manet entered two other major paintings that year in addition to *Le Déjeuner*; rarer still, to the point of vanishing, to be told how they were arranged. A contemporary cartoonist by the name of Fabritzius provided a partial view of the dense hang, each work rendered in crudely mocking caricature, with Manet's three paintings squarely on the central axis, facing down onto the crowd from the third tier [fig. 4]. The top edges of the paintings are aligned, *Le Déjeuner* at the center, flanked on its left by the *Young Man in the Costume of a Majo* [fig. 5] and on the right by *Mademoiselle V. . . in the Costume of an Espada* [fig. 6], both single vertical figures, French models in Spanish dress (now to be found side by side in New York's Metropolitan Museum of Art). There appear to be a striking number of paintings in their vicinity featuring animals, along with several subjects putting female nudes on borderline pornographic display, such that it would have been hard to make the case, even allowing for the parodist's exaggerations, that Manet was purveying any exceptional indecency.[2]

1 See Alan Krell, "Manet's *Déjeuner sur l'herbe* in the Salon des Refusés: A Re-appraisal," *Art Bulletin* 65, no. 2 (June 1983): 316–20; affirmed by Stéphane Guégan in *Manet: The Man Who Invented Modernity*, ed. Stéphane Guégan, exh. cat. (Paris: Musée d'Orsay; Gallimard, 2011), pp. 31–33.

Then purveying what exactly? Any visitor to the exhibition able to pause and puzzle out the quasi-triptych might have spotted the overlap of two models. Both the artist's younger brother, Gustave, as the "young man" and his favorite model, Victorine Meurent, in the guise of the lethal swordswoman present themselves at the sides of the central scene and then appear inside of it, the woman famously naked, her male counterpart still clothed from head to toe in black. Manet had used Gustave, along with their other brother, Eugène, as models for the right-hand member of the quartet. Almost "*en costume de majo*," wrote one of the more astute commentators on the exhibition, who went so far as to discern pungent "*allures espagnoles*" even in *Le Déjeuner*, for all that it depicts Parisians of both sexes: such were the fruits of Manet's "Spanish victories and conquests," he claims, making no mention of the Italian old master references—Giorgione, Titian, Raphael—that have become standard observations about the painting. Not that even these were common at the time, the critics' practiced eye for allusion perhaps disabled by Manet's insistence on such Spanish allusions in his orchestration of his central painting's debut.[3]

The majos and majas of Madrid belonged to a borderline outlaw demimonde in regular overlap with the charismatic entertainers from the flamenco taverns and bullring, an underground indifferent to the rigid proprieties of conventional Catholic society, its denizens visibly

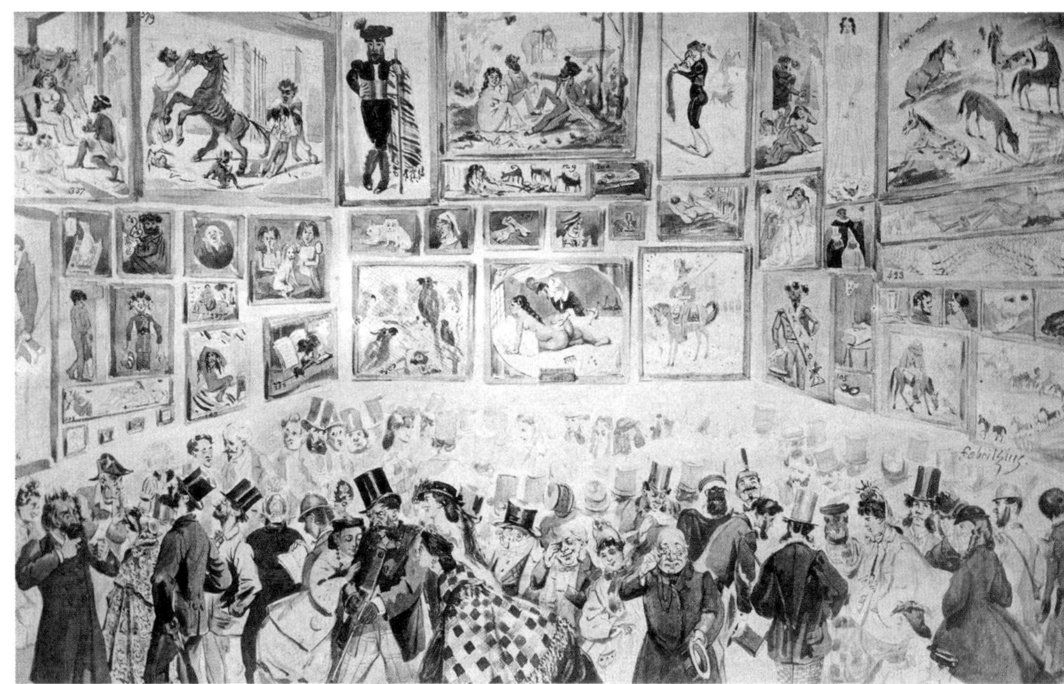

Fig. 4—Lionel Casimir Fabritzius, *Vue caricaturale du Salon des Refusés (Caricature of the Salon des Refusés)*, 1863, Pen and ink on paper, 5 5⁄16 × 8 13⁄16 in. (13.6 × 22.3 cm), Custodia Foundation, Paris

2 On the unique photographic reproduction of the lost ink drawing in brush and pen, with reproduction and key to identified works, see Juliet Wilson-Bareau, "The Salon des Refusés of 1863: A New View," *Burlington Magazine* 149, no. 1250 (May 2007): 309–12.

3 Fernand Desnoyers, *La Peinture en 1863: Salon des Refusés* (Paris: A. Dutil, 1863), p. 41, https://gallica.bnf.frark:/12148/bpt6k108159t. All translations are my own.

4 Ibid., p. 40.

5 Ibid.

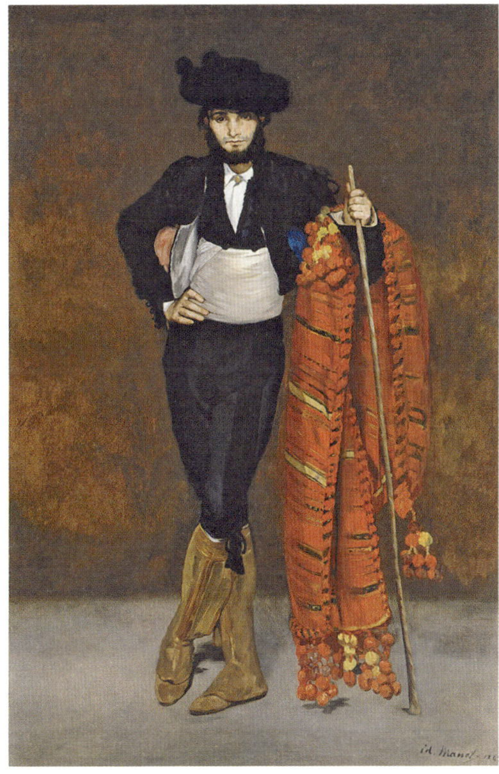

Fig. 5—Édouard Manet, *Young Man in the Costume of a Majo*, 1863, Oil on canvas, 74 × 49 ⅛ in. (188 × 124.8 cm), The Metropolitan Museum of Art, New York

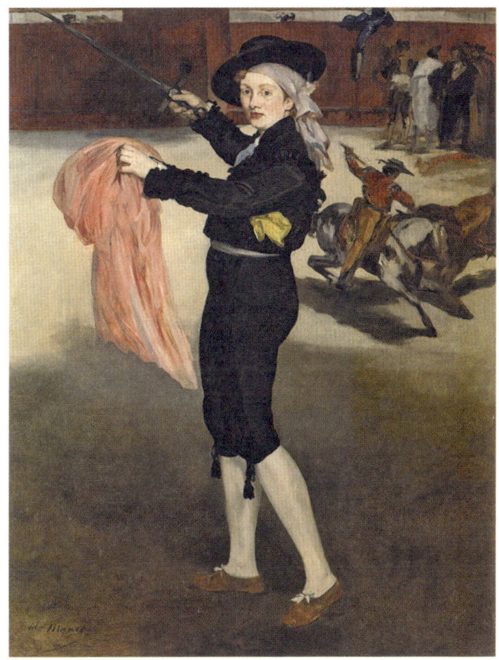

Fig. 6—Édouard Manet, *Mademoiselle V...in the Costume of an Espada*, 1862, Oil on canvas, 65 × 50 ¼ in. (165.1 × 127.6 cm), The Metropolitan Museum of Art, New York

marked out by black garb of both romantic and sinister overtones. Since the later eighteenth century, imitative *majismo* had moreover become a fashion among the more daring or dissolute in Madrid's wealthier classes. Pursuing the theme, this same critic, Fernand Desnoyers, harks back to the previous Salon of 1861, when Manet's portrait of a Spanish guitarist and singer galvanized a group of young artists, who "looked at each other in astonishment, racking their brains for comparisons. And they asked themselves where on Earth, like a stage apparition out of a hidden trapdoor, this Monsieur Manet could have sprung from." The report continues in the same occult vein: "The Spanish musician was painted in a *strange* new manner, to which the astonished young painters believed they alone held the secret key." Even the mode of reaction exceeded customary boundaries. "Some landscape painters," marvels Desnoyers, "acted out their stupefaction in expressive pantomime."[4]

Not content with outlandish antics within the confines of the venue, the group made the spontaneous decision to troop off and pay their respects personally to this mysterious, maligned master: "M. Manet graciously received the delegation, responding to the spokesmen that he was equally moved and flattered and shared with them... all the information they desired. Nor did they stop with this initial visit, even leading a poet and several critics to his door."[5]

One might surmise from this report that Manet had been a reclusive, unknown figure in the firmament of Parisian art, when this notion would have surprised his many prominent social peers who congregated daily at the Café Tortoni on the Boulevard des Italiens, both for lunch and later, after strolling the grand boulevards and gathering under the trees of the Jardin des Tuileries (adjacent to the imperial Palais des Tuileries). Théodore Duret, the art critic and heir to a firm of cognac dealers, described Manet, scion of a likewise well-off family, as something of an exemplar in these routines: "The boulevard was then free of rabble and of an afternoon, an elite more Parisian than any others could meet and stroll, all flâneurs together," adding this personal tribute: "Manet would have been one of the last representatives of this way of living." But the artist added one distinctly professional habit to this daily round, lingering each day in the Tuileries to sketch in the open air, capturing, noted another observer, "the children at play and their nurses as they flop heavily into the chairs."[6]

After these sessions and the requisite sauntering along the boulevards, Manet would return to the Café Tortoni around five or six, gather his regular court around the tables and pass his drawings from hand to hand, doubtless eliciting obligatory compliments from everyone present. That the leading up-and-comers in the painting studios—Henri Fantin-Latour, Alphonse Legros, and Carolus-Duran among them—would have been so baffled by the name "éd. Manet" affixed to *The Spanish Singer* [fig. 7] at the 1861 Salon may attest to the social gulf between their world and the one in which Manet had long been such a prominent participant. The painting was in effect a message from that other world, both in its manner of execution and in its freedom from conventional consistencies, which struck like a blow against the chafing order and discipline imposed by their studio masters. Like magic, they instantly discerned another way forward, but the question remains as to how Manet's mode of existence as posh boulevardier—one of the last of the breed—had yielded this striking artistic synthesis, one so unexpected that his young admirers could at first register its appearance only in supernatural terms.

That was the spring of 1861, but by the same season in 1863, Manet had provided them and all his followers a map of the world that formed his artistic ambitions. In the private Galerie Martinet, on the same Boulevard des Italiens as the Café Tortoni, he mounted something of a retrospective summation of his first maturity as an artist. There were yet no more than a few private galleries in the city, the biannual Salons still serving as the unchallenged, validating showcase for an artist vis-à-vis potential patrons and collectors. One painting in particular, one of his latest and most ambitious, underscored the message that Manet was no striver but a habitué of the privileged class. The work in question is *La Musique aux Tuileries* (*Music in the Tuileries*

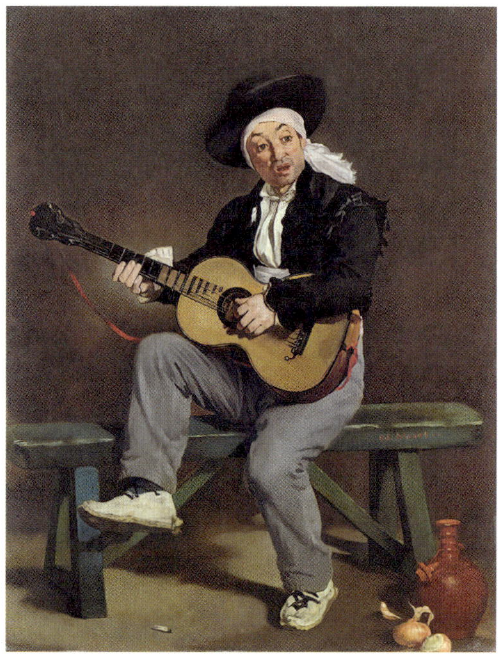

Fig. 7—Édouard Manet, *The Spanish Singer*, 1860, Oil on canvas, 58 × 45 in. (147.3 × 114.3 cm), The Metropolitan Museum of Art, New York

*Gardens*) [fig. 8], which he executed in 1862 as a self-conscious tour de force—self-conscious in a literal sense, as Manet included his own standing likeness at the far left, posed behind his one-time studio partner, the debonair Comte Albert de Balleroy, possessor of the Château de Balleroy in the Normandy countryside. (Proust later used this grand seventeenth-century retreat as his model for the seat of the haughty and remote duchesse de Guermantes, she of the most ancient noble lineage.) A band concert has swelled the gathering, though none of the musicians are visible; at the base of a tree on the right sits the light-opera composer Jacques Offenbach, his mustached, myopic visage an allegory for music that delights a crowd. The left side, by contrast, boasts a much larger constellation of figures from the sphere of the eye rather than the ear. The fact that Charles Baudelaire—Manet's regular companion on his daily visits to the site—is shown engaged in conversation with Théophile Gautier, dean of Parisian critics, underlines the poet's regular role as chronicler of the Salons. With them is Baron Isidore Taylor, the author like Gautier of an Iberian travelogue, the official "inspecteur des musées," and the agent for former king Louis-Philippe in amassing the royal collection of Spanish art (sadly dispersed in 1853). Perhaps the most realized portrait in the painting appears in full face over the shoulder of Baudelaire, but some distance to the rear. It is Fantin-Latour, one of the young painters so moved by Manet's *The*

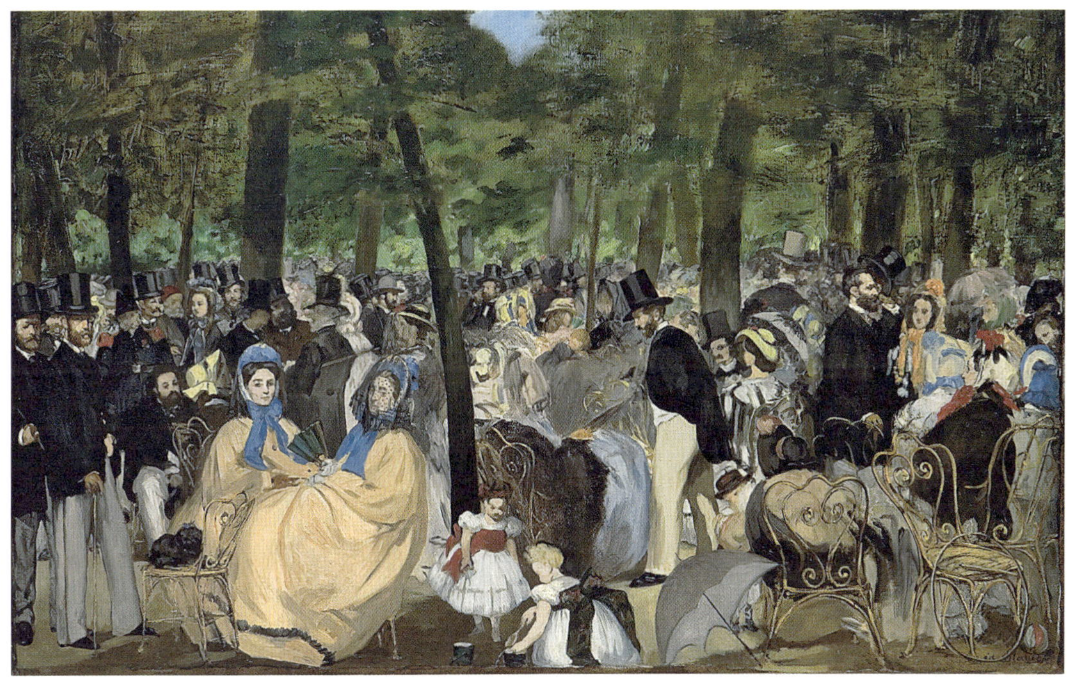

Fig. 8—Édouard Manet, *La Musique aux Tuileries (Music in the Tuileries Gardens)*, 1862, Oil on canvas, 30 × 46 ½ in. (76.2 × 118.1 cm), The National Gallery, London

6 Théodore Duret, *Histoire d'Édouard Manet et de son oeuvre* (Paris: H. Floury, 1902), p. 22.

*Spanish Singer* in the Salon of 1861 and a fast friend ever since.

To key in on the face of Fantin-Latour is to discern the great degree to which Manet relies on the varying sizes of his portrait heads to construct the space that contains the densely packed assembly. No ground plane or framing superstructure creates a proscenium stage; the density of clothed bodies forms a continuous weave of tracks laid down by his blunt brush. Dominating the central zone is a full-length profile view of his brother Eugène, who politely bends to address a pair of seated women, veils lowered from their hat brims such that their persons, right at the heart of the composition, dissolve into an indecipherable crisscross of smeary painted marks. Only the paired younger and older matrons seated at the lower left allow a decoding of what that bravura passage actually might stand for. Such freedom accords with privileged detachment from the demands for servility typically attached to an artistic apprenticeship, not to mention the portrayal of prominent individuals. By family lineage and assured affluence, Manet belongs in the milieu he represents, in the same way that he confidently held court at the Café Tortoni. As might be expected, his jurist father had had strong objections to a son abjuring the professions to keep company with studio *rapins*, raffish menials in their stained rags, while the young Manet had been just as resistant to the role of dutiful pupil, vying for approval and prizes under the watchful discipline of the École des Beaux-Arts. The manifesto that is *La Musique aux Tuileries* declares Manet's success in forging a synthesis unencumbered by either indignity.

The ethos of the painting thus posits polite sociability as fundamental both to Manet's personal identity and to his practice as an artist, here in this informal courtly milieu adjacent to the site of the real imperial one. And this priority visibly impacts the technique and style of the painting. As a first consideration, Manet's daily routine in the Tuileries and on the Boulevard des Italiens would have cut into his time for painting, hence a premium placed on covering canvas with maximum efficiency and impact. While this may sound too flippant an explanation for his broadly flattening application of paint and economy with numbers of strokes, the idea points toward a serious social constraint on what formal effects he could permit himself. His painting could not speak of laborious or overscrupulous effort. Much like the traditional courtier, the nineteenth-century dandy—as Manet certainly was—defined himself by projecting effortless insouciance combined with unforced precision in every endeavor (as the sketches passed round at Tortoni's surely exemplified). He had endured a few years of apprenticeship in the studio of the sought-after historical painter Thomas Couture, a necessary rite of passage if he were to acquire the rudiments of preparing canvas and pigment, along with refining his skills as a draftsman. No doubt he did his time applying the brownish underpainting that his master favored, over

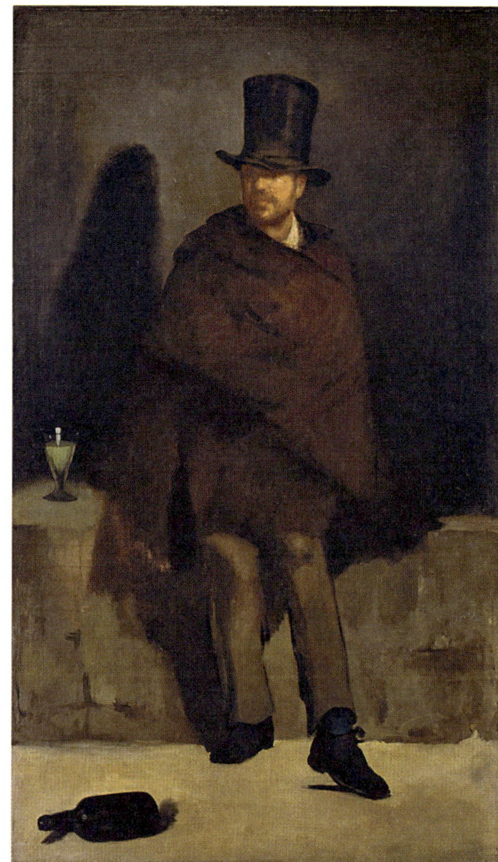

Fig. 9—Édouard Manet, *Le Buveur d'absinthe (The Absinthe Drinker)*, 1859, Oil on canvas, 71 1/16 × 41 5/16 in. (180.5 × 105.6 cm), Ny Carlsberg Glyptotek, Copenhagen

which successive glazes in thinned colors would gradually build up the modeled forms. But none of this labor-intensive gradualism, what Manet called "des ragoûts et des jus" (stews and gravies), would have suited his all-important elite persona.[7]

So where to learn the alternate manner he required? The simple answer was the Louvre, if its offerings were selected with discrimination and care. Frans Hals could supply a template for emphatic, self-evident touches that establish color, contour, and angle all in one decisive gesture, while Titian's example counseled against over-exact modeling. And the Manet family means allowed him to take out time during the 1850s for pilgrimages to the Low Countries, seeking to widen his exposure to the crustier textures of the Dutch and Flemish handling, as well as to Italy, primarily for Venetian color and descriptive abbreviation. Making his first attempt at the Salon in 1859, he mounted an unsuccessful challenge to the jury with *The Absinthe Drinker* [fig. 9], a life-size single figure composed in equal parts from the example of Velázquez, albeit at this point mostly secondhand, and the poetic Parisian underworld of Baudelaire's *Les Fleurs du mal*. The broadly flattened silhouette evokes the Spanish Golden Age, as does the deftly delineated still life attribute, in this case, the last glass of the milky watered liqueur from its discarded empty bottle, addictive consolation for the destitute ragpicker he recruited for his model.

The stone bench and sinister shadow conjure some low, dangerous dive, but the legs of the figure make a contrary impression. Allowing for Manet's abbreviated detail, the trim tailoring and neat hems of the trousers, with his tight blue hose and well-soled, buckled shoes, might befit a boulevard dandy more than they do the destitute scavenger evident in his addict's puffy features and battered hat. But for all that, *The Absinthe Drinker* cuts a figure: his armor against the cold, the blanketlike cloak, may testify to his sleeping rough, but he has thrown it around his shoulders with the flair of a majo sporting a serape. Manet's claim to truth in *The Absinthe Drinker* does not, nor could it, lie in a simple recording of appearances, any more than would his merely flattering the self-regard of the fashionable sorts who populate *La Musique aux Tuileries*. This urban derelict, however recognizable as a type, "figures" the relations between two kinds of undirected occupation of the city's streets and, more significantly, piquant correspondences between them.

So begins Manet's cycle of homages to Velázquez, who offered him not only a model of style as the consummate artist at court, but also a guide to broader human comprehension, as testified in the dignity conferred by the Spanish master on beggars as philosophers and the warmth extended to the companions and entertainers to the royal family. The quasi-court of Parisians at the center of his Galerie Martinet exhibition came surrounded by portraits of Spanish types courtesy of the dancer Mariano Camprubi and his Madrid troupe, who had enjoyed a four-month run of performances at the Hippodrome during the previous year: in advance of Manet's travel to Spain, they had brought Spain to him. The ensuing framing of the French beau monde by at least majo-adjacent figures set the pattern for his own intimates, brother Gustave and model Meurent, donning Spanish costume to serve just a few months later as herald angels on either side of his consummate statement of modern life to date, *Le Déjeuner sur l'herbe*.

Summer fashion for the male habitués of the Tuileries Garden entailed light-colored trousers to accompany their proper black jackets. The corresponding figures in the *Déjeuner*, likewise set in summer, are no exception, yet, as noted above, an alert commentator saw them almost "*en costume de majo*," perceiving in the whole more general "*allures espagnoles*." The flanking portraits for this observer seem to have induced code-switching between the politesse of the French bourgeoisie and the unknown adventures and sensory vividness that were the province of imagined *majismo*. Under their imprimatur, free and easy mingling between naked or semiclad

7 Quoted in Antonin Proust, *Édouard Manet: Souvenirs* (Paris: A. Barthélemy, 1913), p. 24.

women and their clothed male companions becomes plausible. *Majismo* rested on the edge of myth, a liminal zone between contemporary life and the pastoral fantasies of the museum, chiefly Titian's *Concert champêtre* [fig. 10] in the Louvre, a touchstone of refined pastoralism perhaps begun by the enigmatic, deceased Giorgione. An extravagantly dressed courtier and his likewise clothed country companion recreate in a smiling landscape alongside naked naiads, one of whom accompanies the male lutanist on her delicate reed, while an actual shepherd with flock in the middle distance blows into his lustier bagpipes.

The thematic affinity between the *Concert champêtre* and *Le Déjeuner* lifts Manet's loose homage to the Venetian pastoral into the sphere of myth, of the demidivine. Its claim to the out of the ordinary makes itself felt most dramatically in the sheer size of the canvas—207 by 265 centimeters, nearly seven by nine feet, much the largest work he had so far attempted—unveiled in his most prominent showcase to date. When the outsize dimensions of the painting are even discussed, the point is usually to adduce one more provocation on Manet's part, that is, his indecorous expansion of a "mere" genre scene to the proportions of a weighty historical or mythological subject. But there is a way to reverse the terms such that Manet meant to confer on his ostensibly Parisian quartet all the dignity and elevation of the classical pantheon. His original title, simply *Le Bain* (*The Bath*), also fits better in its generality and evocation of classicizing nudes, as opposed to highlighting a parochial French dining custom.

Given that *Le Déjeuner* (to revert to its customary title) shares the same nude model with *Olympia* [fig. 11], the brazenly reclining prostitute attended by her dignified black maid, along with the fact that they were painted in succession during the early months of 1863, has made them something of a dyad and each seemingly the most apposite comparative context for the another. But the later painting is markedly smaller, if by way of compensation, denser in incident and detail. The unsurpassed Manet interpreter Nils Gösta Sandblad speaks for many in extolling the greater coherence of the later painting. He sees the artist's struggle with the heterogeneous parts of *Le Déjeuner* giving way to a sudden burst of decisiveness: "His tension and strain had vanished," observes Sandblad. "All that he had wrestled with in *Le Déjeuner sur l'herbe* is resolved in the long, smooth strokes ending in a little quirk of the brush; and in this painting [*Olympia*] the resolution is spontaneous, and gives to the work what the former, in spite of everything, lacked, the greatness of the self-evident."[8]

It may be, however, that "tension and strain" are more what is wanted in present-day apprehension of the painting. The imperious gamine with her level stare may have been dubbed the "auguste jeune fille" in the accompanying verses by Zacharie Astruc;[9] and Manet may have found the template for *Olympia* in Titian's *Venus of Urbino*, again bestowing an ironic divinity on his contemporary subject. But what Sandblad calls the "greatness" of the work did not compare in physical grandeur to its predecessor, even without the costumed portraits of brother Gustave and Meurent doubling the size of the implied composite work. He may have held *Olympia* back from public view for multiple reasons (surprisingly securing its acceptance in the Salon of 1865), but doing so preserved without distraction the symmetrical coherence of the *Déjeuner* triptych, however loose and additive that ensemble might have been.

It could be said that painting *Olympia* got easier once the multiple kinds of work required by *Le Déjeuner* had been accomplished. Manet could go tighter again once he had gone defiantly bigger. Yet unlike the myriad templates for a reclining nude, there were no real models for work on the scale he had been aiming for at the Refusés. Evidently needing an armature of reassuring stability, he anchored *Le Déjeuner* in perhaps the simplest structural device available: an emphatic equilateral triangle, only slightly tilted; that is to say, he applied the most elementary lesson a young artist might absorb for managing a multifigure composition. Nor did Manet in any way disguise its obviousness and simplicity, thus abjuring with an ironic wink the contorted pictorial arrangements favored by his elders, among them, of course, Couture. And the emblem of that impertinence surely lies in

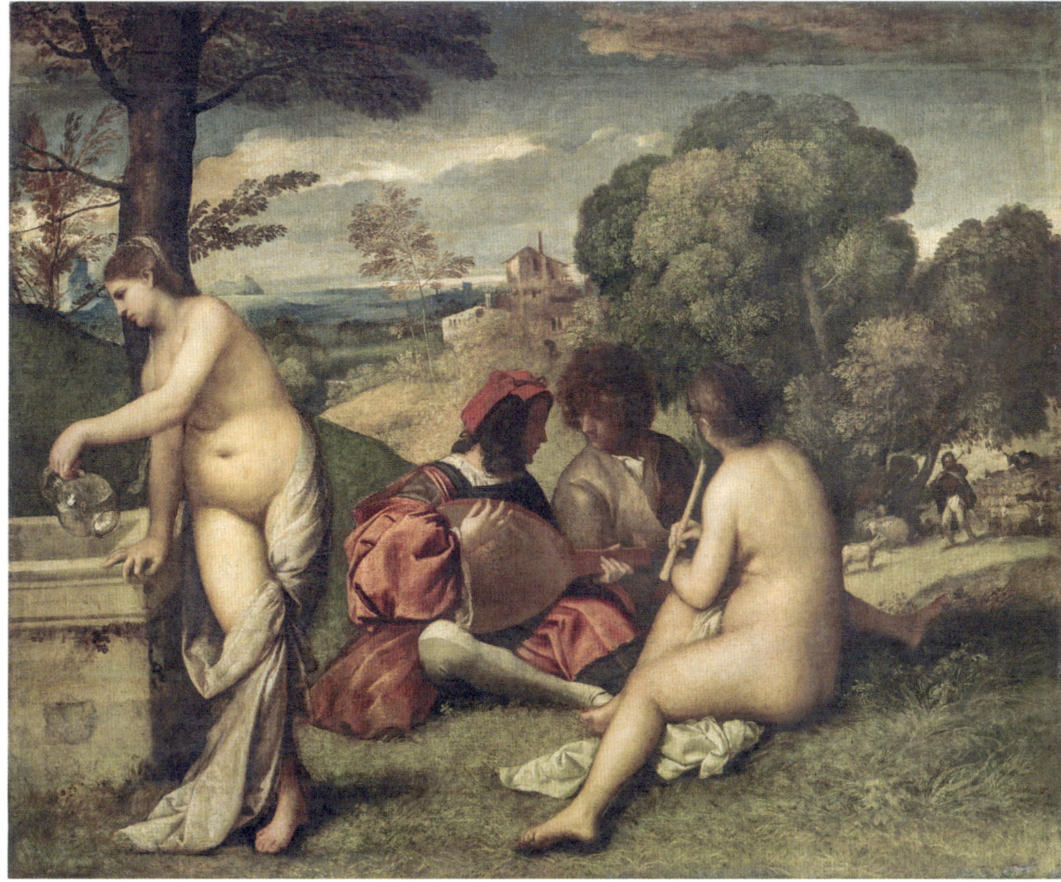

Fig. 10—Titian (Tiziano Vecellio), *Le Concert champêtre (The Pastoral Concert)*, ca. 1500–25, Oil on canvas, 41 5/16 × 53 ½ in. (105 × 136 cm), Musée du Louvre, Paris

the isolated bird hovering in midair just at the triangle's apex.

The creature shows up poorly or hardly at all in reproductions, but catches the light strikingly when one is standing in front of the picture. The brightness of its orange breast exhibits a further internal rhyme with the size, shape, and hue of the peaches in the overturned basket below. It seems as if Manet at first had the idea to hang a peach from one of the boughs above, but the improbability of either botany or season led him to outfit the orange sphere with a beaked head and dark feathers so as to keep that position unequivocally marked. The bird, moreover, signals to its fruit counterpart along a line running through the axis of the nude's torso, which carries one's attention to the virtuoso still life that so arrestingly sprawls across the lower left corner of the canvas, a mélange of the woman's discarded contemporary clothes and the makings of the picnic *déjeuner* that lends the work its enduring title. For an aficionado of Dutch and Spanish

8 Nils Gösta Sandblad, *Manet: Three Studies in Artistic Conception* (Lund, Sweden: C. W. K. Gleerup, 1954), p. 94.

9 As printed in the 1865 Salon *livret* (catalogue):
Quand, lasse de songer, Olympia s'éveille,
(*When weary of dreaming, Olympia awakens,*)
Le printemps entre au bras du doux messager noir.
(*Spring enters in the arms of the gentle black messenger.*)
C'est l'esclave à la nuit amoureuse pareille,
(*It is the slave who, like the amorous night,*)
Qui veut fêter le jour délicieux à voir,
(*Comes to adorn the day, sumptuous to see*)
L'auguste jeune fille en qui la flamme veille.
(*The august young woman in whom the flame keeps watch.*)

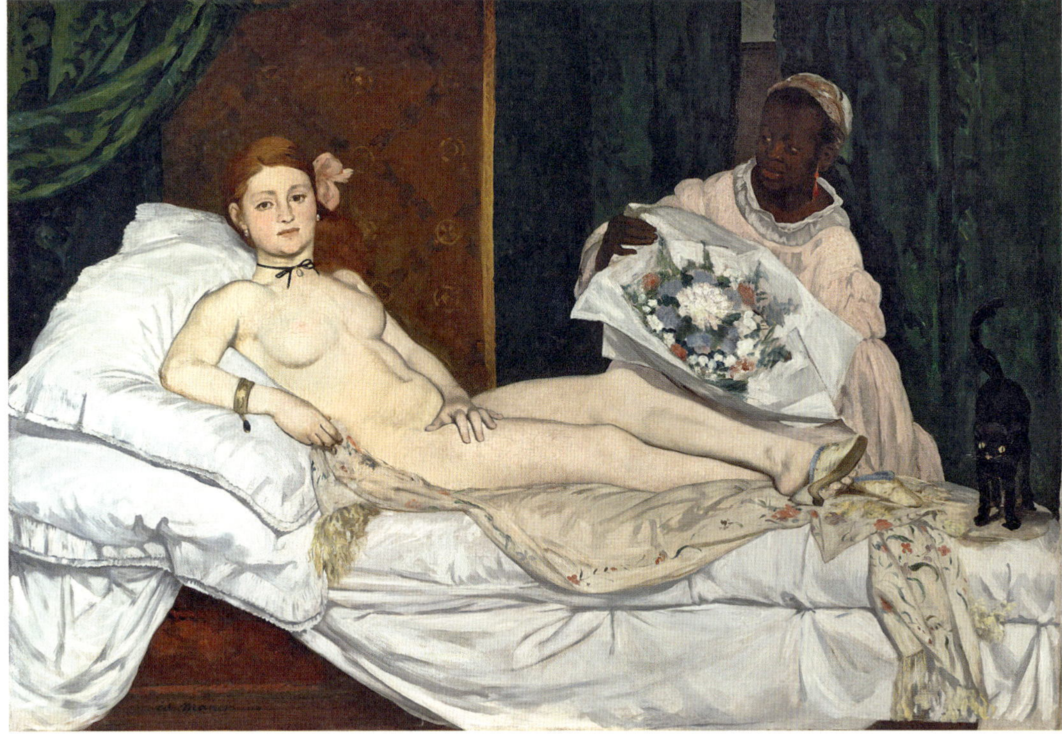

Fig. 11—Édouard Manet, *Olympia*, 1863, Oil on canvas, 51 ⅜ × 74 ¹³⁄₁₆ in. (130.5 × 190 cm), Musée d'Orsay, Paris

prototypes, a Habsburg axis of still life prowess linked the two artistic cultures. Manet's touches retain their somewhat dry bluntness in handling, but his unshowy finesse with rhythmic direction and choices of color conjure from the encounters among objects an animation and unexpected sense of luxury befitting these tokens of intermingled culinary and erotic sensation.

The imposing size of the painting, laden with such generically diverse motifs, carried with it an overarching assertion of mastery by its maker over every facet of art. During the same pivotal year of 1862, Manet made the point explicitly by depicting himself with his future wife, Suzanne Leenhoff, in seventeenth-century costume, surveying with hunting hound a riverine property, rainbow and northern steeple in the distance. Its title, redolent of courtly understatement, is *Fishing* [fig. 12], both for the three men punting with their nets at the center and, more appositely, for Leenhoff's child, Léon, sitting on the opposite bank with his pole. But Manet, more grandly, makes a direct homage to the 1636 pair of paintings by Peter Paul Rubens celebrating his freshly purchased landed estate, where he raised a second family with his much younger second wife, Helena Fourment. Just above the corner position where Manet poses with his own Flemish partner, under a copse of trees, appears a sketchily defined group in which an indistinct but unmistakable nude female looks back over her shoulder in the viewer's direction, a pool of blue water just beyond.

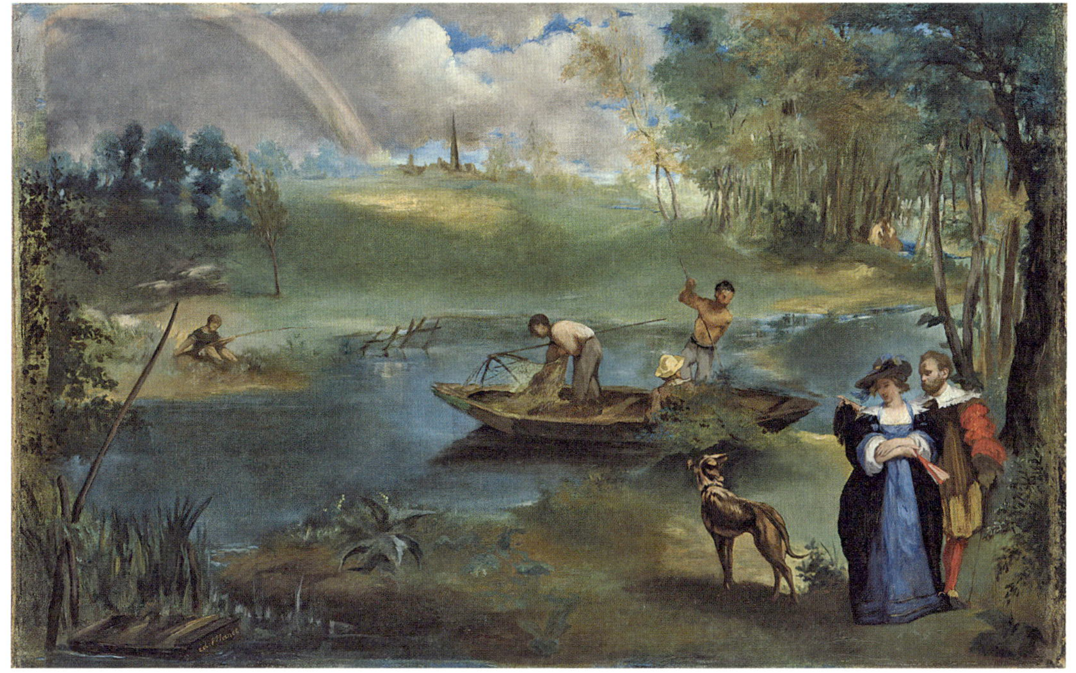

Fig. 12—Édouard Manet, *Fishing*, ca. 1862–63, Oil on canvas, 30 ¼ × 48 ½ in. (76.8 × 123.2 cm), The Metropolitan Museum of Art, New York

Slight as it may seem, this vaguely defined cluster points in two distinct directions. Most literally, it reprises the ambitious nude female figure Manet likewise executed in 1862, *The Surprised Nymph* [fig. 13], now in Buenos Aires, its smoothly sustained flesh tones an explicit acknowledgment of Rubens. Reverse that composition and the pose matches the miniaturized figure in *Fishing* in the modest turning of the back to hide frontal exposure and the backward turn of the head. For the face of his nymph, he melded the features of Fourment and Leenhoff. Sketching in a stagelike wooded setting, he seated his nymph on luxuriantly piled fabrics above a cast-aside Rubensian pearl necklace. The second direction points quite obviously to *Le Déjeuner*, with the open question as to how fully he had at that point imagined his magnum opus—but imagined it was in this easily overlooked vignette.

It is frequently remarked in interpretations of *Le Déjeuner* that the Manet family owned a tract of land along the Seine north of the city at Gennevilliers, industrialized now but bucolic then, where they would spend time in the summers. The stagy landscape in the painting defeats correlation to that actual location, but not to the idea of it, nor to the analogy between his possession and that of Rubens, even more than Velázquez the model of the courtier-artist. Manet makes that shared terrain a site where anything, natural or supernatural, can occur. He had earlier conceived such a place as the banks

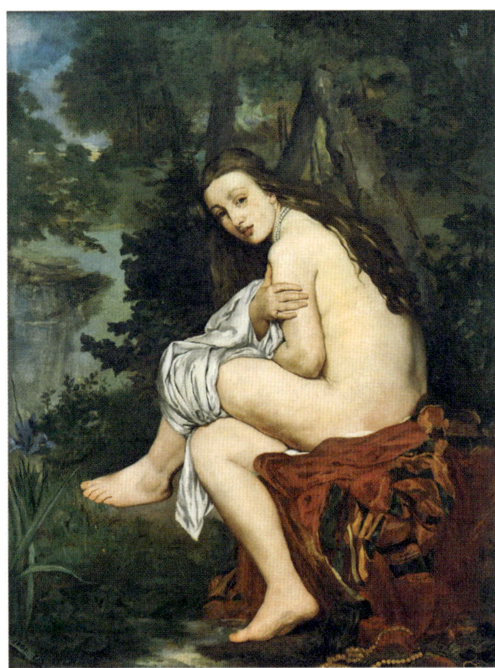

Fig. 13—Édouard Manet, *La Nymphe surprise (The Surprised Nymph)*, 1861, Oil on canvas, 56 ⅞ × 44 5⁄16 in.; frame: 66 13⁄16 × 54 ⅛ × 3 ¾ in. (144.5 × 112.5 cm; frame: 169.8 × 137.5 × 9.5 cm), Museo Nacional de Bellas Artes, Buenos Aires

of the Nile, the setting for a projected *Moses Saved from the Waters*, where the bathing of the seminude Egyptian princess took pride of place—a pose he then isolated in *The Surprised Nymph*. His determination to prove himself with a religious subject, one more of all the genres over which he claimed mastery, waited until he dispatched his remarkable *Dead Christ with Angels* to the Salon in 1865. But his pharaonic maiden announced that intention, even if it was to take a much different turn in 1862 and 1863.

The key point of correspondence between *The Surprised Nymph* and the nude in *Le Déjeuner* can be seen in the way that the uppermost edge of fabric in both just limns with wavering, hesitating overlap the forward hip and buttock in each figure, above which rests the pale acre of flesh. But there the two diverge, with the pose of Meurent transformed by her upright torso and head, accompanied by a gaze that negates any hint of coyness, the figure's contemporaneity secured by the barely visible, close-fitting black hat that she has retained in her disrobing. But Manet, for all that, did not abandon the courtly rendering of the female figure. The second woman, in the middle ground, suspended at the center of his governing triangle, reaches down with exquisite poise and modesty to clutch her shift in a sweeping bow. Though a strap droops over one shoulder, her chitonlike garment carries the wet-drapery effect over from the classical figures in the Louvre. Inside her own distinct wedge of space, she connects to the larger group via the tenuous link between her extended arm and the thumb on the hand of the right-hand male, the portrait amalgam of Manet's two brothers. That pivot point, collapsing the space between them, lends her semicircular silhouette an unstably rocking motion at variance with the solidly grounded foreground trio.

The Manet brother's extended forearm, itself isolated against a flat patch of green, also carries a connotation lying outside fine art; that is, it distinctly resembles a directional pointing shop sign (like the one that Duchamp later employed as a deflating archaism). In the marginal vignette by Raphael of a nymph and river gods [fig. 14] that Manet famously borrowed as a template for his three foreground personages, the corresponding deity grips a bunch of reeds; so the empty pointing hand constitutes a marked departure from the model, such that the pretension of the Renaissance reference (no secret at the time) clashes to ironic effect with this evocation of street-level commerce. For a work that has come to stand for the advent of the modern painting, the allusions and correspondences cultivated by the artist seem largely to point toward the art of the past, the folkloric vernacular, and the shadowy romance of Spain. Nonetheless, the consensus as to the groundbreaking modernity of *Le Déjeuner* is by no means mistaken, but its causes do not lie in prosaic mimicry of its current moment; the aspirations and prohibitions under which Manet was fashioning his anomalous artistic career precluded such a course. As he sought to sum up his ambitions in a grand public statement, the aggregate of those constraints yielded a painting composed out of clashes, discrepancies, and paradoxes, with its sincerities undone by ironies and vice versa. To gain the modern would not lie in any up-to-date spectacle; it would instead entail so thorough an unmooring of the cargo inherited from the past as to prepare a new aesthetic consciousness. Therein lies its enduring shock.

# MANET AS INFLUENCER

Aruna D'Souza

hat is there to say about Manet's *Le Déjeuner sur l'herbe* 160 years after it made its scandalous debut at the Salon des Refusés, an exhibition that launched a thousand art movements, galvanized painters to reject the authority of the official art establishment, and strike out in new directions, build new markets, cultivate new audiences, upend conventional tastes? So much interpretation adheres to the iconic work that I would probably find, if I searched through the literature, that even this opening sentence has been written before, in more or less the same terms.

All writing is citation. All painting, too. "The text is a tissue of quotations drawn from the innumerable centres of culture," as Roland Barthes advised us.[1] This is no less the case for *Le Déjeuner*, though sometimes I manage to convince myself otherwise. I will never not pause in front of this canvas when I visit the Musée d'Orsay, never not revel in the strangeness of it, the pleasures of it, the calm ease that it produces in my body even as it disorients me. For all that I am aware of the ways Manet has used history as his medium—as much as he manipulated oil paint and canvas—I totally buy the hype around the work's utter originality.

Four people in a glade, a strange picnic scene. A woman, naked save for some fabric twisted around her bottom and her ankle, with arm not quite propped on knee, hand on chin, face turned toward me, meeting my eyes. An auburn-haired gentleman looking off into my direction, though with a thousand-mile stare, as if I am not here. Another man, leaning back against the grass, one hand grasping a walking stick (why is he holding it, since it's clear that he's been sitting for a while, that this is a gathering that has been going on for some time?). He makes a pointed, pointing gesture, as if he is trying to emphasize whatever he's saying, but his mouth is closed, and his companions pay him no particular attention. A woman, half dressed in a chemise, bending over into a pond that seems to hover above the central grouping, not quite settling into space. A sunlit field of hay in the distance. A rowboat peeping out from between some trees. A pile of women's clothes—blue gown and blue-bowed straw hat, some white undergarments—but only one, which is odd because both women lack them. Some peaches and cherries, a brioche, an empty bottle. There are even a couple of discarded oysters at the bottom edge.

*Le Déjeuner sur l'herbe* operates in many ways, on many levels. Perhaps this is how we can measure the success of a work—the number of convincing readings it generates, the way that it ushers in new ways of thinking of both art and the world. By such a standard, it's a wildly successful painting.

*This is a work about the privilege of the flâneur*[2]—the bourgeois man who strolls through urban and suburban landscapes with a sense of entitlement. The simultaneous invisibility and

1 Roland Barthes, "The Death of the Author," in *Image, Music, Text*, trans. Stephen Heath (London: Fontana Press, 1977), p. 146.

2 On the flâneur as artist, see Charles Baudelaire, "The Painter of Modern Life," in *The Painter of Modern Life and Other Essays*, trans. and ed. Jonathan Mayne (London: Phaidon, 1995). On Manet as flâneur, see T. J. Clark, *The Painting of Modern Life: Paris in the Art of Manet and His Followers* (Princeton, NJ: Princeton University Press, 1999); and Linda Nochlin, "Manet's *Masked Ball at the Opera*," in *The Politics of Vision: Essays on Nineteenth-Century Art and Society* (New York: Harper and Row, 1989), pp. 75–94.

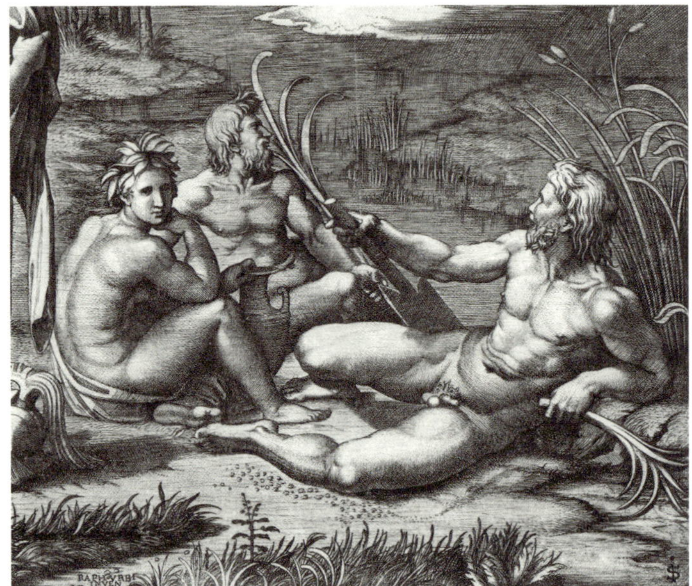

Fig. 14—Marcantonio Raimondi, after Raphael, *The Judgment of Paris* (detail)

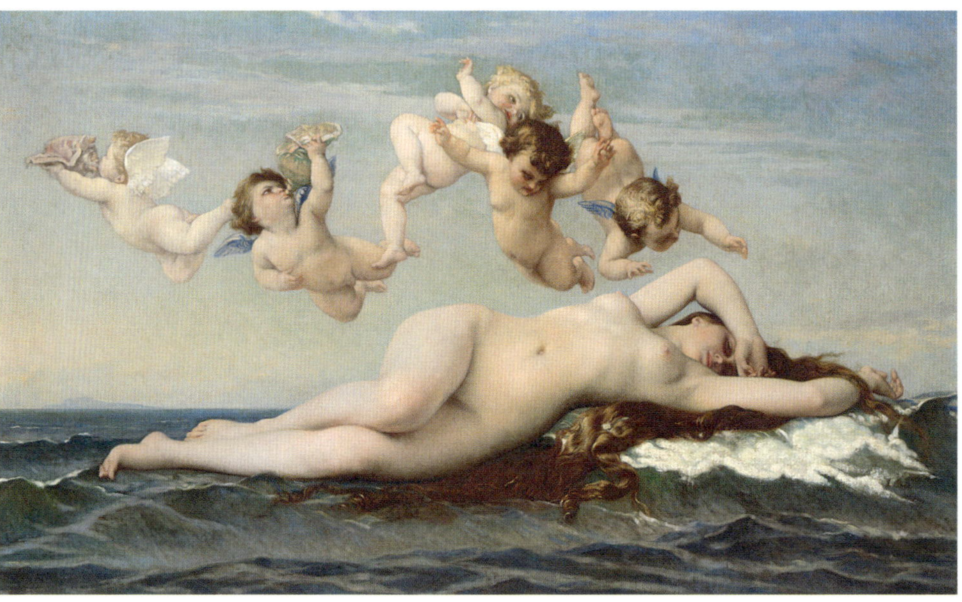

Fig. 15—Alexandre Cabanel, *The Birth of Venus*, 1875, Oil on canvas, 41 ¾ × 71 ⅞ in. (106 × 182.6 cm), The Metropolitan Museum of Art, New York

authority conferred by his fashion and bearing allow him to occupy any space effortlessly. Manet was the quintessential *flâneuriste* painter, his personal elegance giving him access to the most elite salons and the demimonde at once. For Walter Benjamin, the flâneur was also defined by his predilection for seeing the city as a commodity—all interactions in the streets were forms of window-shopping, and anything in his path, including women, was understood through this lens of consumption.[3] Those men at the center of *Le Déjeuner*, relaxed and at ease even as they are surrounded by delectable half- and fully undressed women, as if this is a nonevent, an ordinary occurrence? They are flâneurs.

*This is a work about the power and interruption of the male gaze.* It is an image that has it both ways: it offers up its women to viewers' hungry looks while at the same time makes us uncomfortably aware of our creepiness. The nude woman in the foreground, posed by Victorine Meurent, frustrates our expectations of looking without consequences. It's not that such a stare is entirely withering, though; her frankness can equally be read as a form of titillation.

*This is a work about its relationships to other works*[4]—to a group of sea gods in an early sixteenth-century engraving by Marcantonio Raimondi [fig. 14], based on Raphael's *Judgment of Paris*; to *Concert champêtre* (ca. 1500–25), once attributed to Titian; to Giorgione's *The Tempest* [fig. 17]; and to one of Manet's other paintings hung at the Salon des Refusés, next to *Le Déjenuer*, which also featured Meurent, and even teased her name in its title—*Mademoiselle V... in the Costume of an Espada.*

*At the same time, this is a work about a rejection of that past*, in the way it uses its art historical sources as mere pastiche, as bits and pieces that can be combined any which way, as easily to shock viewers as to placate them. In defiance of Titian, Raphael, Giorgione, Raimondi—and so many of his contemporaries at the official Salon, like Alexandre Cabanel, who were busy painting naked Venuses [fig. 15], fulfilling the market's desire for a kind of highbrow soft porn—Manet had no time for mythology or pretense. He was all about the now and about forthrightness when it came to sexuality and desire—he didn't paint goddesses; he painted prostitutes or lovers or friends. This was part of his realism, no less a sign of that artistic approach than the way he rendered the figures, especially Meurent, as slightly flattened, with apparent shadows and dark outlines, without the "licked," completely blended and varnished surfaces of academic painting. *Le Déjeuner* reflected Manet's determination to use art history only so far as it served his purpose: to paint his moment, his modernity.

*This is a work about artistic rivalry.*[5] It is a shot across the bow to Gustave Courbet, at the time the most notorious bad boy of the Parisian art world, who in the mid-1850s had exhibited works like *Les Demoiselles des bord de la Seine*, depicting garishly dressed, overly made-up

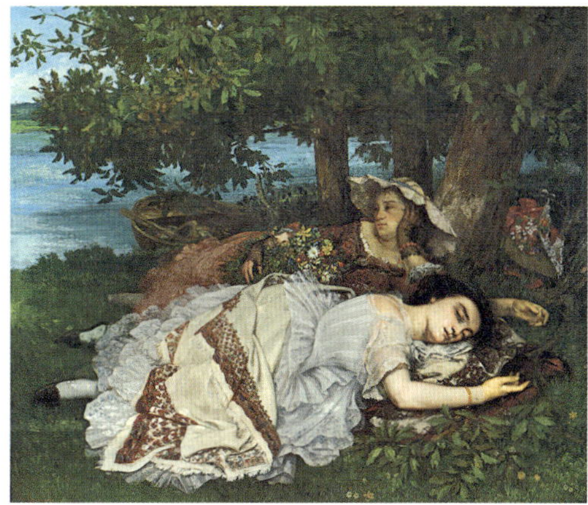

Fig. 16—Gustave Courbet, *Les Demoiselles des bords de la Seine (Young Ladies on the Banks of the Seine)*, 1857, Oil on canvas, 68 ½ × 81 ⁷⁄₁₆ in. (174 × 206 cm), Petit Palais, Musée des Beaux-Arts de la Ville de Paris

3 On Benjamin's notion of the flâneur, see Martina Lauster, "Walter Benjamin's Myth of the 'Flâneur,'" *Modern Language Review* 102, no. 1 (January 2007): 139–56.

4 The search for iconographic sources in this painting is an industry unto itself, but one of the most important examples of the endeavor is Michael Fried, "Manet's Sources: Aspects of His Art, 1859–1865," *Artforum* 7, no. 7 (March 1969), republished as "Manet's Sources, 1859–1869" and accompanied by his reevaluation, "'Manet's Sources' Reconsidered," in Fried, *Manet's Modernism, or, The Face of Painting in the 1860s* (Chicago: University of Chicago Press, 1996). See also Theodore Reff's response to Fried's original article: "Manet's Sources: A Critical Evaluation," *Artforum* 8, no. 1 (September 1969).

women on a riverbank sleeping off last night's debauchery [fig. 16]; Manet replaces Courbet's rough, working-class, shocking tawdriness with an equally shocking elegance, announcing in the process a new, cooler, more cosmopolitan, and urbane avant-garde point of view.

*This is a work about artificiality*, about the clash between the conceit—that we are seeing a group of people out in nature—and the overt theatricality of the setup, including the strange unnaturalness of the poses and the fact that we know (no less than the visitors to that 1863 exhibition knew) that Meurent was a model for many of Manet's paintings. "What if a group of classical gods and goddesses were plopped into the middle of the Bois de Boulogne?," Manet seems to ask. And then he dares us to laugh at the absurdity of the result.

*This is a work about the gender binary*, showing women as nature (thanks to their nudity, in part) to men's culture. The trope is as old as Western culture itself, and I'll leave it up to others to decide if Manet does much to unravel it.[6] That said, it always struck me that in relation to this particular binary, the women were much better off, no matter how much patriarchy wanted to insist otherwise.

*Perhaps most interestingly, this is a work about silence.* It's not just that none of the figures speaks, that mouths are closed. It's that each point of this pyramidal grouping looks past and through one another. The half-dressed woman is occupied with her bathing. (I always think I see her laughing at a private joke.) Meurent looks out at us. The glassy-eyed man looks inward. The leaning man holds forth, but soundlessly, his hand emphasizing a point that remains unsaid. (The oddness of the gesture is related to Manet's treatment of one of his sources. In Raimondi's print, the sea god on which this figure is based holds a long reed; Manet keeps the pose but discards the original meaning of it, thereby introducing a kind of illegibility into his composition at the very point that we expect communication to occur.)[7] This is an image of elegant sociability in which no social interaction seems to take place. It's interesting to me that when Manet showed it in 1863, he called it *Le Bain*, or *The Bath*—focusing the viewer's attention on the solitary activity in the background rather than the supposed conviviality in the foreground.

As ever, Meurent's gaze stops me in my tracks: she looks at me as if I've interrupted something. She appraises me, she questions my presence with her cool, though not hostile, glance. It's not the startled, even frightened reaction of Manet's *Surprised Nymph* (which is related, it seems clear, to the biblical story of Susanna and the Elders, in which a bunch of old men creep up on a young woman at her ablutions). It's not even the unimpressed, hardened look of *Olympia* (also posed by Meurent). In the face of *Le Déjeuner*'s nude woman, I'm thrown back to my high school self, stumbling into a conversation among the cool kids who respond by falling quiet, waiting for me to leave. Despite the openness of the men's

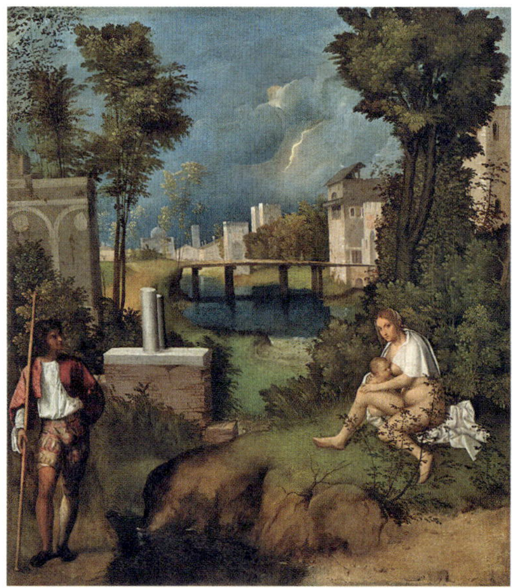

Fig. 17—Giorgione (Giorgio da Castelfranco), *La Tempesta (The Tempest)*, ca. 1506–8, Oil on canvas, $32\frac{5}{16} \times 28\frac{3}{4}$ in. (82 × 73 cm), Gallerie dell'Accademia di Venezia, Venice

poses—they don't withhold themselves from the viewer—they don't quite engage us, either. And despite Meurent's nudity—a sign, in a lot of nineteenth-century painting, of her availability to the viewer (sexually, psychically, optically)—her bent leg, the arm that barely sits on knee, the temporary twist of her head away from her companions, all point to the fact that she is not for us, or we are not for her.

This push and pull of *Le Déjeuner*—on one hand, the picnic whose guests seem so sophisticated and at ease, a scene of *luxe, calme, et volupté*, and on the other, the signs that I am not to be part of the fun—make this, for me, the perfect painting for the Instagram age. I am held ever so slightly at bay, just at arm's length, from this life. That this life is simultaneously ever so slightly artificial only adds to my sense of longing, of unbelonging.

*Le Déjeuner* is a nod to a bourgeois elite in 1863 who recognized the models in the painting—not only Victorine Meurent, but also one of Manet's brothers (it's not clear whether we're seeing Eugène or Gustave) and his brother-in-law, the Dutch sculptor Ferdinand Leenhoff. Those viewers could understand themselves as part of this exclusive club. For petit bourgeois viewers in 1863—the French Salons, including the Salon des Refusés, were mass cultural events, drawing hundreds of thousands of visitors of all classes—it might have reminded them of their own Sunday afternoons on the Grande Jatte or Grenouille or other Seine-side parks where they threw off the labors of the week to indulge in a newish kind of activity, that of leisure. Perhaps they hoped they looked as soigné as this group when they went out into the suburbs to bathe and bask. But faced with Meurent's unimpressed gaze, how could they not squirm, knowing that they would never be mistaken for this elegant crowd.

The painting is, in this way, aspirational—we are faced with a kind of longing, of wanting to be included.

Manet portrays in *Le Déjeuner sur l'herbe* a lifestyle that is theatrical, constructed, citational, devoid of real sociability, and—crucially—just out of reach. If it sounds like I'm describing him as some kind of Instagram influencer—well, let's just say I'm not NOT describing him that way. Manet proposed modernity as pastiche—if we're now living in a world where objective standards and unchallenged authority no longer hold sway, where there are no more academicians to tell us how to paint or monarchs to tell us how to live, we are free to create a world that we want out of bits of past, present, and even future. If those bits don't quite hold together, if they defy correct perspective or look not fully knit into the painting's surface because of their black outlines or just don't quite make sense, that's okay, too, because it tells viewers that they are equally free to build their world in this way.

This world—theatrical, constructed, citational—is an Instagram world. All those lifestyle videos, the makeup tutorials, the travel photos just as aspirational as *Le Déjeuner* and also as devoid of real sociability—they only give us the impression or spectacle of it. (It's like an endless stream of "women laughing alone with salad" stock photos.) The difference between what all those Instagram influencers create and what Manet did was that Manet proposed modern life as a form of pastiche, and they proffer in the form of the meme. Pastiche requires an endless reorganization of the elements that go into its making, where a meme requires endless replication. He may have to learn a few new tricks, but I suspect Manet would be quite at home in our new world.

5 On the question of artistic rivalry between Courbet and Manet (and later, Cézanne), see Nanette Salomon, "Courbet's *Woman with a Parrot* and the Problem of 'Realism,'" in *Tribute to Lotte Brand Philip: Art Historian and Detective*, ed. William W. Clark et al. (New York: Abaris, 1985), pp. 144–53; Laurence des Cars, "A Legacy of Truth: The Reference to Courbet, from Manet to Cézanne," in *Gustave Courbet*, ed. Dominique de Font-Réaulx, exh. cat. (New York: The Metropolitan Museum of Art, 2008), pp. 59–69; and Aruna D'Souza, *Cézanne's Bathers: Biography and the Erotics of Paint* (University Park, PA: Penn State University Press, 2008), pp. 51–56.

6 Marcia Pointon argues that the painting creates conditions "in which gender is deeply unsettled and in which the binaries...disintegrate, leaving a semantic void." Pointon, "The Fascination with This Rendezvous Does Not Diminish...," in *Manet's "Le Déjeuner sur l'herbe,"* ed. Paul Hayes Tucker (Cambridge: Cambridge University Press, 1998), p. 157.

7 On the question of illegibility in *Le Déjeuner*, see Nancy Locke, "Manet's *Le Déjeuner sur l'herbe* as a Family Romance," in Tucker, *Manet's "Le Déjeuner sur l'herbe,"* pp. 119–51.

# MANET AND THE REINVENTION OF HISTORY

Marina Molarsky-Beck

Artist Sam McKinniss paints images with "in-built cultural power," a term he borrows from Gary Indiana.[1] He scours the Internet for memorable stills from film and television, publicity photos, works of art—any visual form is potential fodder for his painterly reinterpretation. Two such paintings reproduce some of the most memorable scenes from the 1999 film *Cruel Intentions*. Directed by Roger Kumble, *Cruel Intentions* is a raunchy romantic teen drama of the kind that proliferated at the millennium, replete with punchy one-liners delivered by twenty-something starlets playing adolescents.

The film adapts and modernizes *Les Liaisons dangereuses* (*Dangerous Liaisons*), a 1782 epistolary novel by Pierre Choderlos de Laclos. Both the original novel and the 1999 film tell a tragic tale of seduction and betrayal, centering on a bet made between a pair of master manipulators as to whether notorious playboy Valmont can seduce a seemingly impossible target, a woman as renowned for her virtue as Valmont is for his vice. While the novel explores (and exposes) the culture of libertinage among the French nobility in the period shortly before the Revolution, *Cruel Intentions* transposes the action to modern-day New York City and makes its characters privileged—but ethically impoverished—Upper East Side teenagers who spend less time attending school than they do taking drugs and plotting schemes.

The two stills from *Cruel Intentions* that McKinniss has selected for his paintings evoke nineteenth-century French painting, despite their apparently modern subject matter. *Picnic (Cecile and Kathryn)* (2021) bears an immediate resemblance to Édouard Manet's famous *Luncheon on the Grass*—its composition hinges on figures lounging on a grassy expanse, water and lush foliage visible behind them, though McKinniss substitutes Central Park for French woodlands. In McKinniss's painting, as in Manet's, the figures are positioned centrally, in a kind of tableau that seems aware of its own status as image—just as Manet's model, Victorine Meurent, turns toward the viewer, looking out, so too does McKinniss's Kathryn Merteuil, as portrayed by Sarah Michelle Gellar. Meanwhile, beside her, Cecile Caldwell (Selma Blair) remains absorbed in a just-interrupted kiss, eyes still closed as she leans toward Kathryn, seemingly unaware that Kathryn has pulled away from her. She thus parallels the figure of the hatted man at the right of the *Luncheon on the Grass*, whose face in profile is angled away from the viewer and toward his companions. The picnic that spread around the figures, too, recalls Manet's, with its sumptuously rumpled blue fabric, reflective glassware, and picturesquely arrayed fruits.

If the female bather in the background of Manet's *Luncheon* is absent from the picnic scene in *Cruel Intentions*, that figure of the bather is displaced, instead, to another scene, the subject of McKinniss's second painting, *Bather (Sebastian)* (2021). Here, Manet's female bather is substituted by a male bather who turns away to towel himself off after a swim. His pose echoes that of Gustave Caillebotte's *Man at His Bath* (1884), each painting making a display of the muscular male nude, seen from behind.

One is left wondering whether the cinematographer of *Cruel Intentions*, Theo van de Sande, and its art director, David Lazan, have

1 Sam McKiniss, interview by the author, May 1, 2022.

deliberately drawn from the visual arsenal of French painting in order to produce a Y2K teen drama that pays aesthetic homage to its own point of origin—the eighteenth-century novel *Les Liaisons dangereuses*, on which it is based. Certainly, the interiors in which the teenage protagonists swan around are appointed in a late-1990s pastiche of Rococo style, replete with gilded molding and rich brocades. The film's antagonist, Kathryn, sprawls frequently across a chaise longue like the one made famous by Jacques-Louis David's *Portrait of Madame Récamier* (1800). They may live on the Upper East Side and vacation in the Hamptons, but the characters that populate *Cruel Intentions* are modern-day libertines, with the trappings to match.

In the film's bathing scene, Sebastian is drying himself in front of Annette Hargrove (Reese Witherspoon), the virginal Kansas transplant who becomes the object of his seductive pursuit. The still McKinniss paints, though, is visually divorced from that context—only Sebastian is in the frame, and Annette is nowhere to be found. McKinniss's painting amplifies the homoerotic potential of the male bather, thus picking up a thread found both in Caillebotte's bather and in Manet's *Luncheon*.[2] Indeed, the *Luncheon* illustrates the cover of Eve Kosofsky Sedgwick's landmark book *Between Men: English Literature and Male Homosocial Desire* (1985).[3] Though the book itself discusses literary representations of homosociality, rather than visual ones, its cover memorably demonstrates that in Manet's famous painting, despite the presence of a starkly nude female figure, the two men seated on the grass seem more in rapport with each other than with their companion. The man seated at right, in particular, turns toward his fellow; his gaze, averted from the picture plane, seems to be fixed not on the nude woman but on the other man beside her.

McKinniss's paintings from *Cruel Intentions* preserve the eroticism—and homoeroticism—for which the film is most notable. The kiss scene between Selma Blair's and Sarah Michelle Gellar's characters appeared at a time when love scenes of any kind between two women were rare in mainstream Hollywood productions and certainly in those targeted at young people. A recent article published on the occasion of the twentieth anniversary of the film's release claimed it "sparked a generation's sexual awakening."[4] A 2022 music video released as a beverage brand's Pride Month promotion features a cameo by Sarah Michelle Gellar—who shouts "Gay rights!"—and a playful re-creation of the *Cruel Intentions* kiss.[5] Ryan Phillippe, the actor who plays Sebastian Valmont, remarked in an interview that his nude scene, depicted in McKinniss's *Bather (Sebastian)*, is often cited by men as "the moment I knew I was gay."[6] The "in-built cultural power" of the stills that McKinniss portrays, then, lies partly in their quasi-cult status as representations of queer desire. In this way, the paintings seem to respond to the gender and sexual dynamics of Manet's *Luncheon*, offering reversals of the roles in the original painting: McKinniss's nude bather is male, rather than female, and the moment of intimate connection that he alludes to is one between two women.

By the time *Cruel Intentions* was released in 1999, Laclos's *Les Liaisons dangereuses* had itself been adapted endlessly, into stage plays, operas, ballets, television productions, and radio plays, among other formats. In 1988–89 alone, it became two separate films, one directed by Stephen Frears and starring Glenn Close, John Malkovich, Michelle Pfeiffer, and Uma Thurman, another directed by Miloš Forman and starring Annette Bening and Colin Firth. A decade later, Kumble modernized Laclos's story to make *Cruel Intentions*, taking an approach akin to that of Amy Heckerling's *Clueless* (1995)—which makes Austen's Emma a present-day Valley girl—and Gil Junger's *10 Things I Hate about You* (1999)—which relocates Shakespeare's *Taming of the Shrew* to twentieth-century Seattle. *Cruel Intentions* appears, today, a document of its time, a particularly brash and clever example of the late-1990s taste for modernizing classic plots and turning them into widely marketable teen movies. The movie is indicative, too, of culture's seemingly unquenchable thirst to reinterpret familiar material.

Like *Cruel Intentions*, Manet's *Luncheon on the Grass* is a symbol of adaptation and reinvention. The *Luncheon* has become an icon of modernist painting, a point of departure artists have returned to time and again over the century and a half since its first display. And yet, crucially, Manet's composition also iterated on tradition, taking the poses of the central figures from Marcantonio Raimondi's engraving *The Judgment of Paris* (ca. 1510–20), a print itself made after Raphael's design.[7] McKinniss, then, in drawing out the similitude between the *Cruel Intentions* picnic scene and Manet's famous *Luncheon*, layers reference upon reference. His painting depicts a scene from the 1999 film adaptation of a 1782 novel, while paying simultaneous visual homage to Manet's 1863 painting, which itself reuses a figural group from Raimondi's print of about 1510–20 after Raphael. With such densely accumulated references, the painting seems not merely to draw from history, but to explore the very question of how art can take up the old and make it new again. McKinniss's painting shuttles through time, across six centuries—and further back, even, if one considers the mythological subject matter for Raphael and Raimondi's *Judgment of Paris*.

Of the artists in the *Luncheon on the Grass* exhibition, several address Manet slantwise, through prior representations of his painting. Manet's *Luncheon* often comes already mediated. Take, for instance, Cecily Brown, whose approach to the work is informed not only by the painting itself, but also by the band Bow Wow Wow's album cover for *The Last of the Mohicans* (EP, 1982) that photographically restages the *Luncheon*. Brown's paintings metabolize at once the original painting and its later reimagining as album artwork. The title of one such work, *Go Wild in the Country*, makes direct reference to a Bow Wow Wow single of the same name, cementing the relationship between Brown's painting, Manet's masterpiece, and Bow Wow Wow's reimagining.

The traces of Bow Wow Wow are also visible in Brown's compositions, which feature the lounging male figure on the right attired in brilliantly red trousers, just like the band member who occupies that position in the album cover. Various other slippages occur: in Brown's *Le Déjeuner sur l'herbe*, two nude figures are visible in the background of the scene, rather than the one present in Manet's painting—perhaps an echo of the two figures in the background of the Bow Wow Wow photograph. Brown uses a saturated, vivid color palette very different from Manet's, but akin to that of the photograph. The resultant paintings Brown has made thus bear the marks of Manet and Bow Wow Wow, perhaps in equal measure. And, indeed, it takes careful study to begin to unravel which compositional elements might be drawn from each source—and which are invented anew, the artist's own interpolations.

As Brown has recounted in an interview for this volume, Bow Wow Wow's riff on Manet constituted a scandal, in some ways akin to that caused by the *Luncheon* itself, so many years before. The controversy stemmed, most centrally, from the inclusion of the central nude female figure, who in the Bow Wow Wow photograph was the band's

2 On Caillebotte and homoeroticism, see Norma Broude, "Outing Impressionism: Homosexuality and Homosocial Bonding in the Work of Caillebotte and Bazille," in *Gustave Caillebotte and the Fashioning of Identity in Impressionist Paris*, ed. Norma Broude (New Brunswick, NJ: Rutgers University Press, 2002), pp. 117–74.

3 Eve Kosofsky Sedgwick, *Between Men: English Literature and Male Homosocial Desire* (New York: Columbia University Press, 1985).

4 Shannon Keating, "It's Been 20 Years since 'Cruel Intentions,' and There's Never Been Another Movie Quite Like It," BuzzFeed News, March 5, 2019, https://www.buzzfeednews.com/article/shannonkeating/cruel-intentions-20th-anniversary-1999-sarah-michelle.

5 Glenn Garner, "Sarah Michelle Gellar on How She Speaks to Her Children about Gender and Sexuality," *People*, June 1, 2022, accessed July 20, 2023, https://people.com/parents/sarah-michelle-gellar-how-she-speaks-to-children-about-gender-sexuality.

6 Shirley Li, "Exclusive: *Cruel Intentions* Cast Spills All the Details on Making the Seductive Teen Drama," *Entertainment Weekly*, EW.com, March 21, 2019, accessed July 20, 2023, https://ew.com/movies/2019/03/21/cruel-intentions-oral-history.

7 Ernest Chesneau, *L'Art et les artistes modernes en France et en Angleterre* (Paris: Didier, 1864), p. 190; Michael Fried, *Manet's Modernism, or, The Face of Painting in the 1860s* (Chicago: University of Chicago Press, 1998), p. 131.

singer, Annabella Lwin—then a girl of fourteen, who nonetheless posed nude for the shoot. Her mother later pursued legal recourse, although Lwin herself continued playing with the band and remains a key member to this day. The initial album cover was replaced with a photographic rendition of Courbet's *Young Ladies on the Banks of the Seine* upon its release in the United States, in an apparent attempt to skirt controversy while nonetheless retaining a focus on Lwin, posed suggestively, though this time clothed.

Bow Wow Wow was formed by one of the foremost architects of punk, Malcolm McLaren, former manager of the Sex Pistols—and it was McLaren who conceptualized the album cover's homage to Manet. McLaren had studied art and was likely familiar with the history of Manet's *Luncheon*—and, moreover, with its scandalous reception.[8] Even if he was unaware of the painting's role in art history, the album cover effectively draws on that history, generating a new scandal in place of the historic one.

Much critical attention has been devoted to untangling exactly why Manet's two most famous masterpieces, *Olympia* and the *Luncheon on the Grass*, elicited such strong responses from the nineteenth-century public. Both shocked audiences, and, according to prevailing narratives, that shock gave rise to modern art as we know it—what Pierre Bourdieu called a "symbolic revolution."[9] Manet's importance is therefore inseparable from his scandalousness—and from his persistence in the face of critical disdain, which led him to exhibit the *Luncheon* at the Salon des Refusés after it was refused entry to the official state-sponsored Salon. Though art historical interpretations differ, most agree that the *Luncheon* was provocative as much for its depiction of sexuality as for its formally daring approach to the medium of painting. The nude female body was commonplace in academic French painting of the nineteenth century, but Manet's depiction of Victorine Meurent was intensely provocative—in part because of its unusual depiction of the naked body as contemporary, rather than safely historical or mythological.[10] With the Bow Wow Wow cover, McLaren, and the photographer Andy Earl, may have been quite intentionally courting a similar kind of succès de scandale.[11] Despite, or possibly because of, the controversy surrounding the album cover, Bow Wow Wow had a hit on its hands with "Go Wild in the Country," which entered the top ten in the UK charts.

In Brown's *Déjeuner*, the man sitting at left appears trouser-less. His naked leg is an element unfamiliar, neither from Manet's nor from Bow Wow Wow's iterations of the scene, and thus all the more striking. With this unsettling moment of partial nudity, as with the doubling of the female bathers in the background, Brown hints at the complex gender and sexual politics of the *Luncheon*, so pivotal both for Manet and for Bow Wow Wow. To unravel the possibilities suggested by this errant leg, one must consider not only the nudity of Manet's painting but also the potentially exploitative nudity of Bow Wow Wow's cover. As with McKinniss's paintings, Brown's must be read in concert with Manet and with the succession of responses to Manet that have led us to today.

Like Brown, Jill Mulleady explores the gendering of the nude body in Manet's *Luncheon* with her *Suddenly, Last Summer* (2022). Here, Mulleady condenses two Manet paintings representing the same model, Victorine Meurent. Mulleady reproduces the distinctive seated pose adopted by Meurent in the *Luncheon*, with some changes: Mulleady's model, Nicole-Antonia Spagnola—herself an artist and musician—turns more fully toward the viewer than does Meurent, and she raises one hand to her mouth, holding a strawberry, in an echo of Manet's *Street Singer*, in which Meurent is pictured eating cherries. Mulleady portrays Spagnola not starkly naked, as Meurent was so famously in the *Luncheon*, but attired in a boyish suit, its browns and grays bringing to mind not only the coat Meurent wears in *The Street Singer*, but also the dark jackets of the men lounging fully clothed in the *Luncheon*. Those men, Meurent's companions in the *Luncheon*, are absent from Mulleady's composition, the picnic becoming a solitary one. As in Manet's *Luncheon*, Mulleady includes a bather in the distance, but hers is male, rather than female, and nude against the foaming waves. Through these transformations and reversals, Mulleady reorients the mechanics of gender and desire in her painting—the female model, no longer exposed for the viewer's gaze or for those around her, is now a consumer, eating the titular picnic left untouched in Manet's masterpiece. And, naturally, this inversion of Manet's portrayal of gender cannot be disentangled from the long afterlife of the *Luncheon* in art and in criticism. We might think, here, too, of Nina Chanel Abney, Caitlin Cherry, and Christina Quarles, who make the latent eroticism of the *Luncheon* impossible to ignore in their own rejoinders to Manet. Each of these artists seems in dialogue not only with Manet, but with his place in the story of modern art, as we receive it.

Manet's *Luncheon* is so ubiquitous as to be haunted by its own representation—few of us can likely see the painting without recalling some reinterpretation of it. Even in the Musée d'Orsay, where the work hangs prominently today, it faces Claude Monet's answer to Manet—his own *Luncheon on the Grass*, a sprawlingly large and unfinished composition that the artist cut into fragments following damage to its surface. Two such fragments of Monet's work accompany Manet's *Luncheon*, an ever-present reminder of the work's status as a kind of art historical starting point, ripe for reinvention—as much today as it was already in 1865.

Perhaps Manet's *Luncheon on the Grass* remains such a crucial reference for today's contemporary artists in part because of this long arc of the painting's history, from Raphael and Raimondi through to Manet himself and on to Monet, Picasso, and all the subsequent reinterpreters of the painting's theme. Manet's painting stands not merely for itself, but for artistic appropriation and reassembly as a model for creation. Paintings like those by McKinniss, Brown, and Mulleady explore the accretion of meaning as visual ideas are presented and re-presented over time and across media, transforming with each turn. Manet's *Luncheon* has, perhaps by an accident of history, come to signify the possibilities of revisiting the past in order to produce decisively new art. His painting embodies this strategy, in its deployment of a reused figural grouping, but it also provides a demonstration of how a work of art can create a dialogue that unfolds over generations.

8 Ian Chapman, "Luncheon on the Grass with Manet and Bow Wow Wow: Still Disturbing after All These Years," *Music in Art* 35, nos. 1–2 (2010): 96.

9 Pierre Bourdieu, *Manet: A Symbolic Revolution* (New York: John Wiley & Sons, 2018).

10 See, for instance, Anne McCauley, "Sex and the Salon: Defining Art and Immorality in 1863," in *Manet's "Le Déjeuner sur l'herbe,"* ed. Paul Hayes Tucker (Cambridge: Cambridge University Press, 1998), pp. 37–74.

11 As Ian Chapman has discussed, McLaren's investment in a punk ethos of rebellion and unorthodoxy is difficult to separate from his engagement in a series of projects involving the sexualization of adolescents, including the Bow Wow Wow cover shoot. See Chapman, "Luncheon on the Grass with Manet and Bow Wow Wow": 95–104.

# PLATES I

Nina Chanel Abney
*Outdoor Dining #1*, 2022
Spray paint on canvas
60 × 60 in. (152.4 × 152.4 cm)

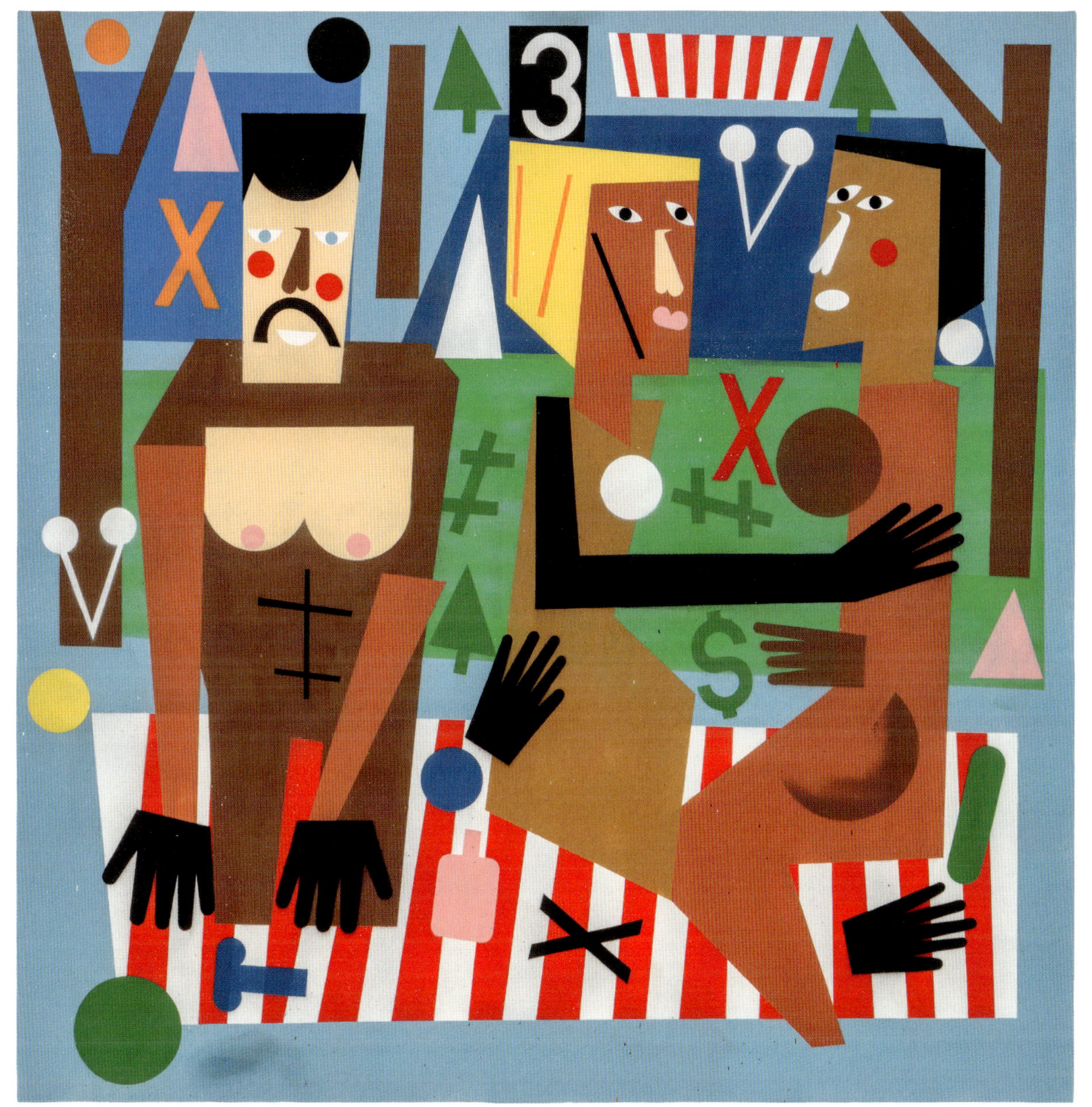

Diane Arbus
*A family one evening in a nudist camp, Pa. 1965*
Printed by Diane Arbus 1966–69
Gelatin silver print
Sheet: 20 × 16 in. (50.8 cm × 40.5 cm)

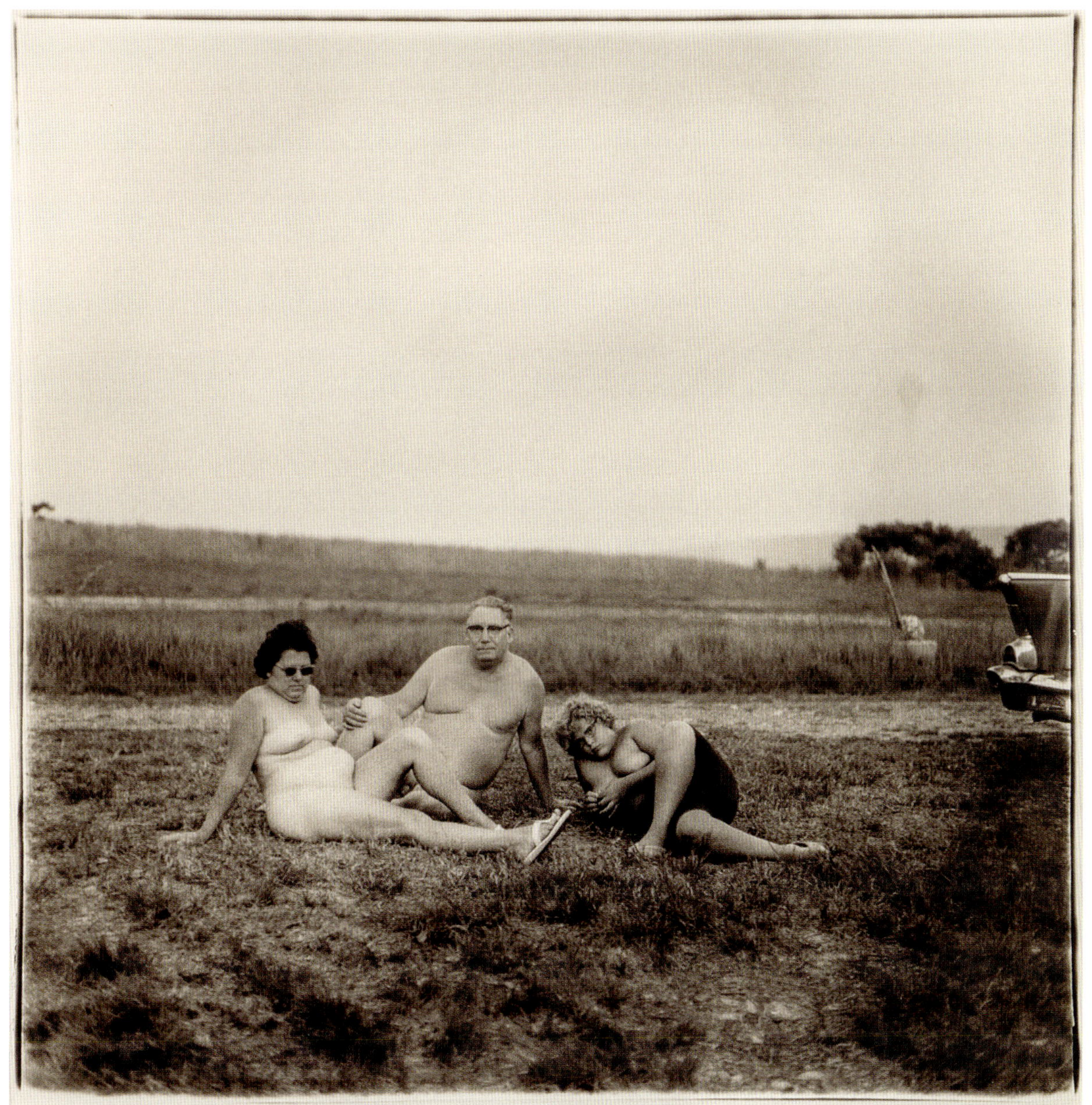

Vanessa Beecroft
Jeffrey Deitch and Deitch Projects artists posing in a set inspired by Paul McCarthy's *The Garden* (1991–92) for *Harper's Bazaar* in 2000
Photo by Jason Schmidt

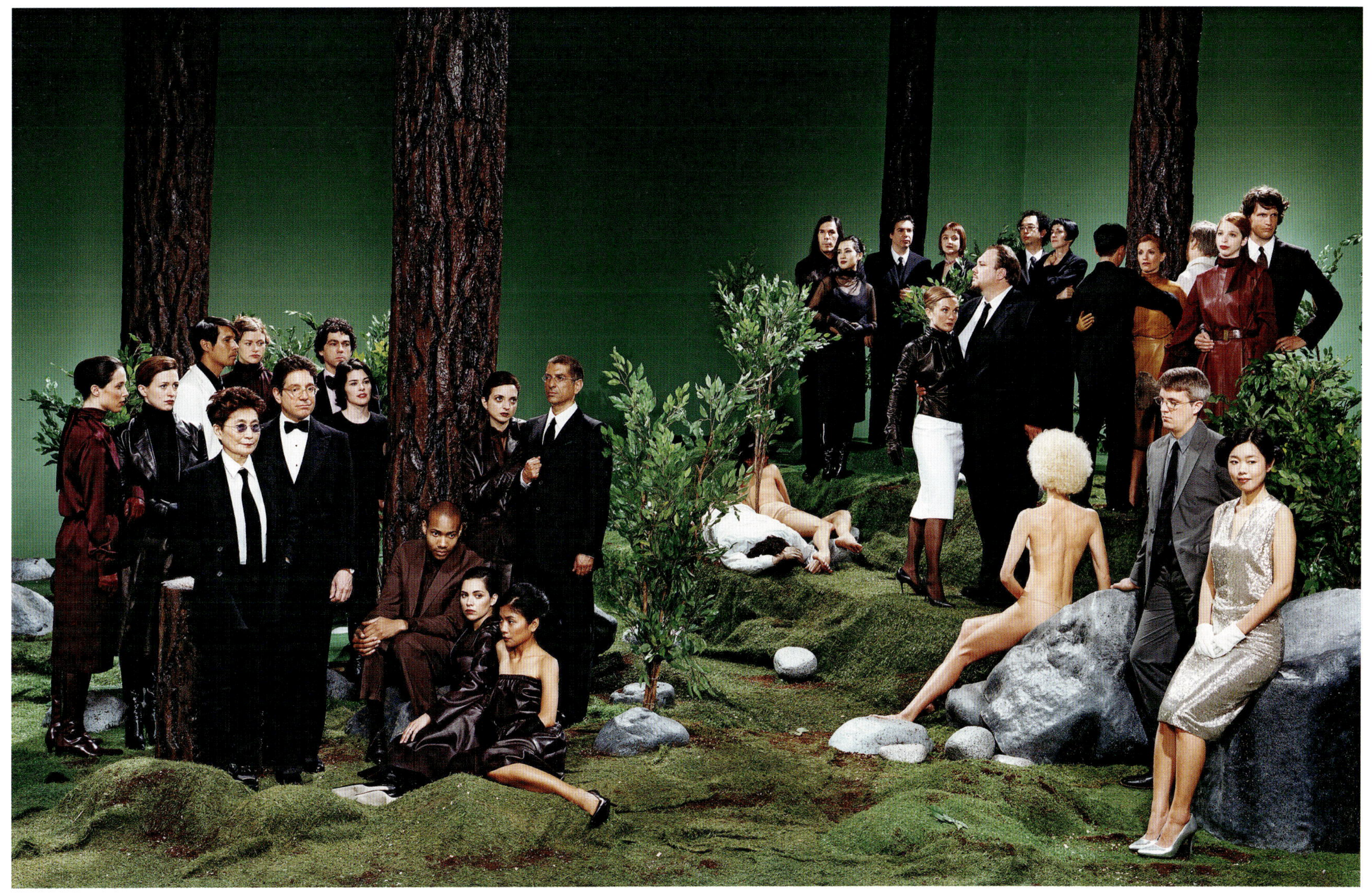

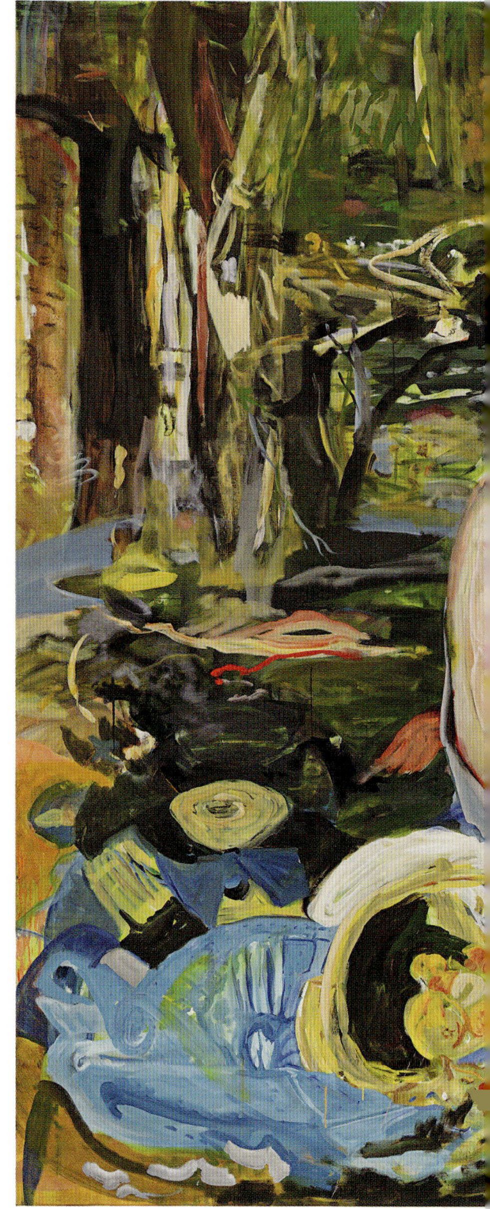

Cecily Brown
*Le Déjeuner sur l'herbe*, 2021–22
Oil on linen
Diptych, overall: 105 ½ × 211 in.
(268 × 535.9 cm)

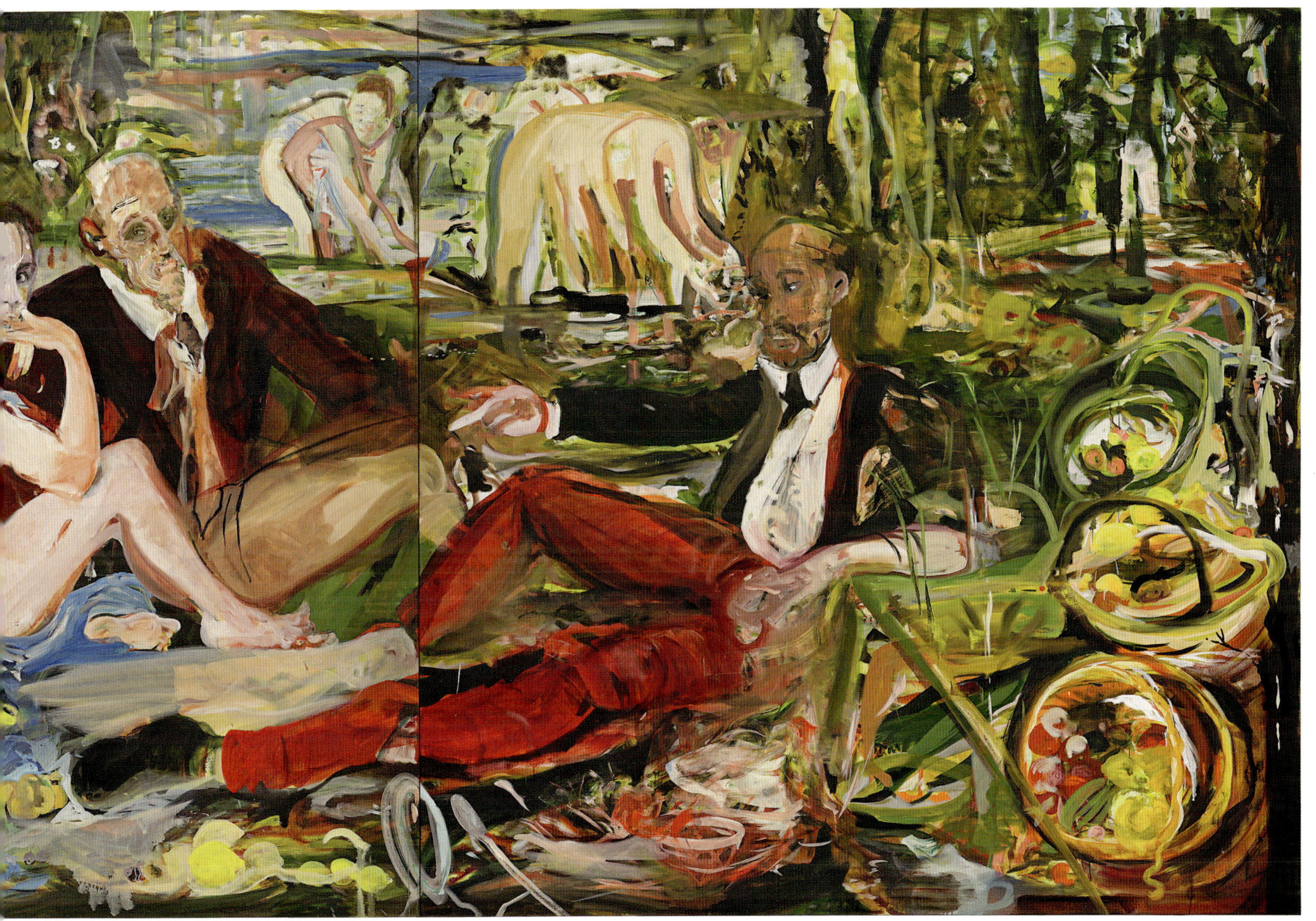

Cecily Brown
*Luncheon on the Grass*, 2021–22
Oil on linen
73 × 83 in. (185.4 × 210.8 cm)

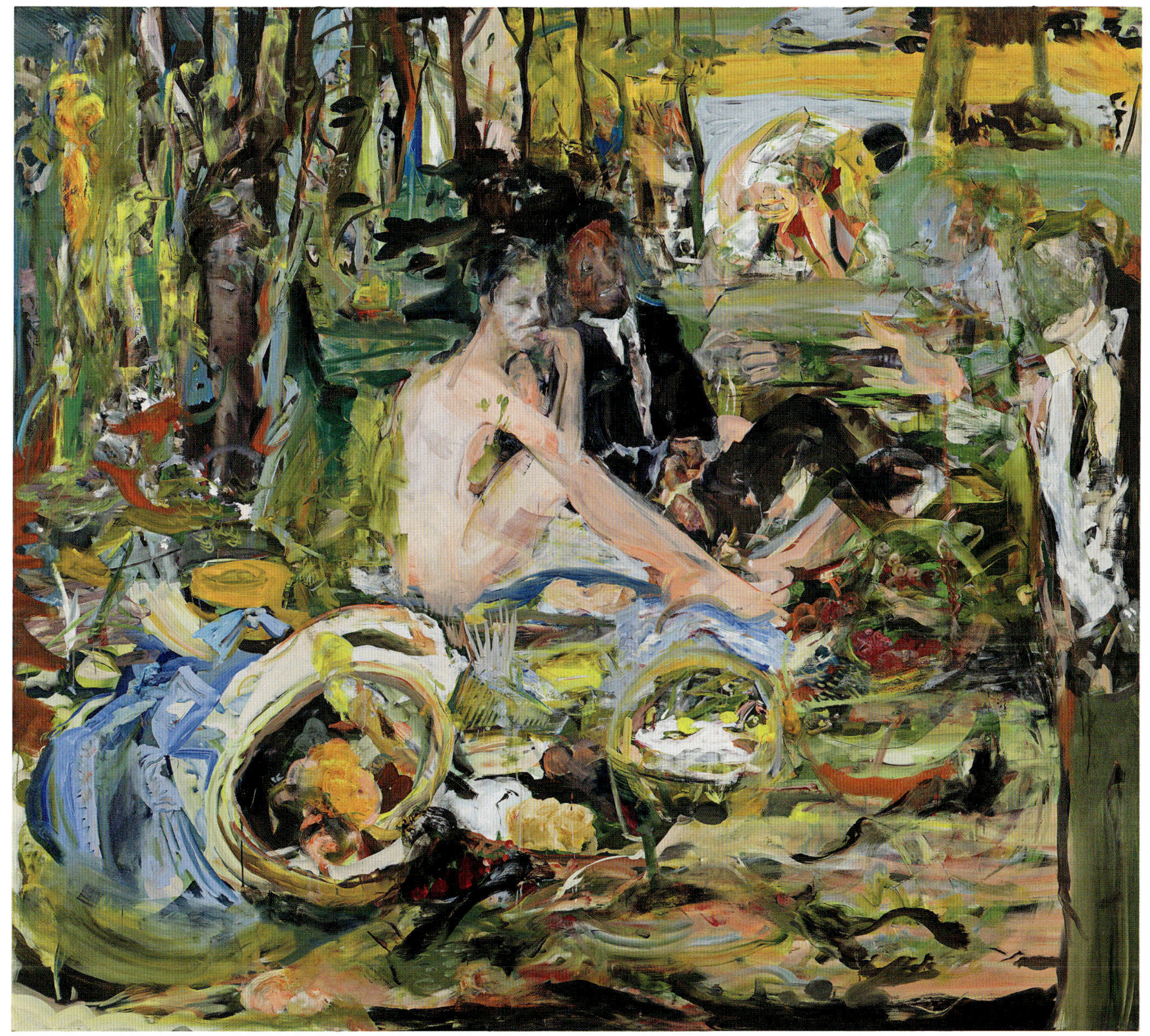

Cecily Brown
*Go Wild in the Country*, 2021–22
Oil on linen
73 × 83 in. (185.4 × 210.8 cm)

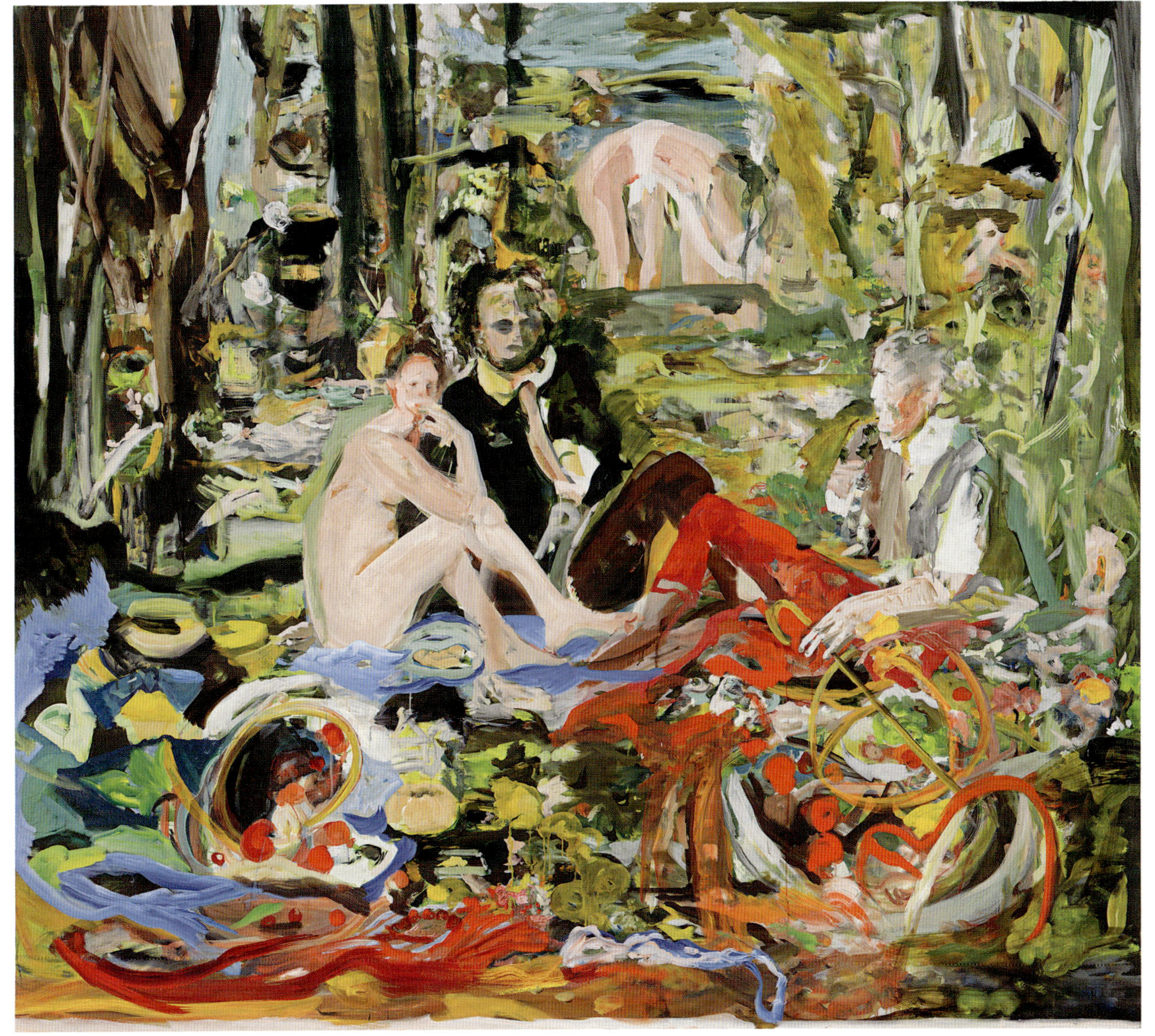

Caitlin Cherry
*Mixed Clout Relationships (Feast of the Ass)*, 2022
Oil on canvas
59 × 102 in. (149.9 × 259 cm)

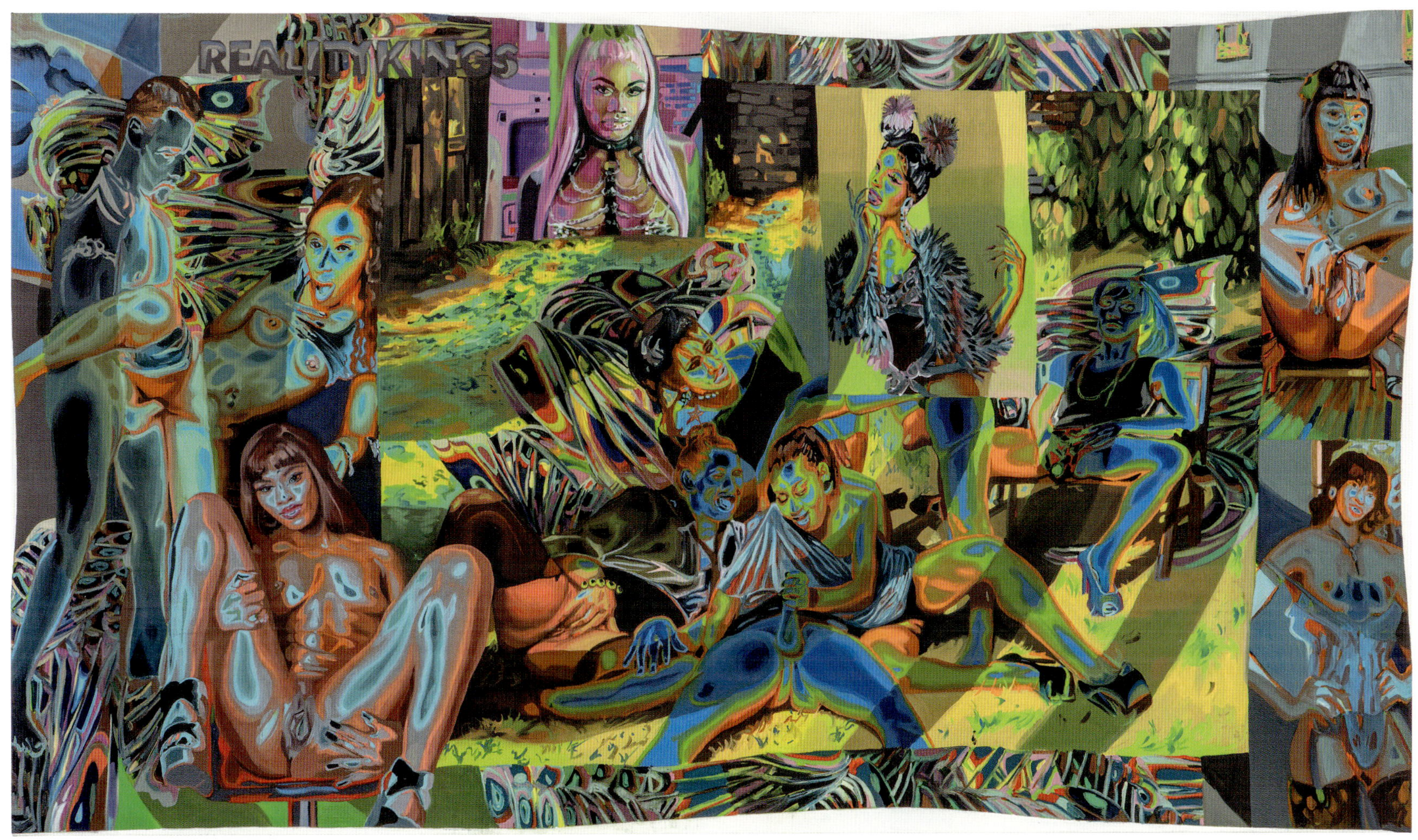

Joe Coleman
*Le Déjeuner sur l'herbe avec la Dieu Fée Mère de l'Avant-garde (Luncheon on the Grass with the Fairy Godmother of the Avant-garde)*, 2020
Acrylic on panel
14 × 11 in. (35.6 × 27.9 cm)

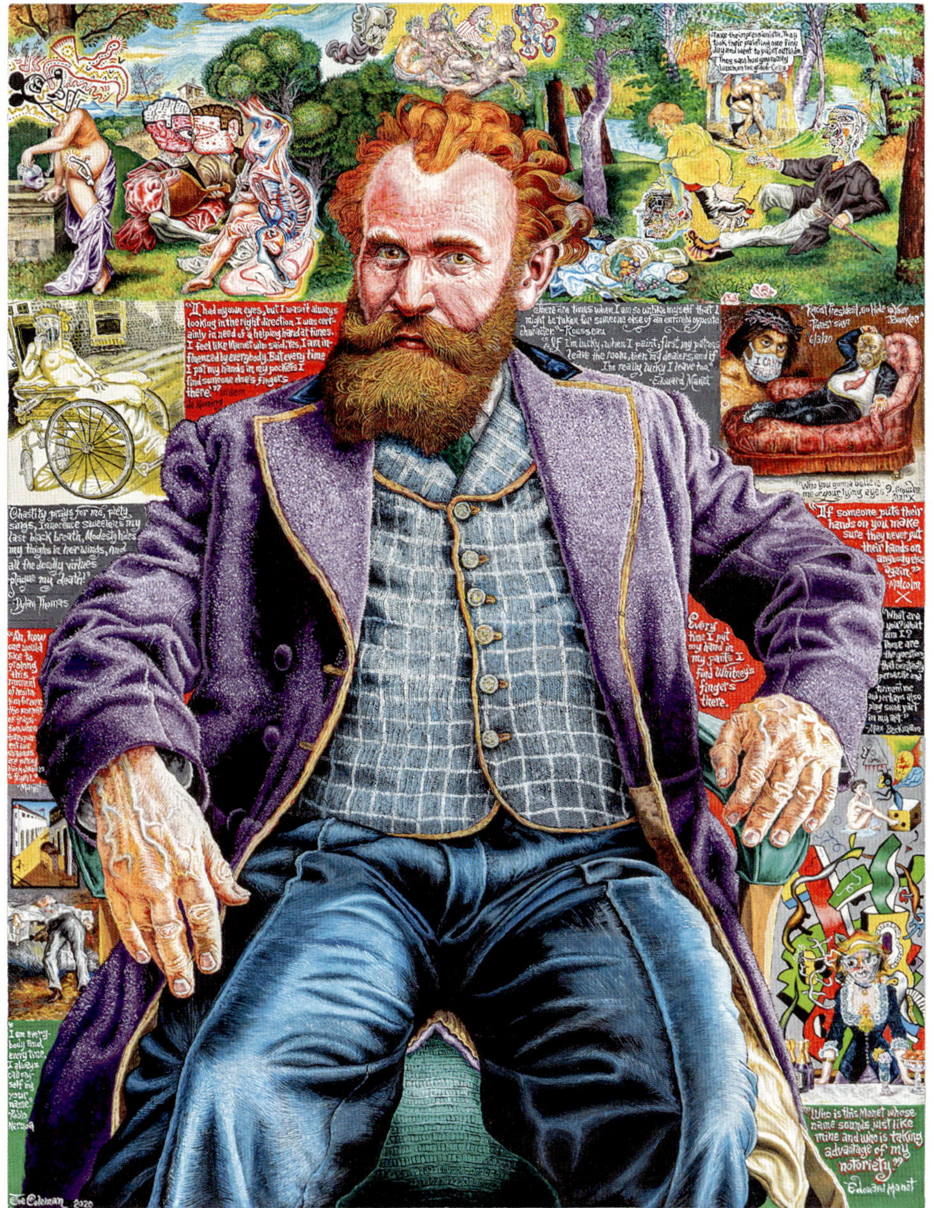
"Take the impressionists. They took their painting one fine day and went to paint outside.
"I had my own eyes, but I wasn't always looking in the right direction. I was certainly in need of a helping hand at times. I feel like Manet who said, Yes, I am influenced by everybody. But every time I put my hands in my pockets I find someone else's fingers there." Willem de Kooning
"There are times when I am so unlike myself that I might be taken for someone else of an entirely opposite character." -Rousseau
"If I'm lucky, when I paint, first my patrons leave the room, then my dealers, and if I'm really lucky I leave too." -Edouard Manet
"Racist President, go Hide in Your Bunker" -Protest sign 6/3/20
I CAN'T BREATHE
"Who you gonna believe - me or your lying eyes?" -Groucho Marx
"Chastity prays for me, piety sings, Innocence sweetens my last black breath, Modesty hides my thighs in her wings, And all the deadly virtues plague my death!" -Dylan Thomas
"If someone puts their hands on you make sure they never put their hands on anybody else again." -Malcolm X
Every time I put my hand in my pants I find Whitney's fingers there.
"What are you? What am I? These are the questions that constantly persecute and torment me and perhaps also play some part in my art." -Max Beckmann
"I am everybody and every time. I always call myself by your name." -Pablo Neruda
"Who is this Monet whose name sounds just like mine and who is taking advantage of my notoriety?" -Edouard Manet
Joe Coleman 2020

Robert Colescott
*Sunday Afternoon with Joaquin Murietta*, 1979
Acrylic on canvas
Framed: 73 × 85 in. (185.4 × 215.9 cm)

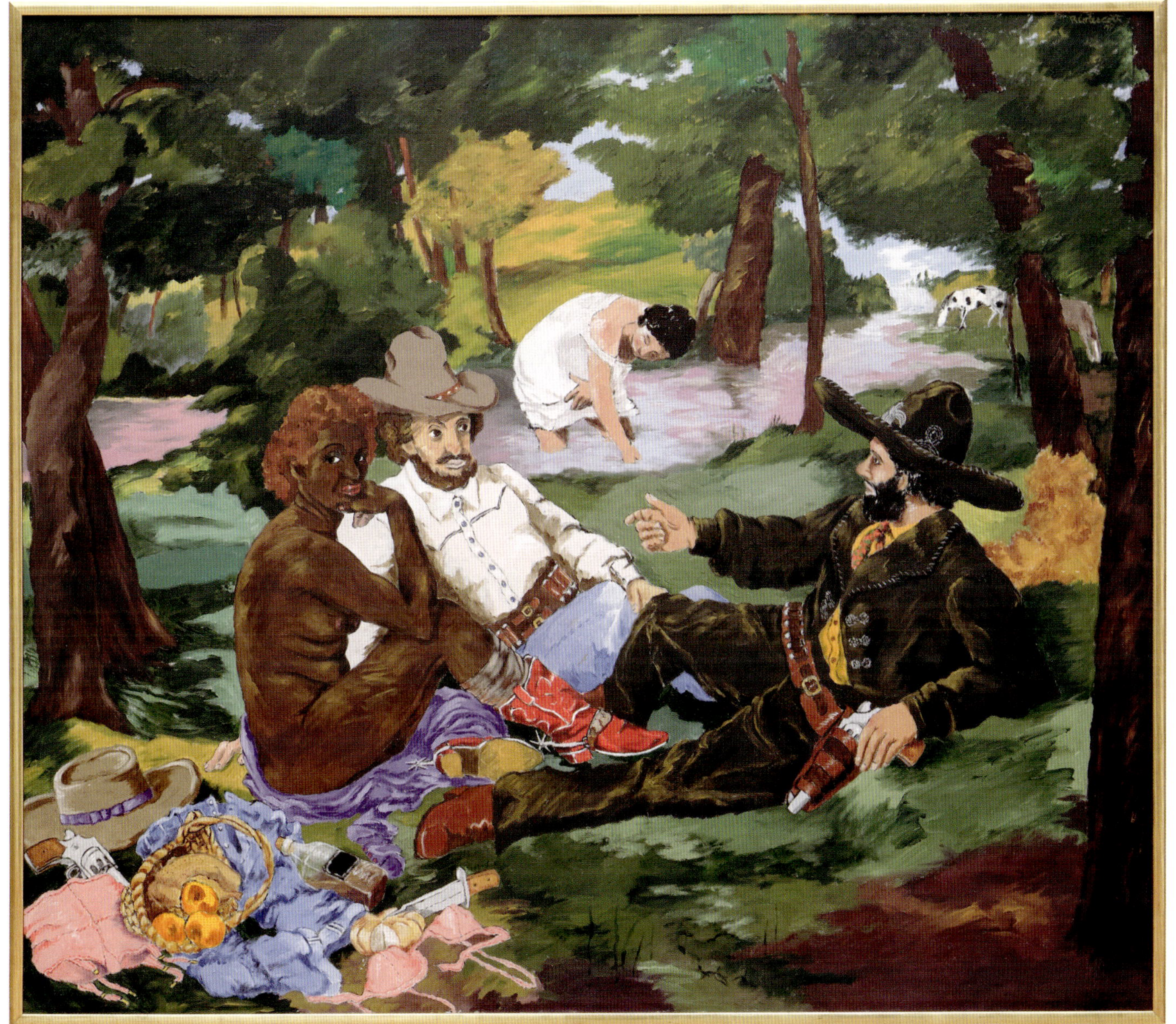

Somaya Critchlow
*Mr. Peanut! (The Picnic)*, 2020–21
Oil on linen
35 ½ × 27 ¾ in. (90 × 70.4 cm)

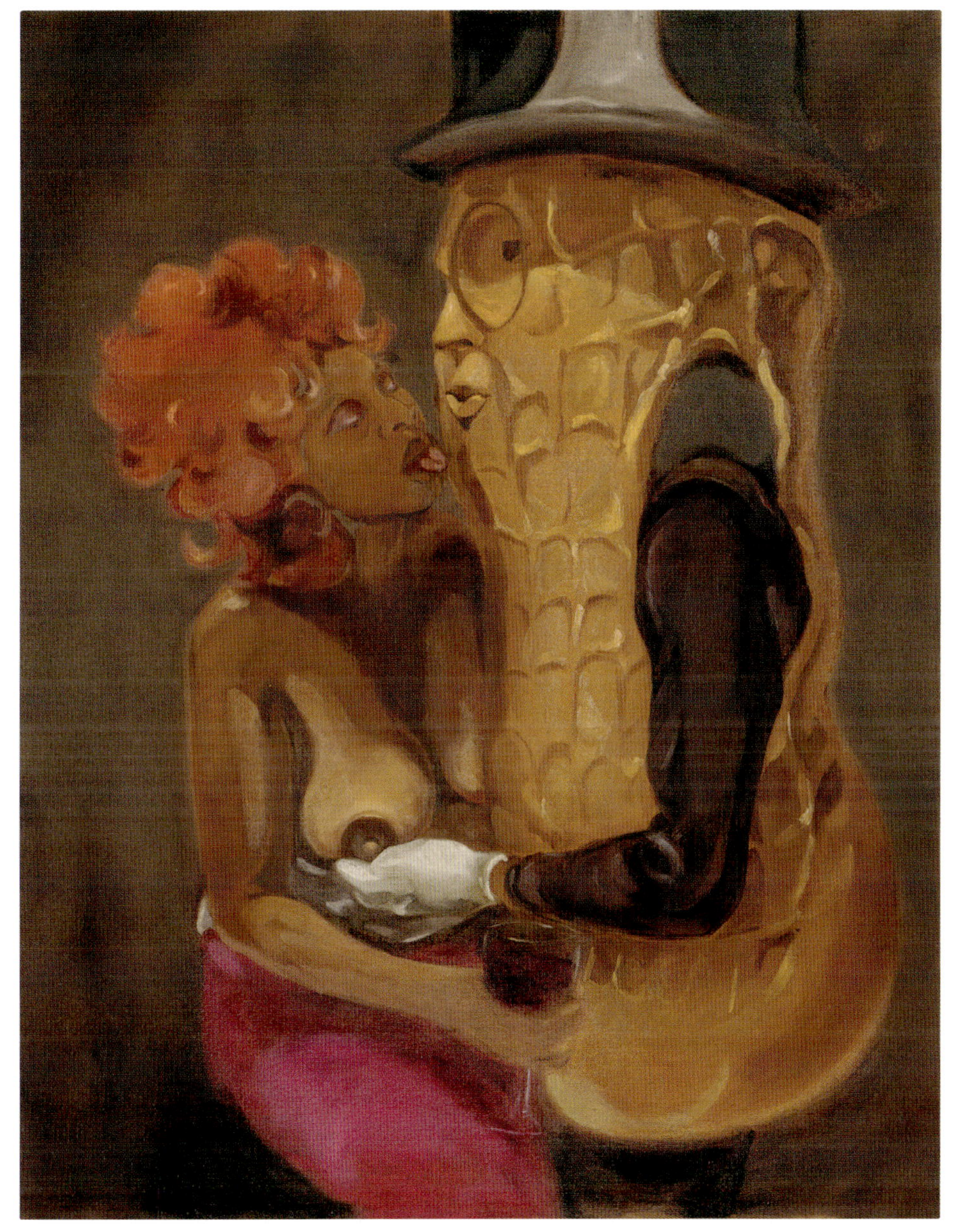

Celeste Dupuy-Spencer
*Ode to Enjoyments*, 2022
Oil on linen
70 × 60 in. (177.8 × 152.4 cm)

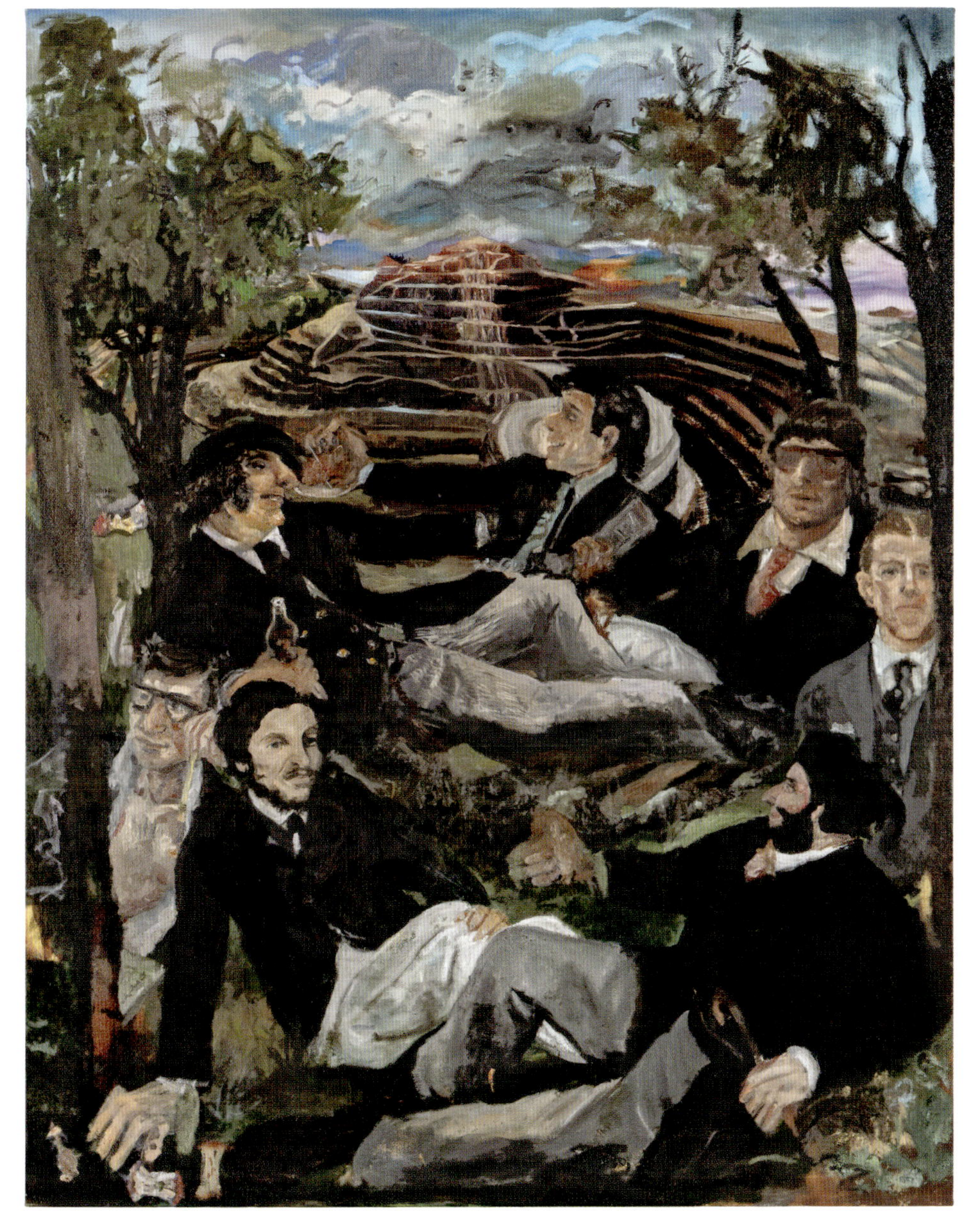

Dominique Fung
*Sans Les Mains*, 2022
Oil on canvas
81 ⅞ × 104 ⅛ in. (208 × 264.5 cm)

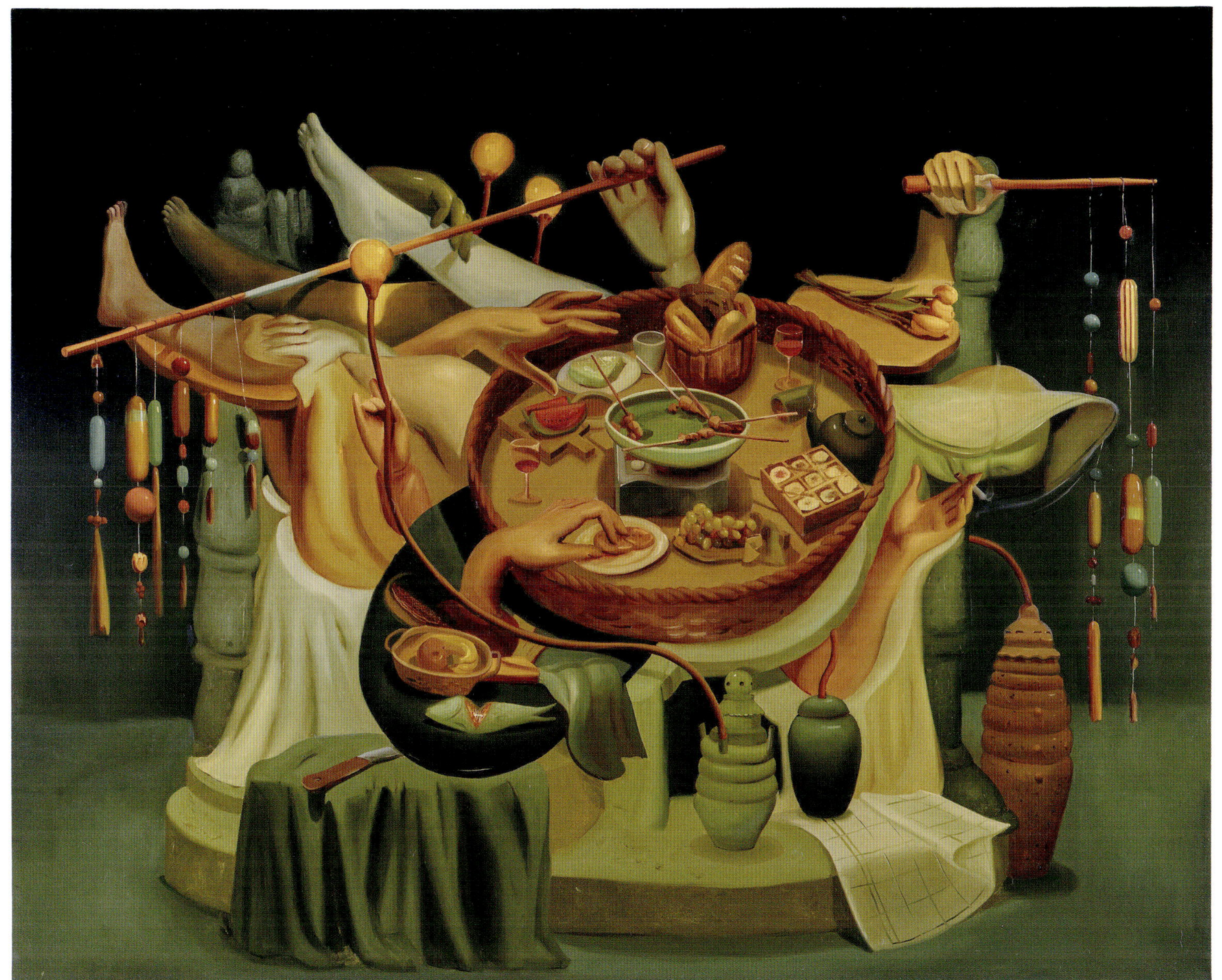

Alain Jacquet
*Le Déjeuner sur l'herbe*, 1964
Silkscreen on canvas
68 ⅞ × 76 ¾ in. (175 × 195 cm)
Unique variant (in a series estimated at 100)

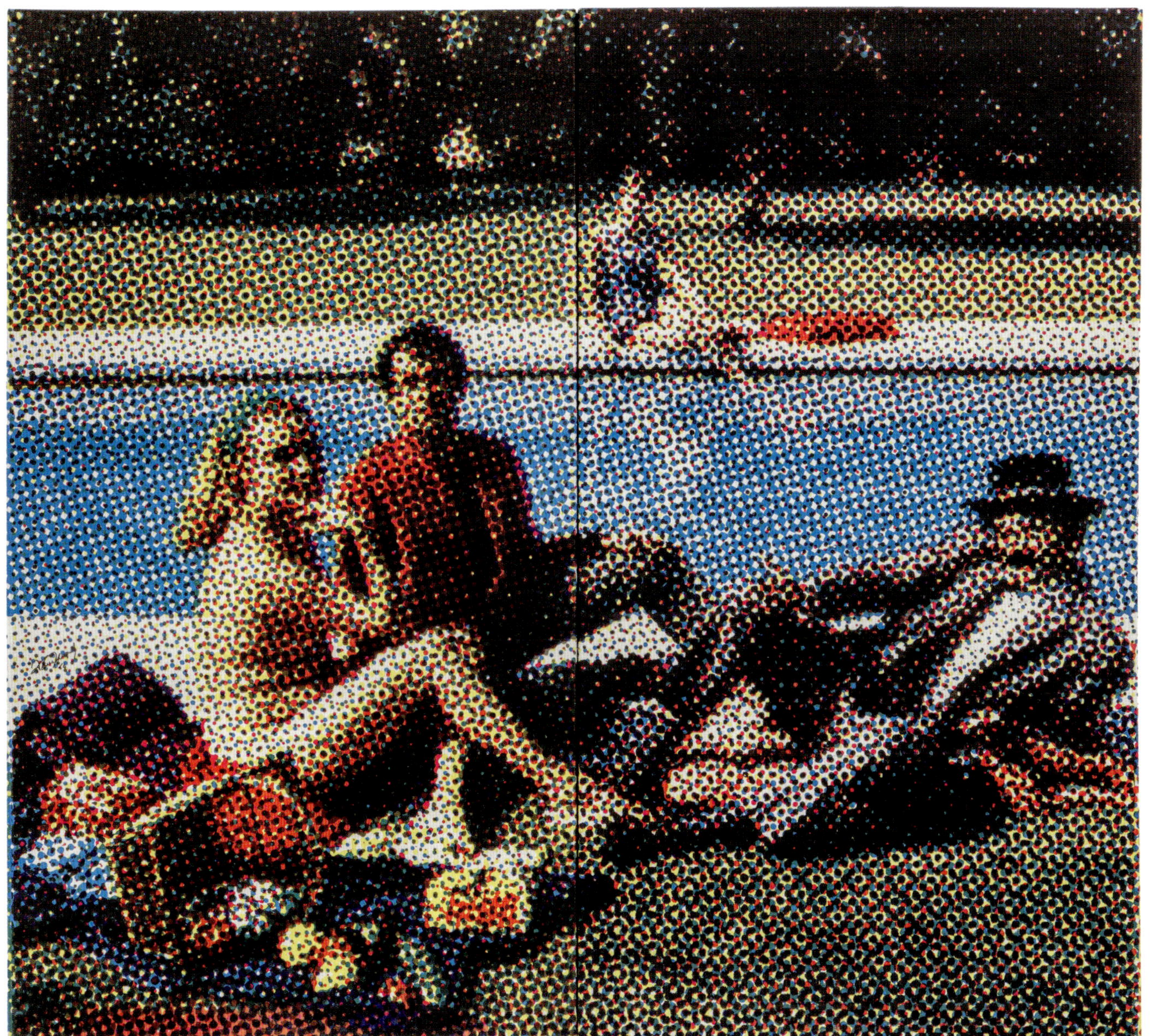

Sophie Matisse
*Be Right Back*, 2003
Gouache on paper
Framed: 14 × 16 in. (35.6 × 40.6 cm)

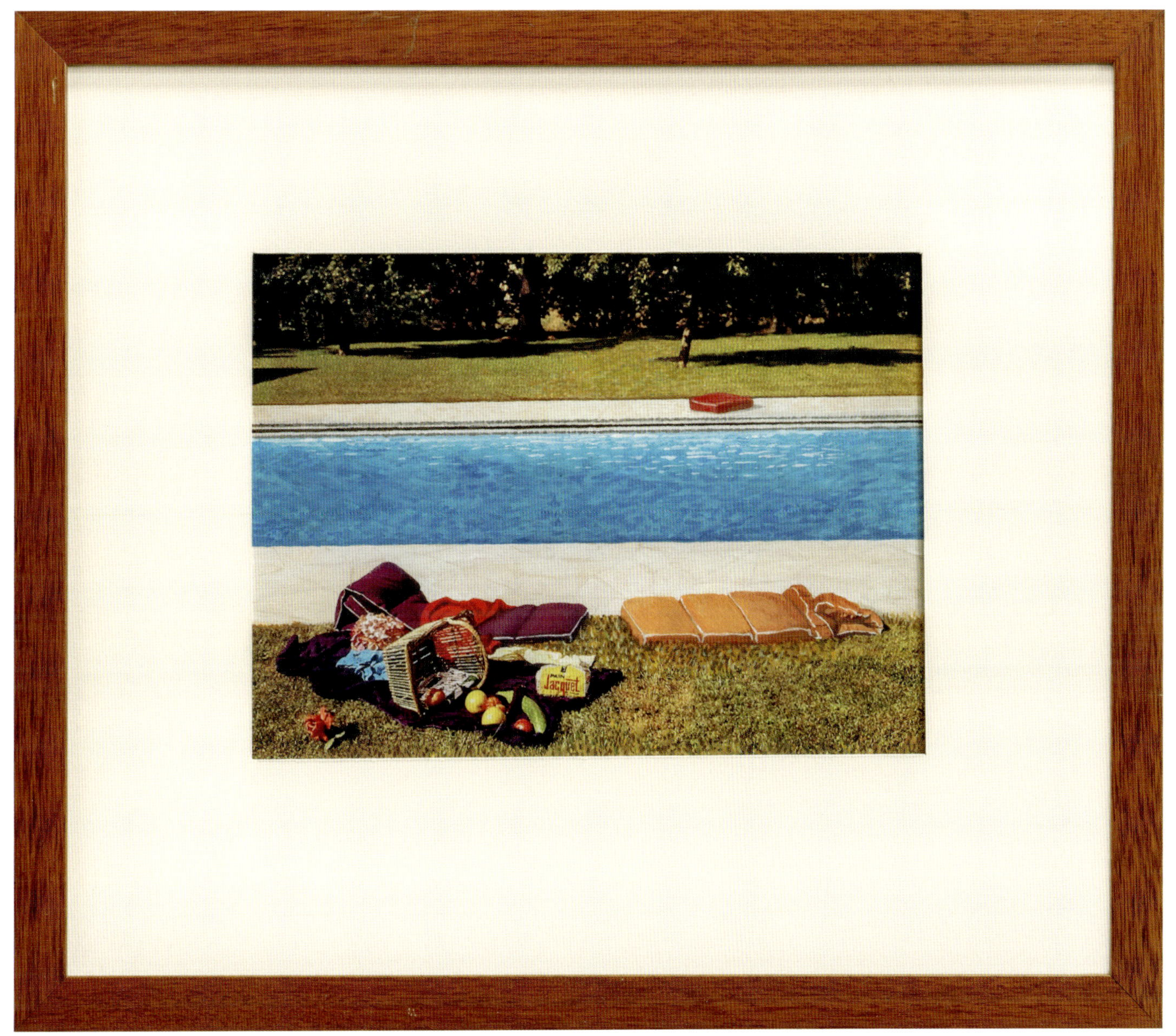
PAIN
Jacquet

Kurt Kauper
*Men in the Park*, 2022
Oil on dibond
36 × 48 in. (91.4 × 121.9 cm)

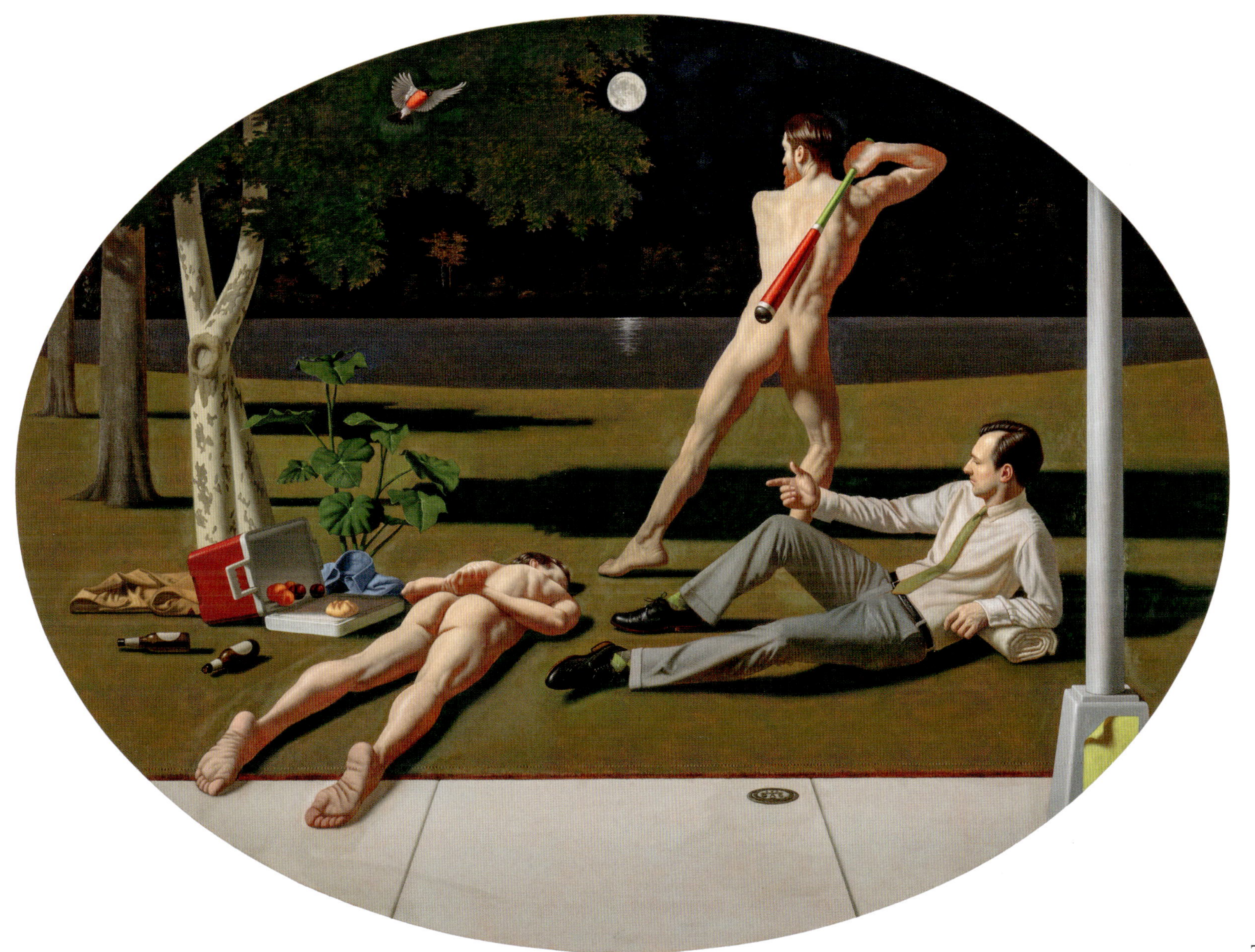

Karen Kilimnik
*La Fôret*, 2021
Water-soluble oil color on canvas
14 × 18 in. (35.5 × 45.5 cm)

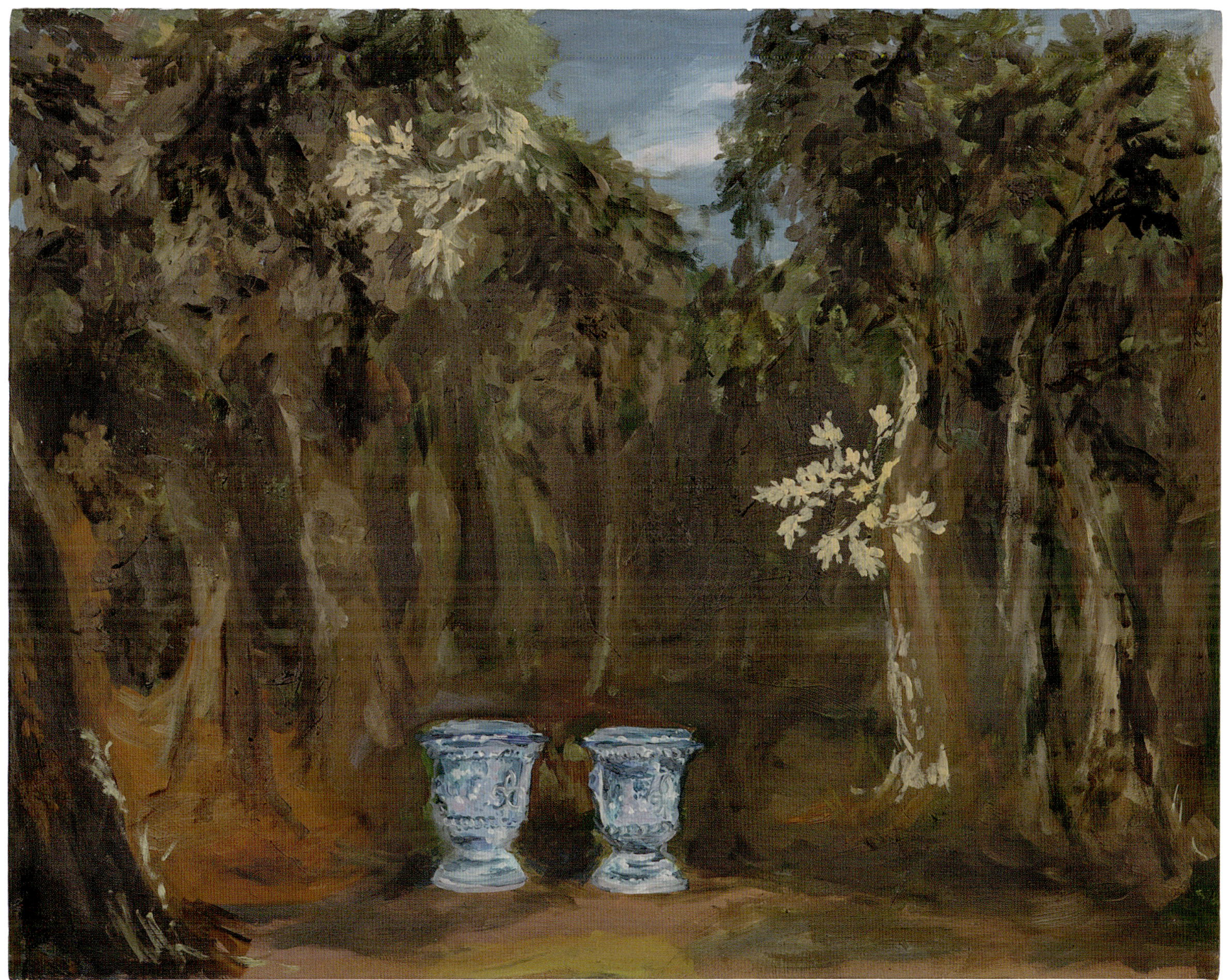

Cindy Ji Hye Kim
*Luncheon on the Grass, after Manet*, 2022
Graphite and acrylic paint on wall
82 × 104 in. (208.3 × 264.2 cm)

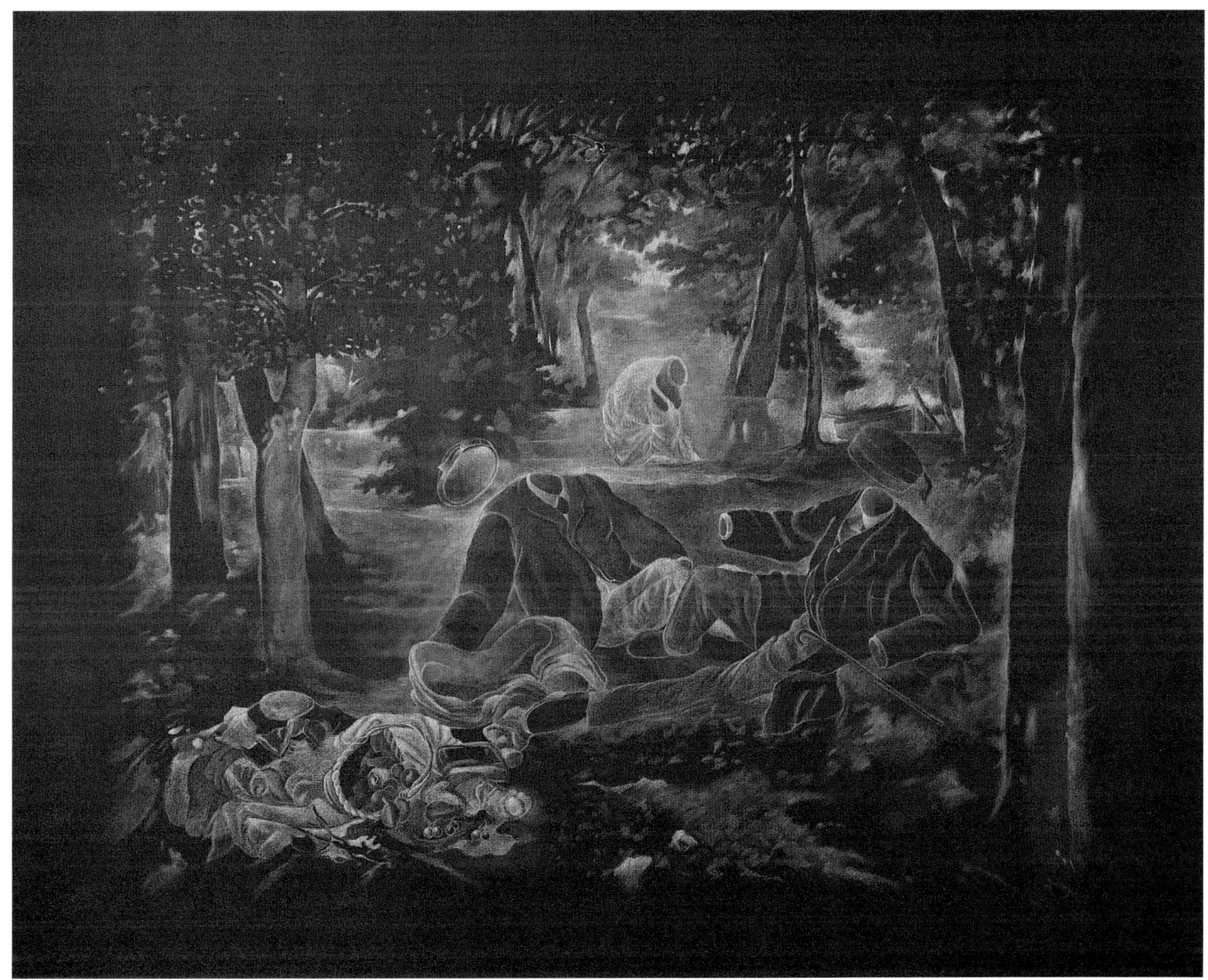

Jeff Koons
*Gazing Ball (Manet Luncheon on the Grass),*
2014–15
Oil on canvas, glass, and aluminum
63 × 81 ¼ × 14 ¾ in. (160 × 206.4 × 37.5 cm)

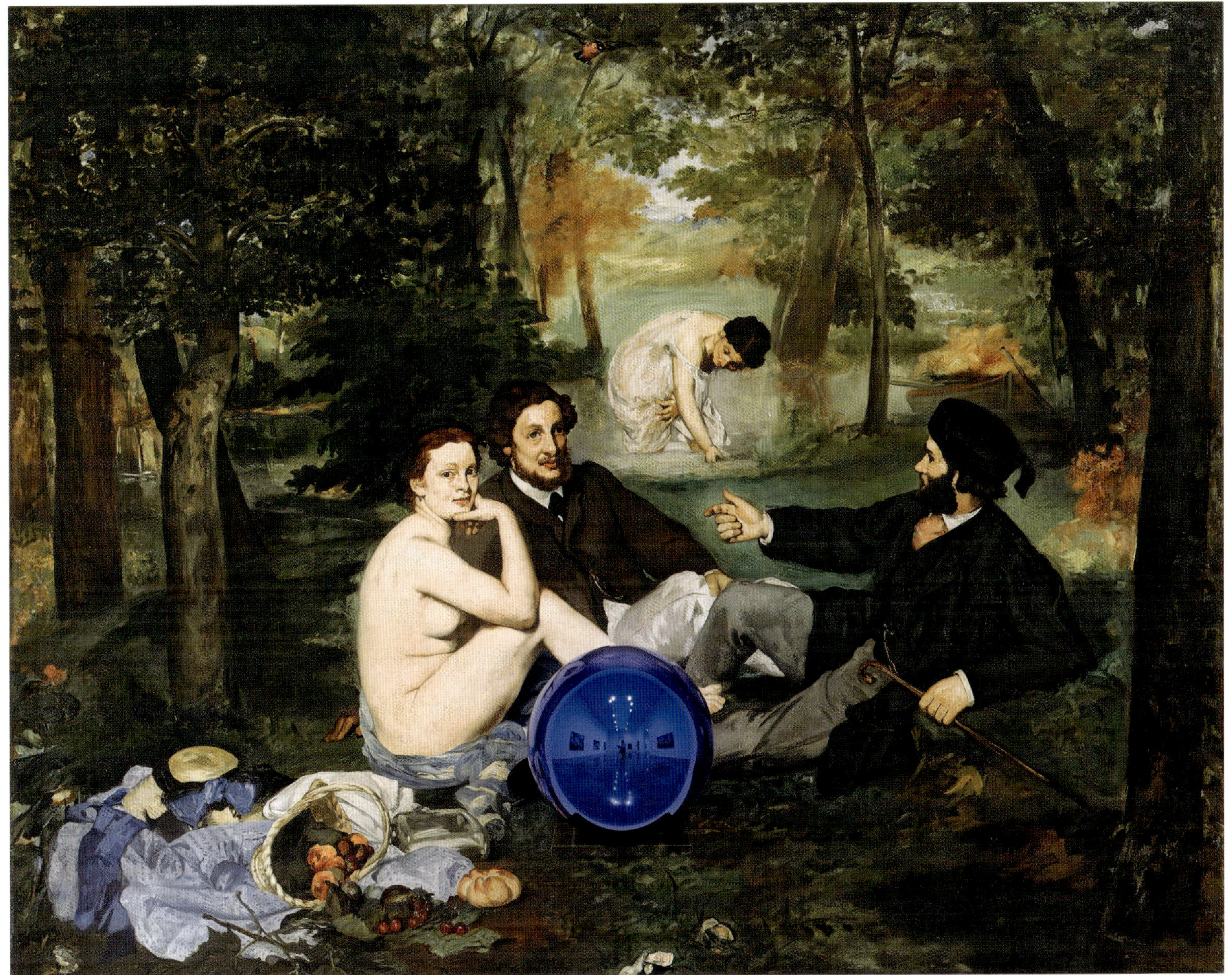

Ella Kruglyanskaya
*The Rug and the Blinds (Red)*, 2022
Oil on linen
82 × 64 in. (208.3 × 162.6 cm)

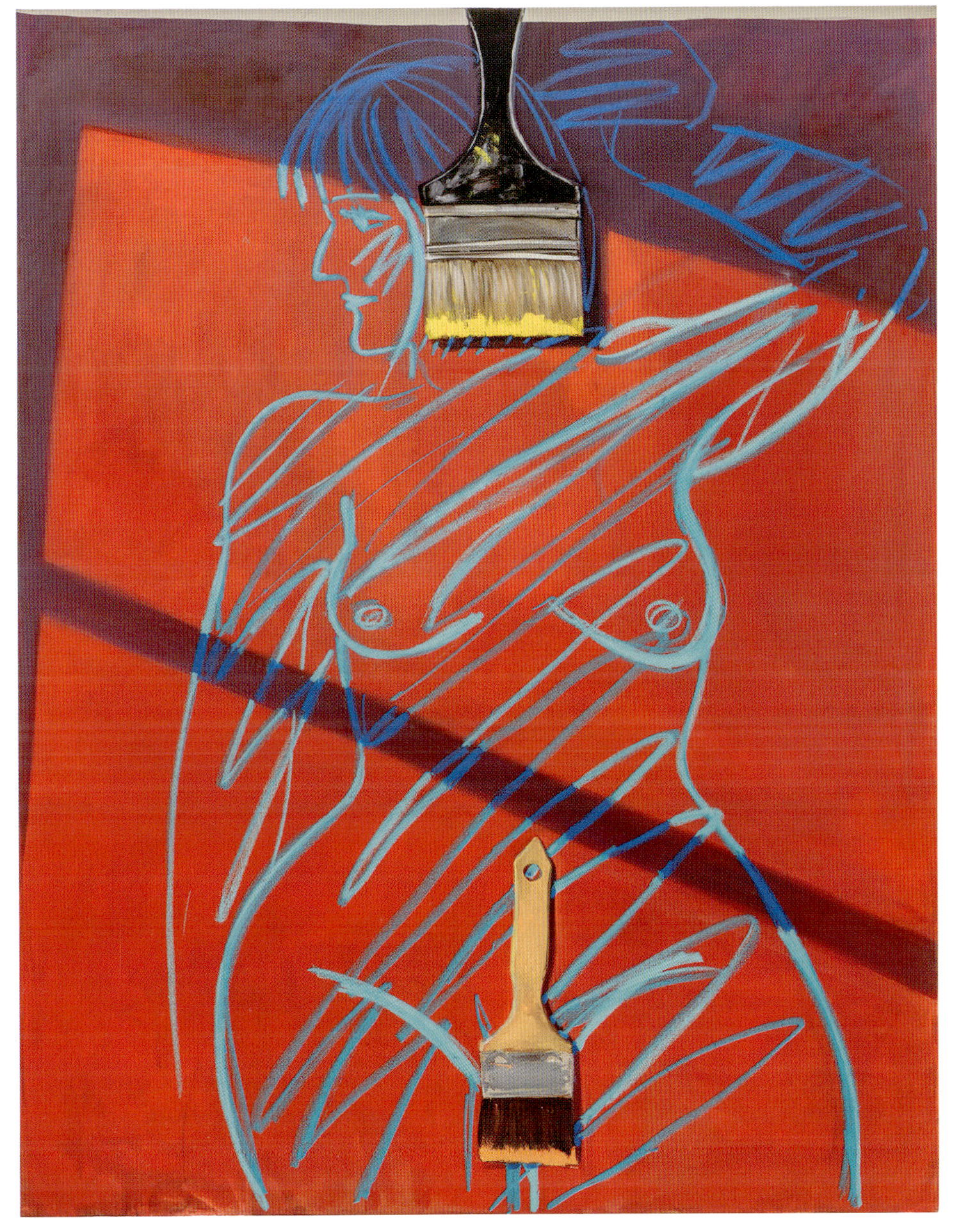

Liu Xiaodong
*Newcomers in the Village—Response to Manet*, 2021
Oil on canvas
98 ⅜ × 118 in. (250 × 300 cm)

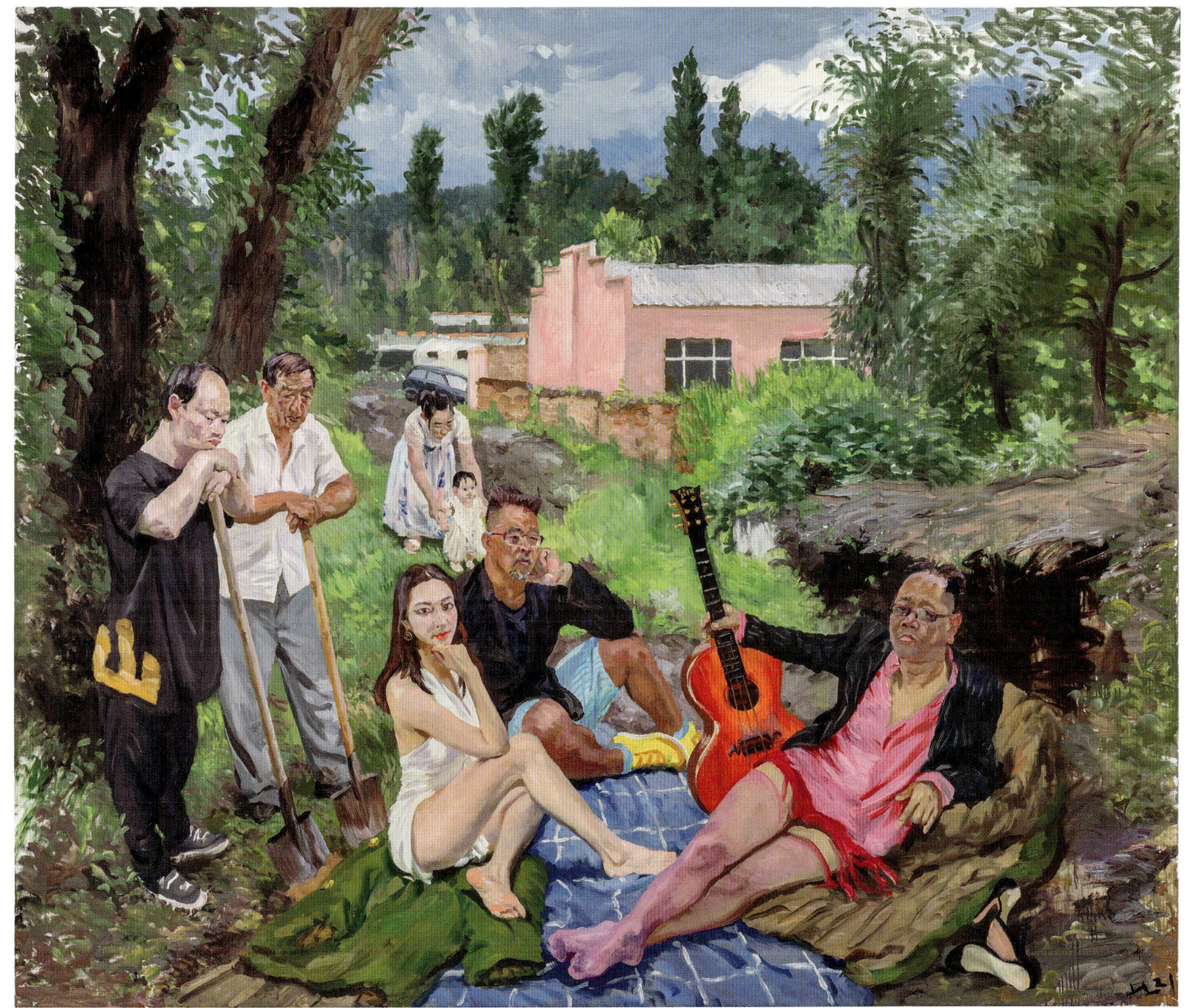

Liu Xiaodong
*Coming across a scene like this one cannot but think of Manet's Le Déjeuner sur l'herbe*
*2020.06.12*, 2020
Watercolor on paper
10 ¼ × 14 ⅛ in. (26 × 36 cm)

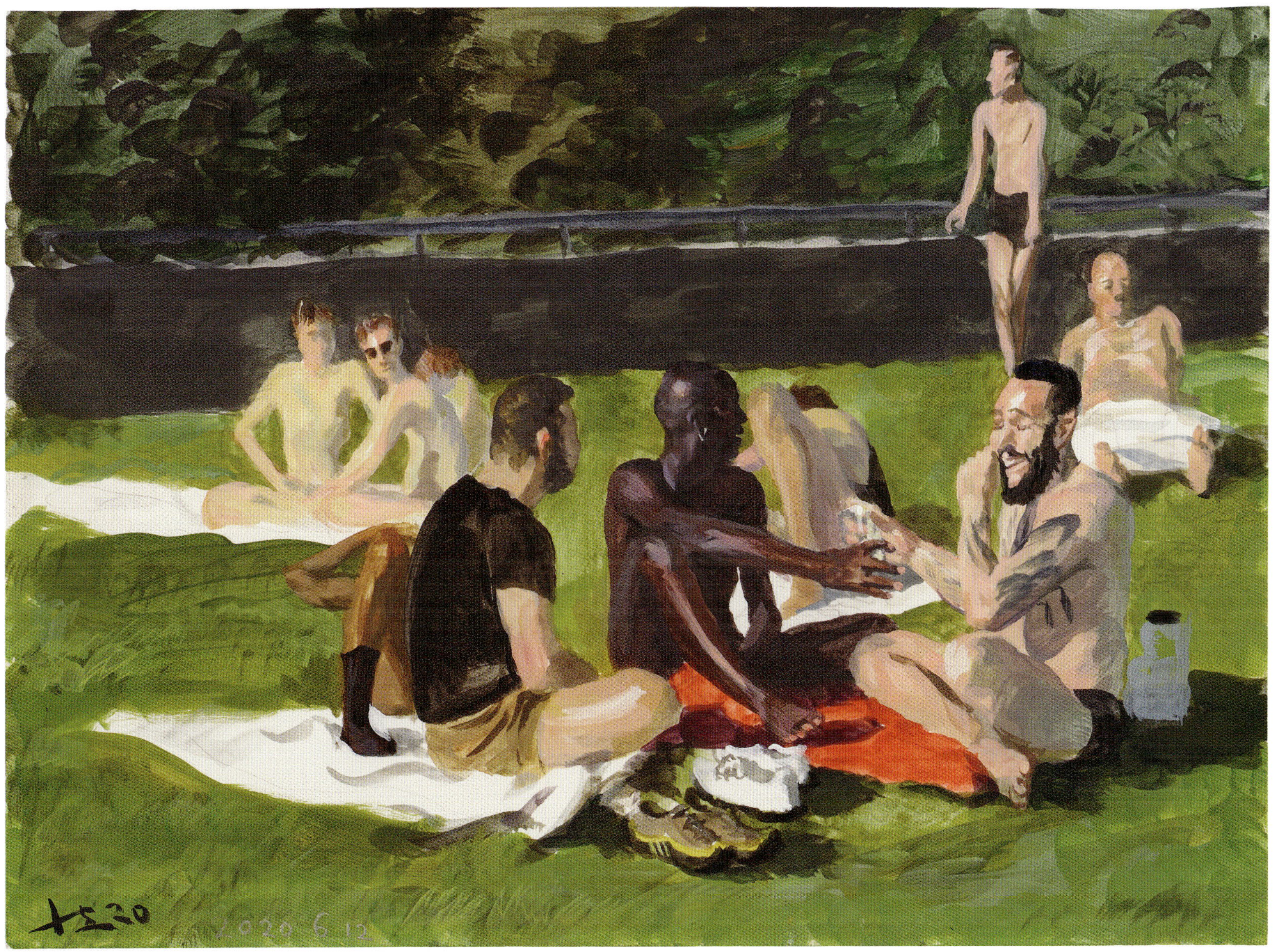
2020 6 12

Tala Madani
*Pickled*, 2022
Oil on linen
15 × 12 in. (38.1 × 30.5 cm)

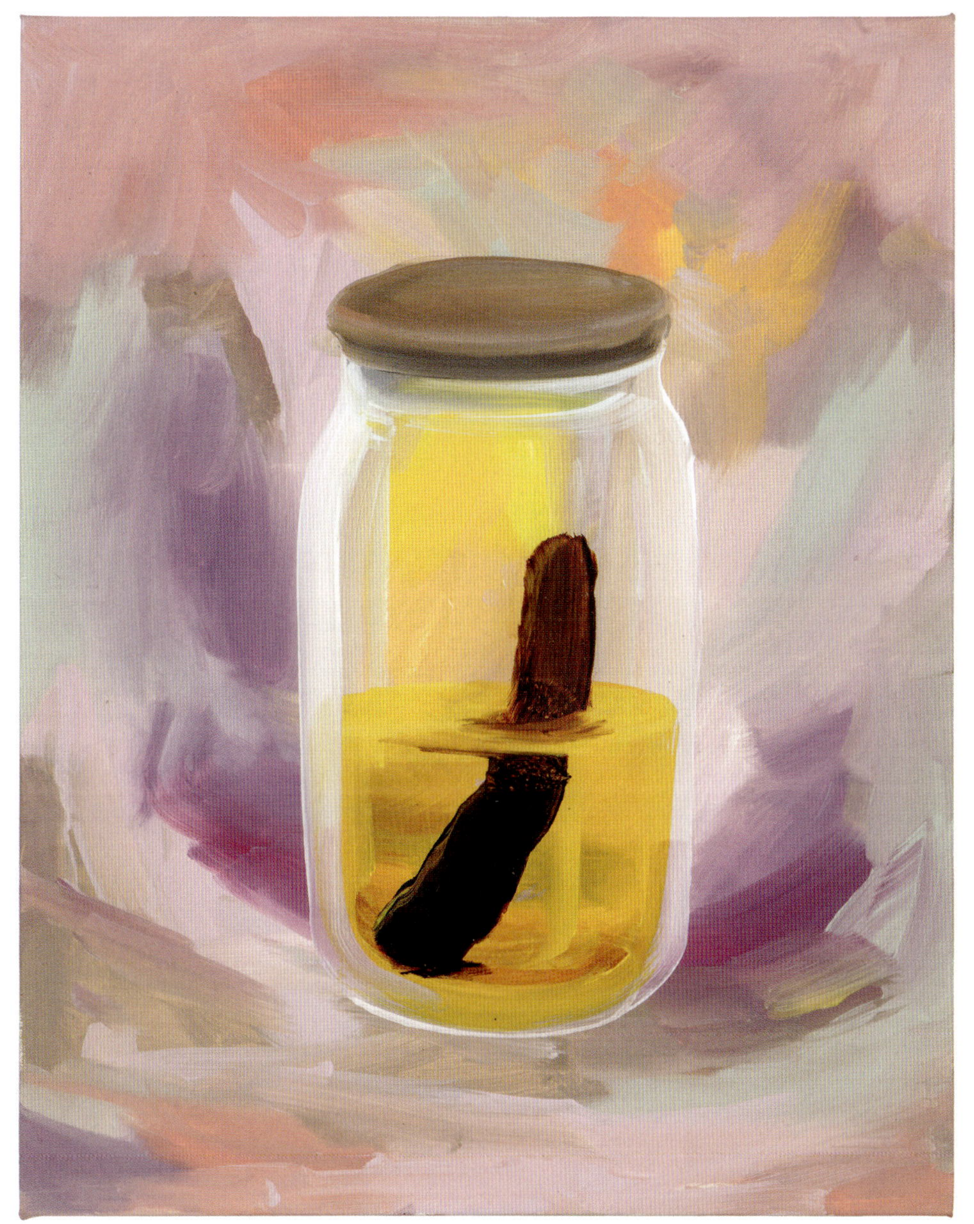

Paul McCarthy
*CSSC, Luncheon on the Grass, Mary, Ronald, Adam, and Eve*, 2019
Lightjet print
40 × 60 in. (101.6 × 152.4 cm)
Edition of 3, 2AP

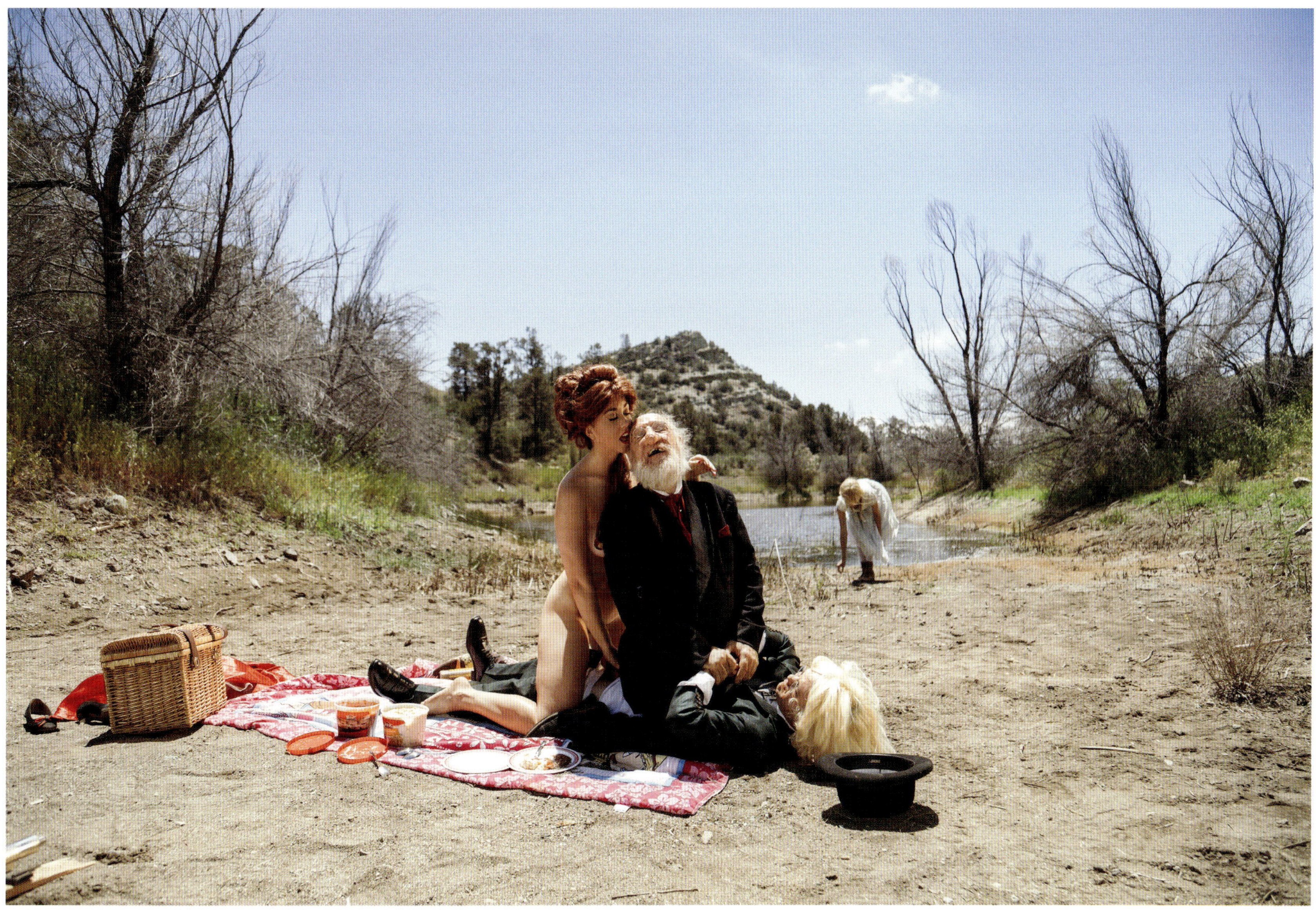

Paul McCarthy
*CSSC Luncheon on the Grass*, 2018
5 lightjet prints
Print 1: 27 × 21 5/8 in. (68.5 × 54.9 cm)
Prints 2, 3, 4: 21 5/8 × 27 in. (54.9 × 68.5 cm)
Print 5: 27 × 18 in. (68.5 × 45.7 cm)
Edition of 3, 2AP

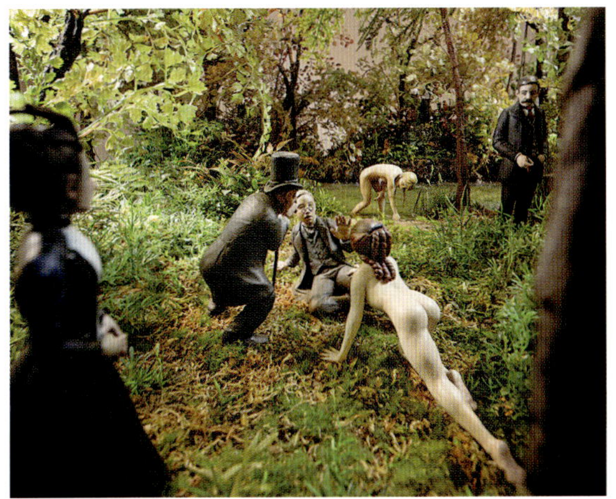
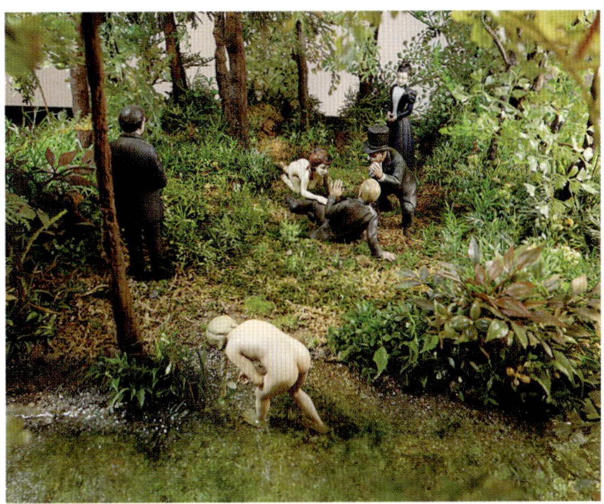
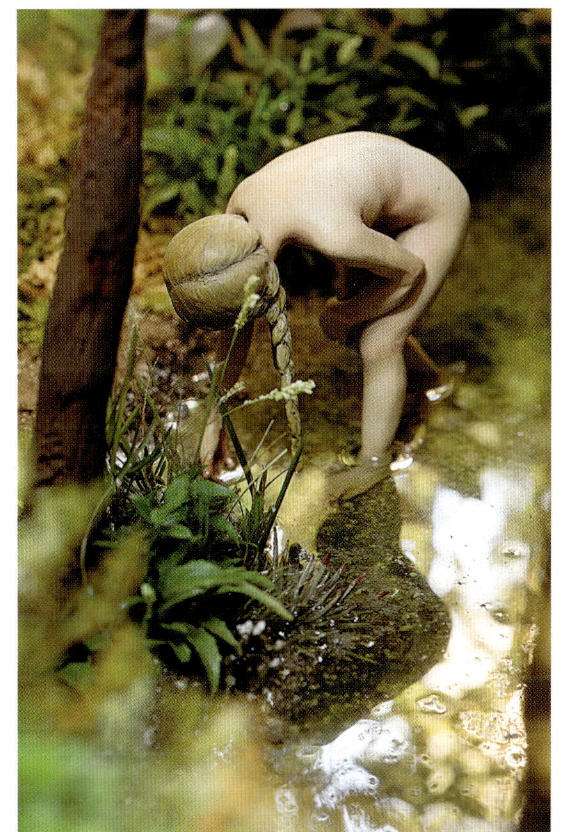
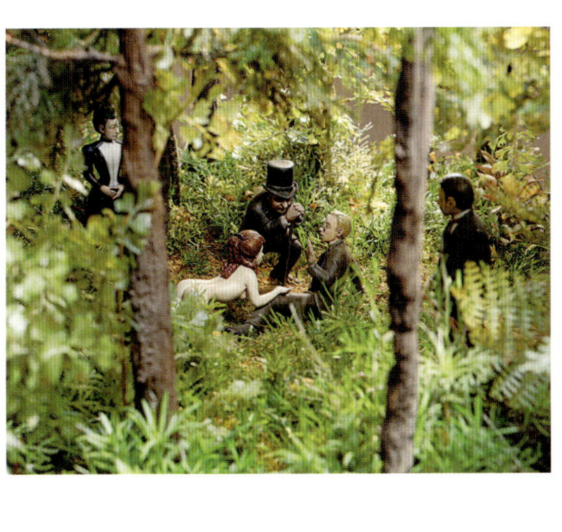
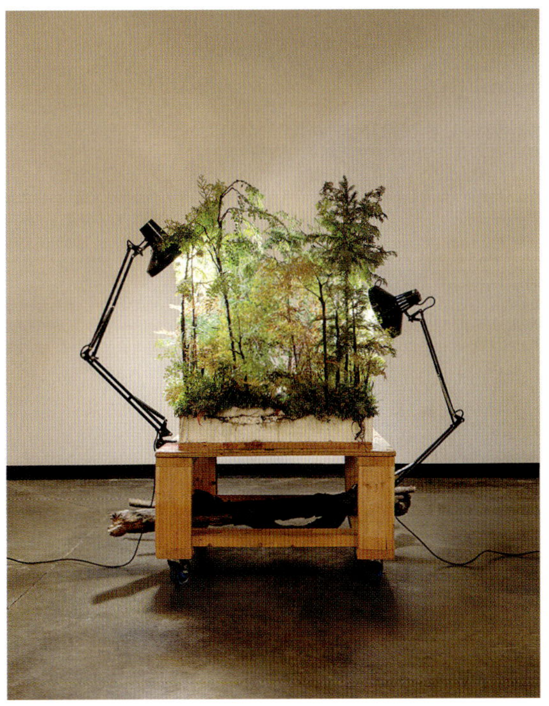

Paul McCarthy
*Mary and Adam, Study for CSSC Luncheon on the Grass*, 2013
Clay, paint, artificial foliage, wood, and light
37 × 30 × 27 in. (94 × 76.2 × 68.6 cm)

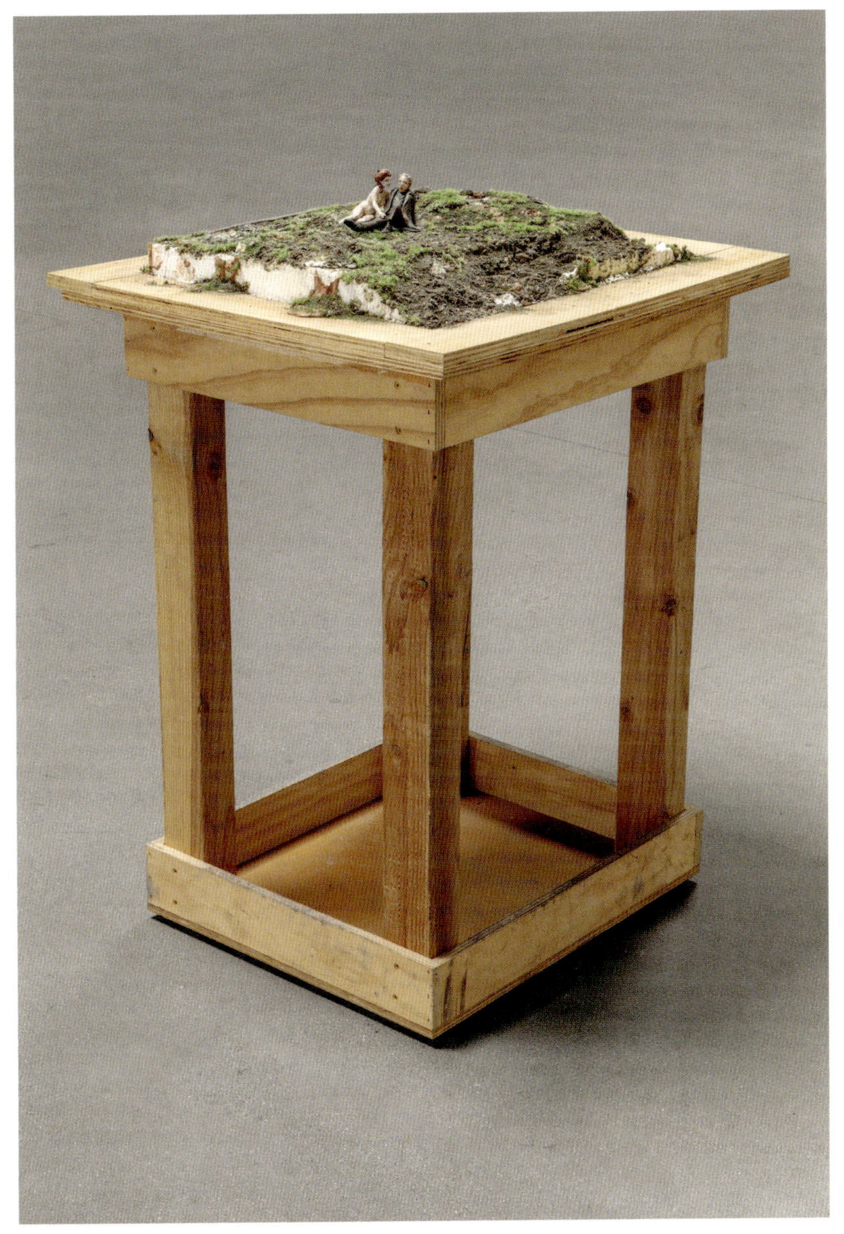

Sam McKinniss
*Picnic (Cecile and Kathryn)*, 2021
Oil and acrylic on linen
42 × 77 in. (106.7 × 195.6 cm)

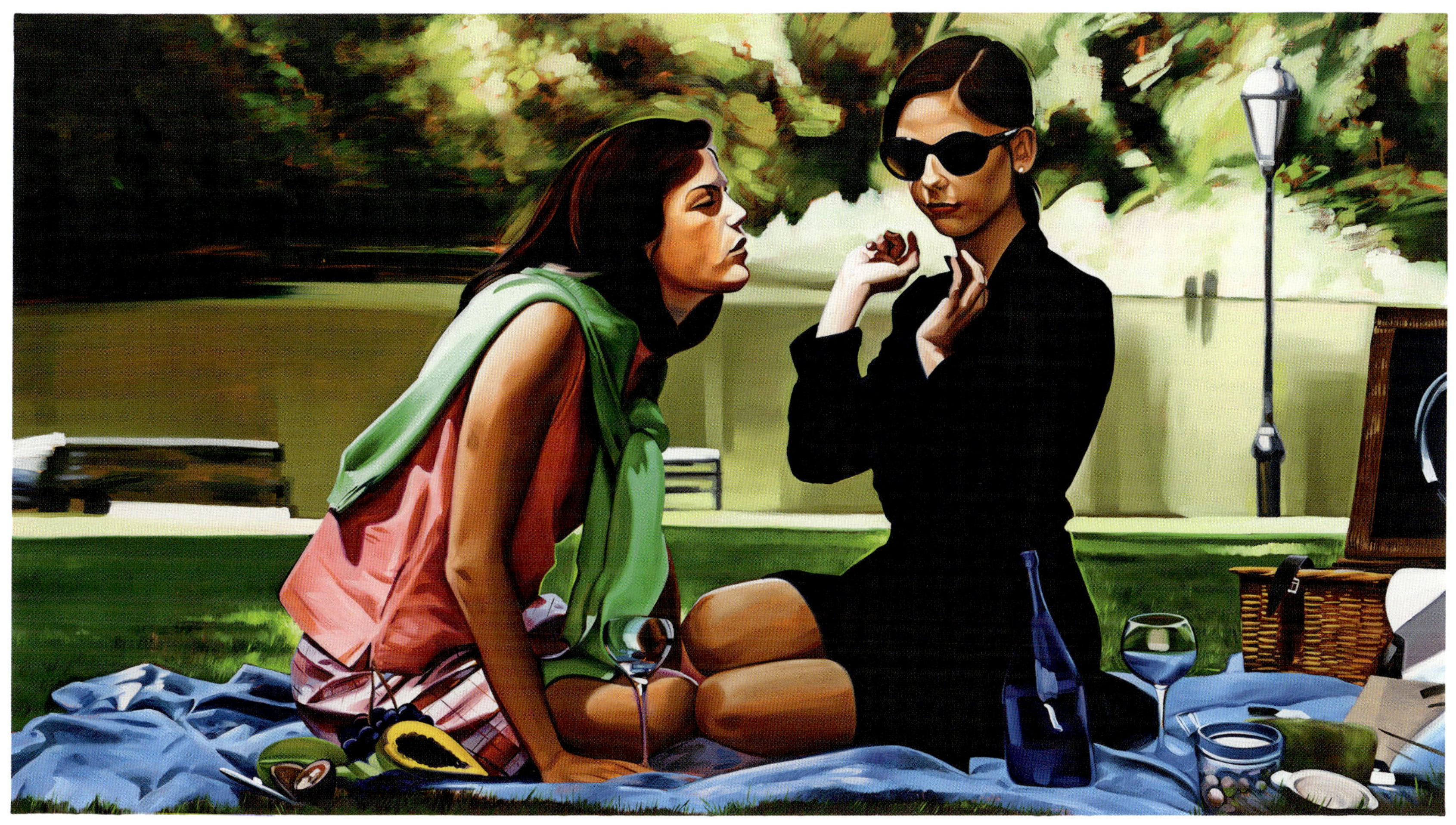

Sam McKinniss
*Bather (Sebastian)*, 2021
Oil on linen
54 × 99 in. (137.2 × 251.5 cm)

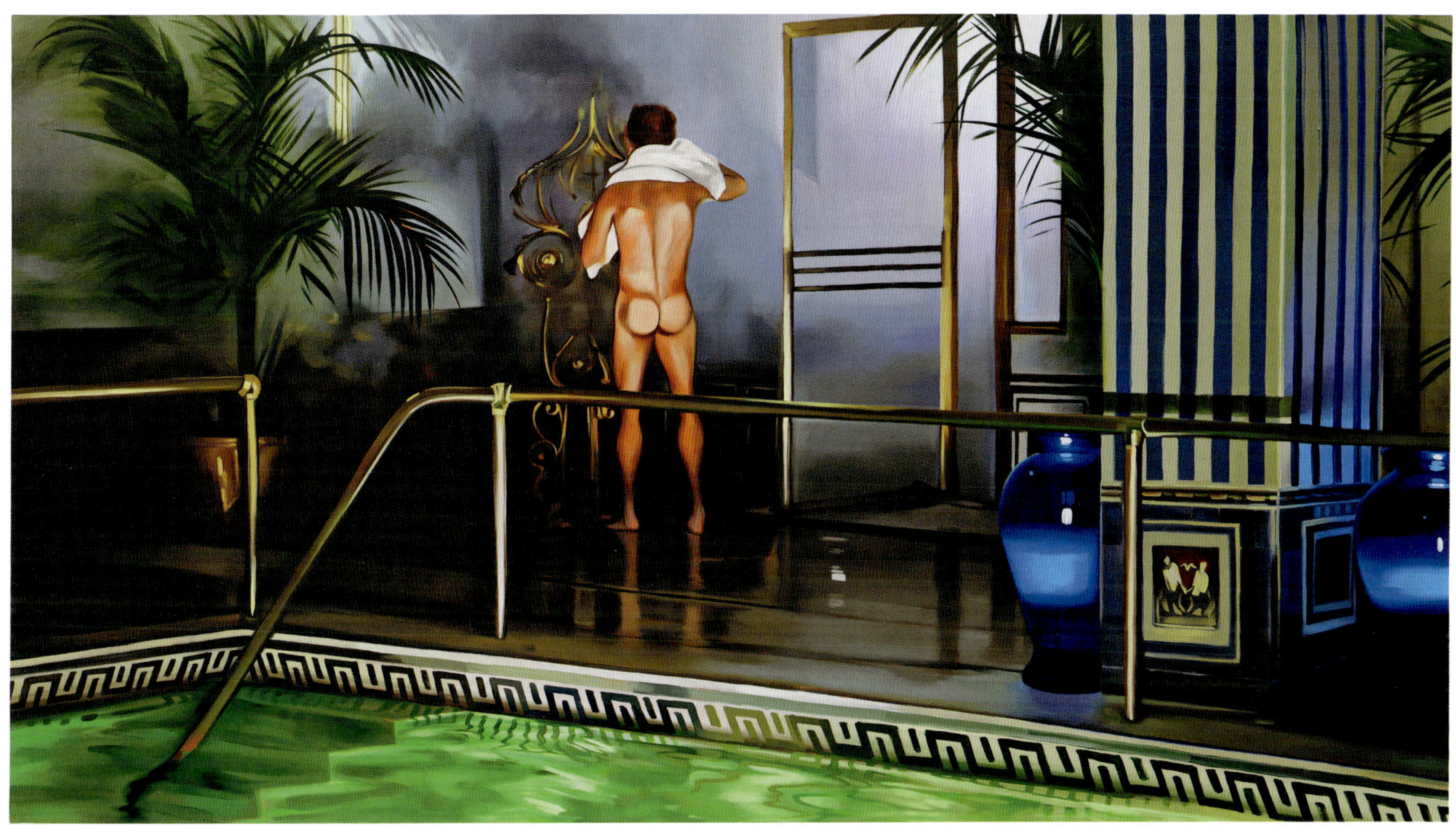

Jill Mulleady
*Suddenly, Last Summer*, 2022
Oil on linen
66 × 58 in. (168 × 147 cm)

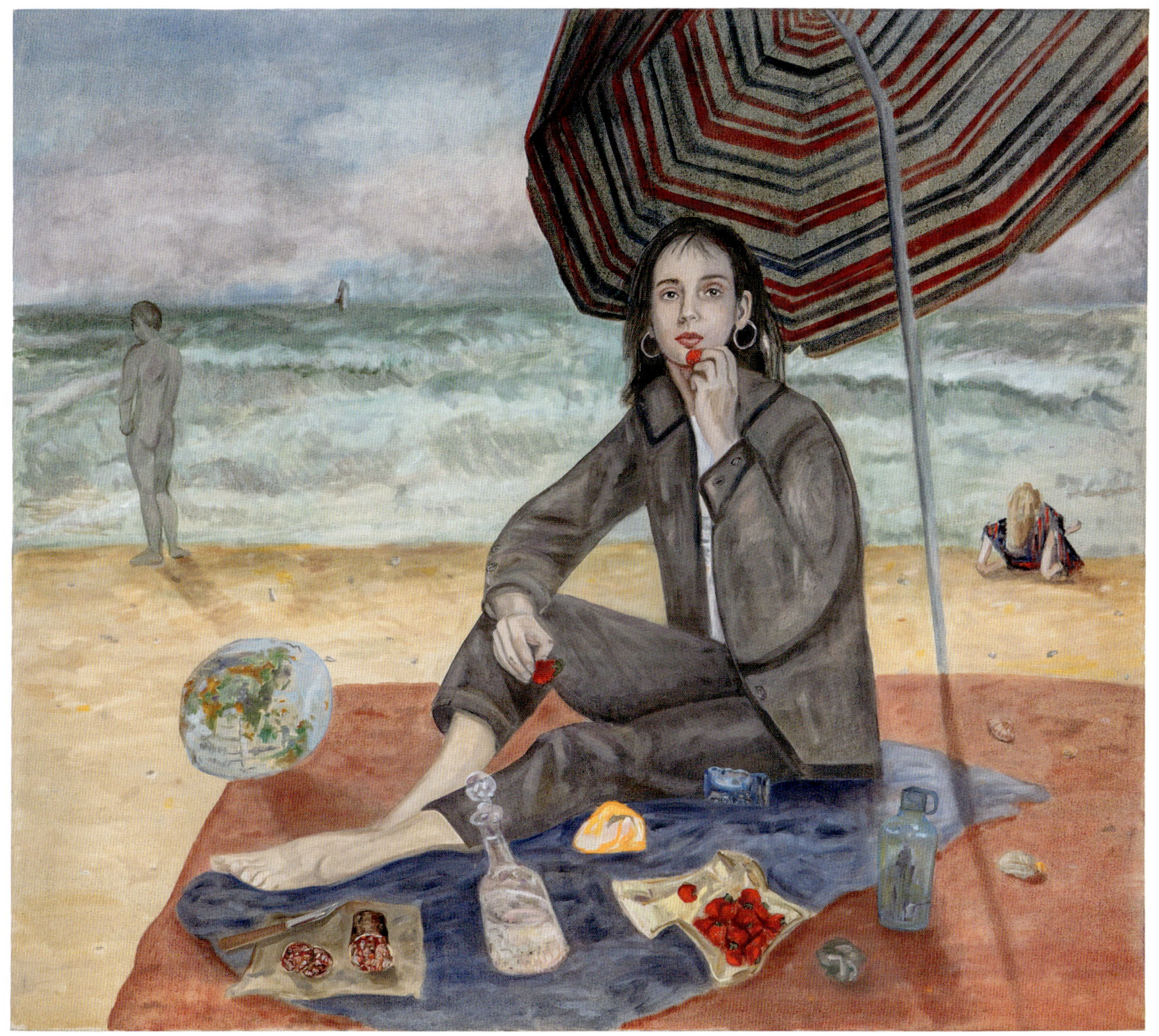

Ariana Papademetropoulos
*It Becomes Blurry in That Moment*, 2022
Oil on canvas
92 × 79 in. (233.7 × 200.7 cm)

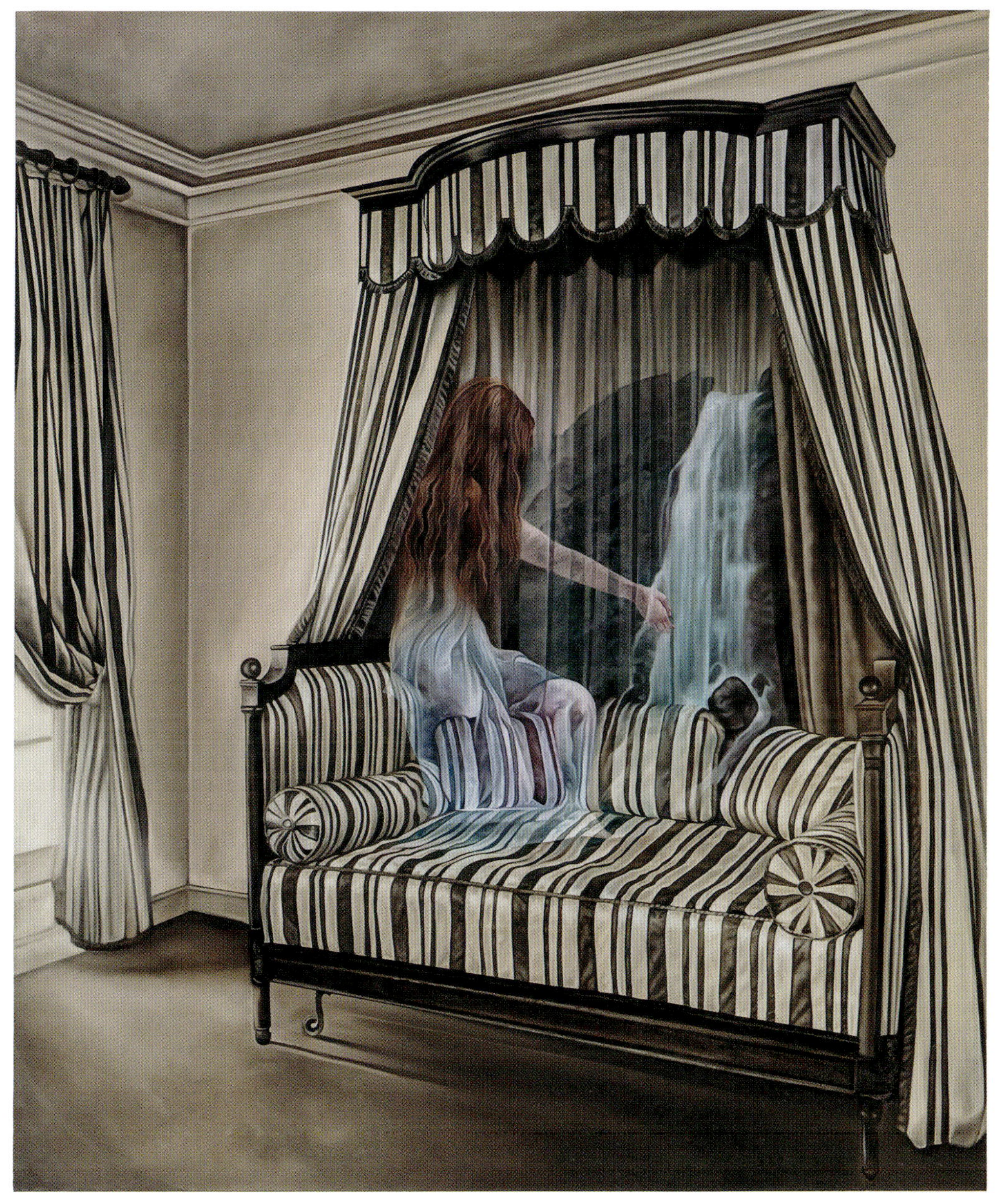

Naudline Pierre
*In Our Midst*, 2022
Oil on canvas
60 × 36 in. (152.4 × 91.4 cm)

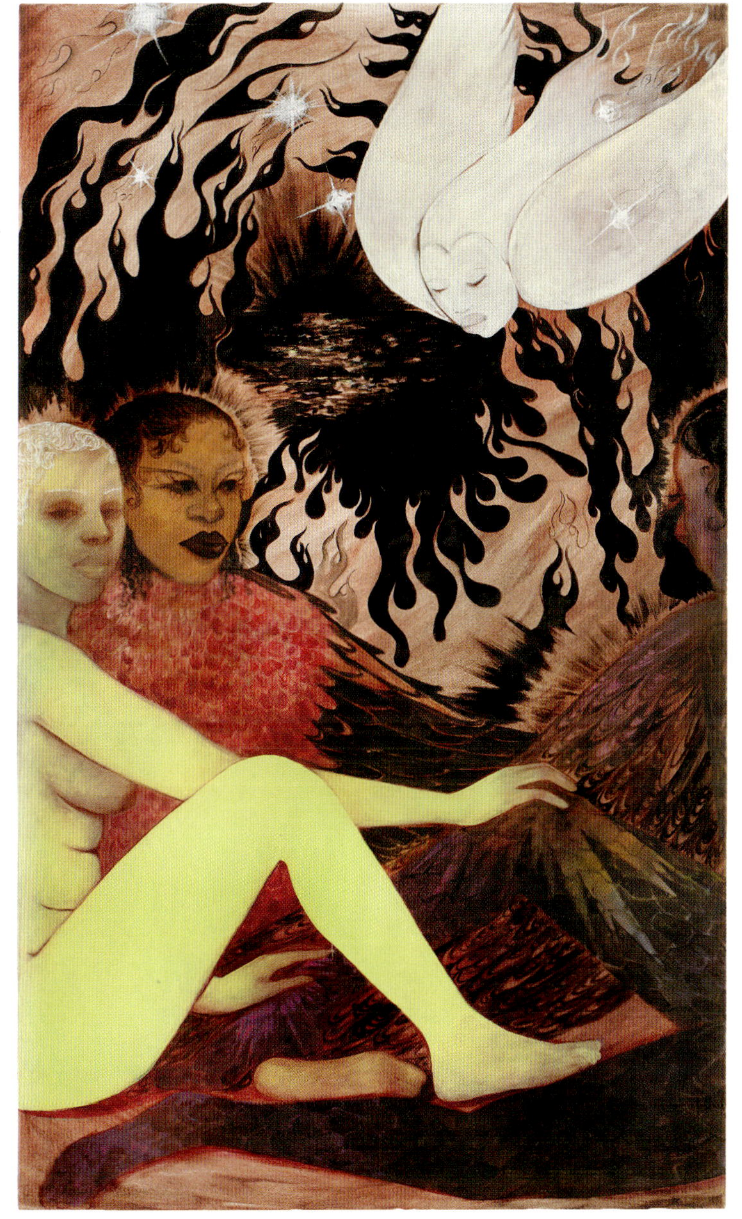

Christina Quarles
*Yer Apart of Everything*, 2022
Acrylic on canvas
60 × 72 × 2 in. (152.4 × 182.9 × 5.1 cm)

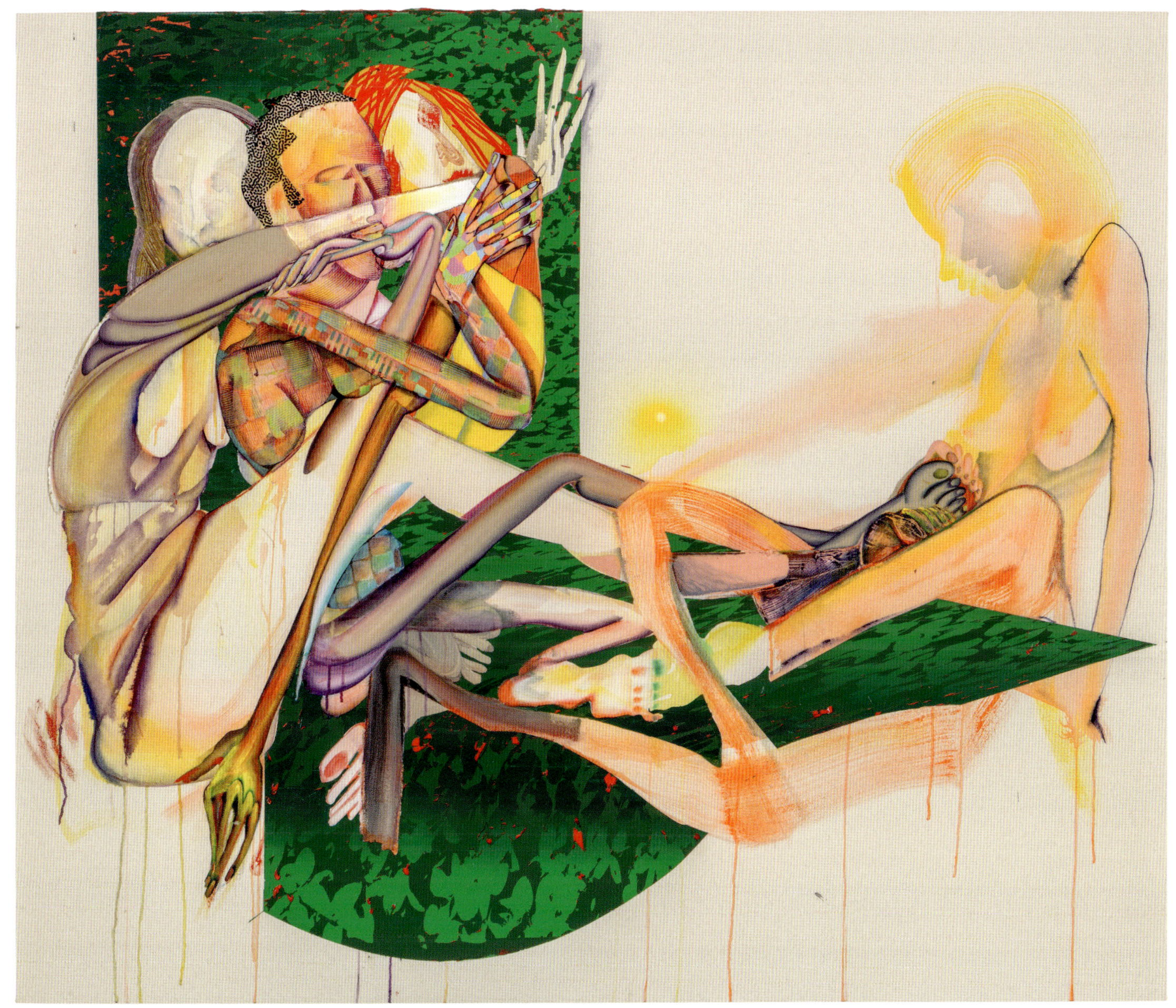

Walter Robinson
*Affronter sur l'herbe*, 2021
Acrylic on canvas
80 × 60 in. (203.2 × 152.4 cm)

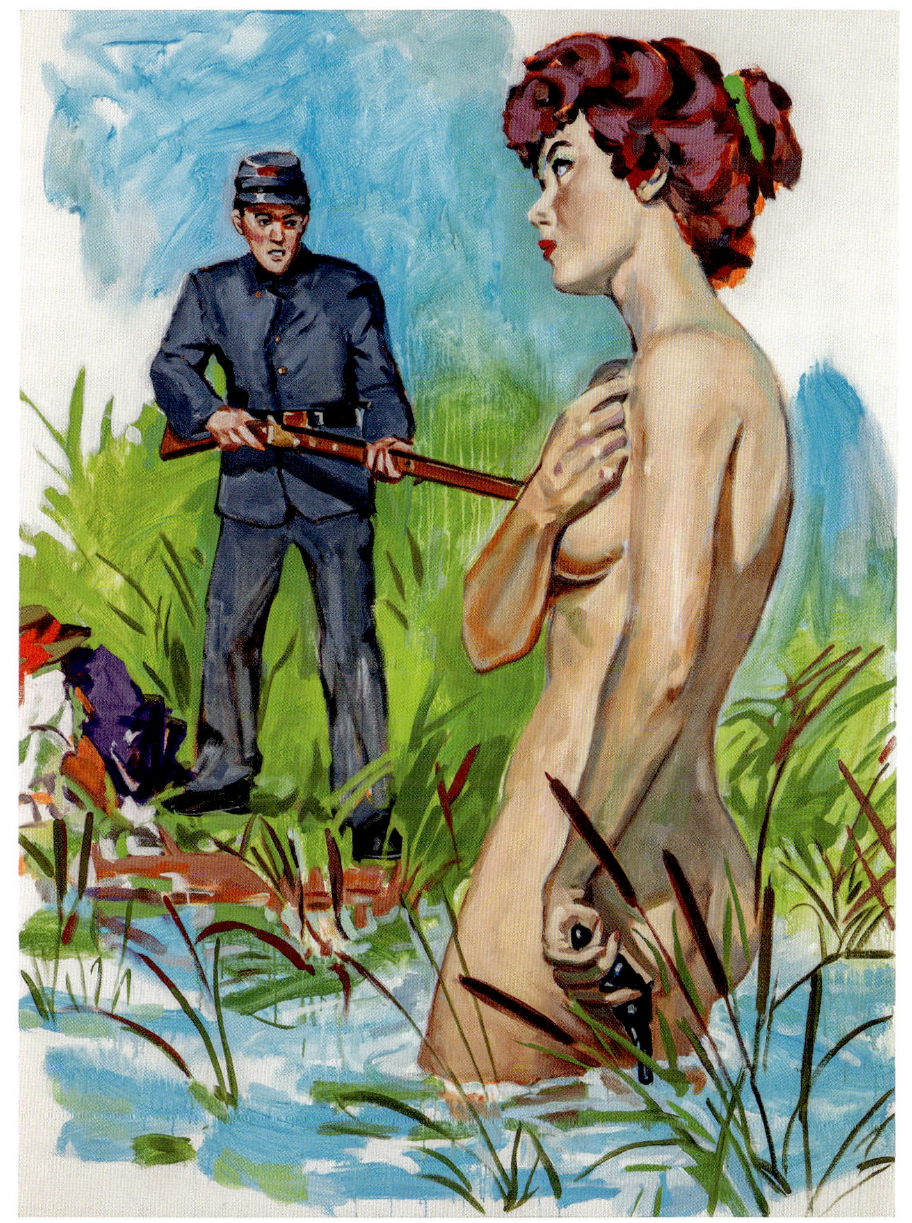

Giangiacomo Rossetti
*New Year*, 2023
Oil on panel
19 11/16 × 27 ½ in. (50 × 70 cm)

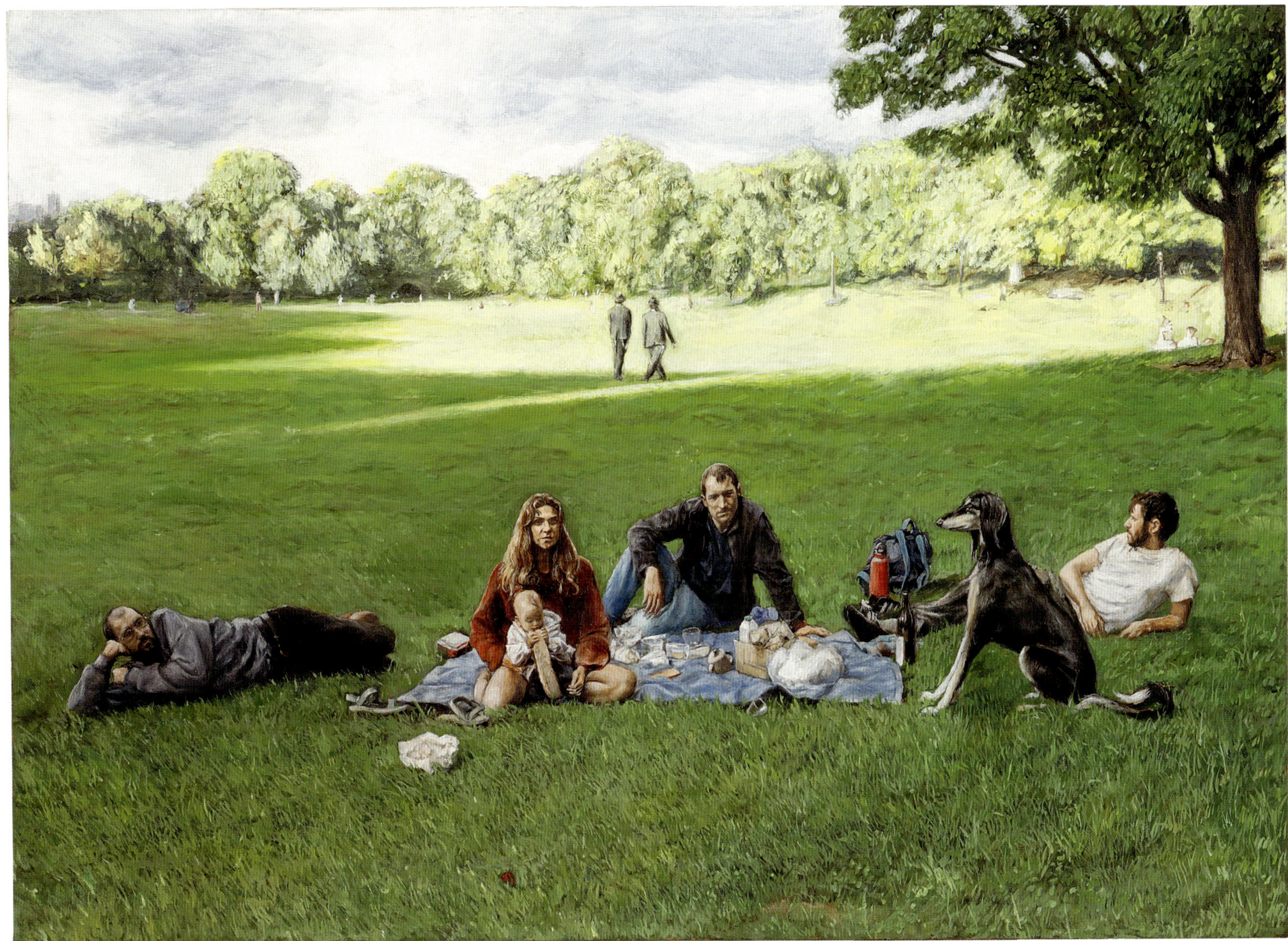

David Salle
*Tree of Life (After Manet)*, 2021–22
Oil and acrylic on linen
96 × 72 in. (243.8 × 182.9 cm)

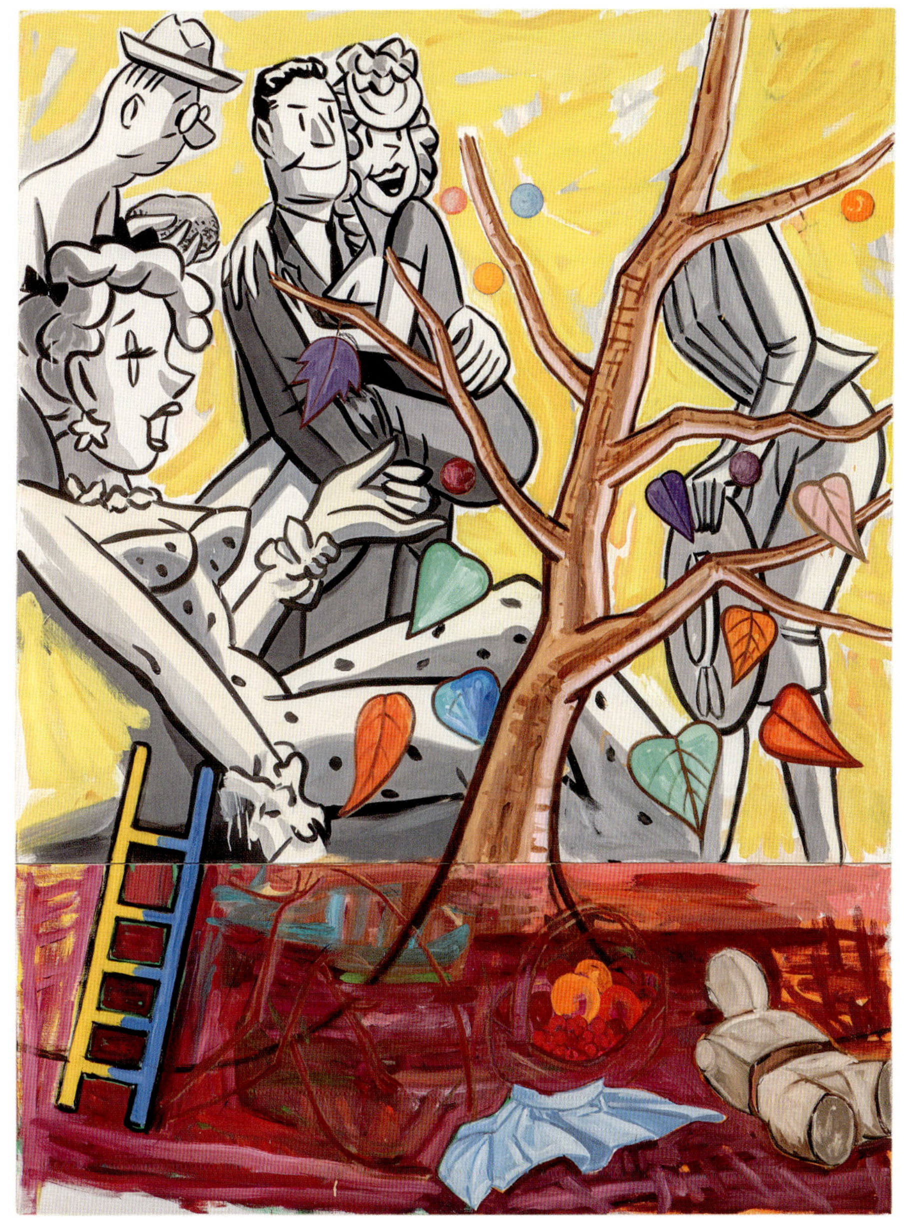

Katja Seib
*A Picnic Inside*, 2021
Oil on canvas
96 × 66 in. (243.8 × 167.6 cm)

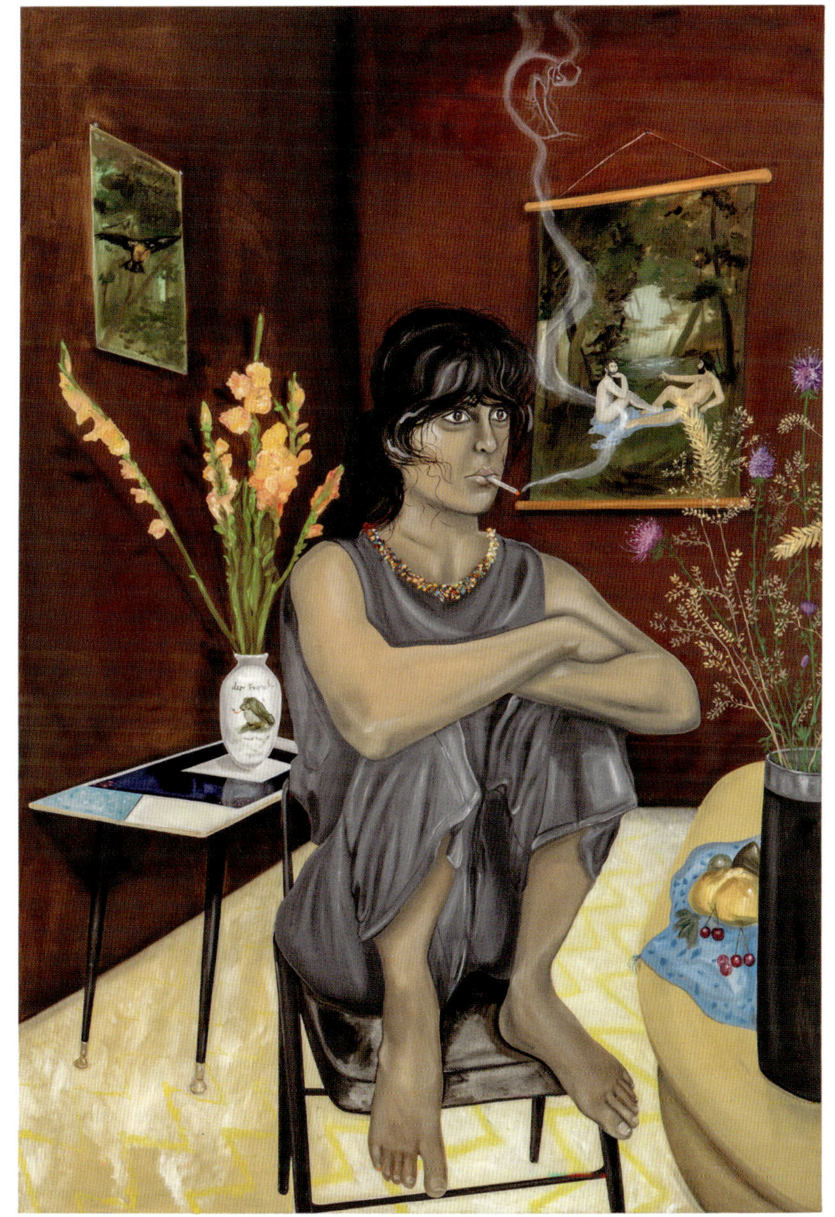

Tschabalala Self
*12pm on 145th*, 2019–21
Jean fabric, digital printed T-shirt, velvet, lace, tulle, painted canvas, dyed canvas, acrylic, and Flashe on canvas; three parts
Overall: 96 ⅛ × 228 in. (244 × 579 cm)

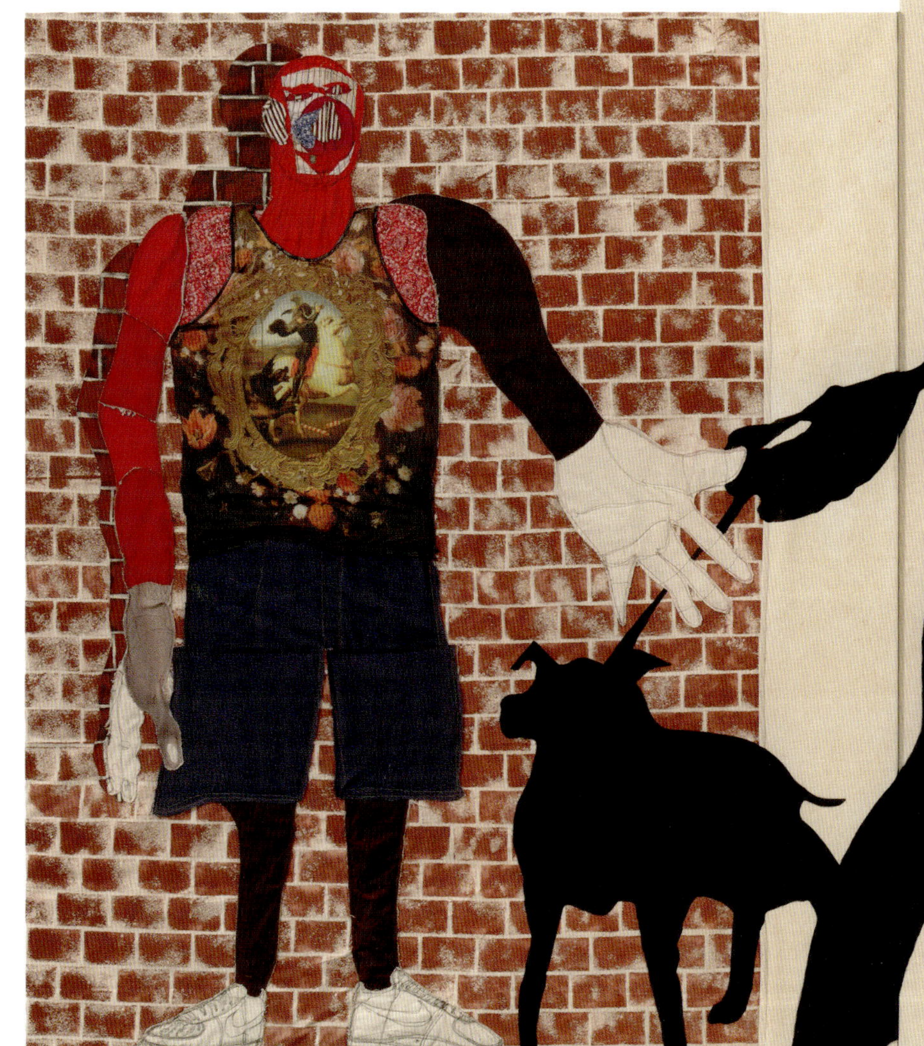

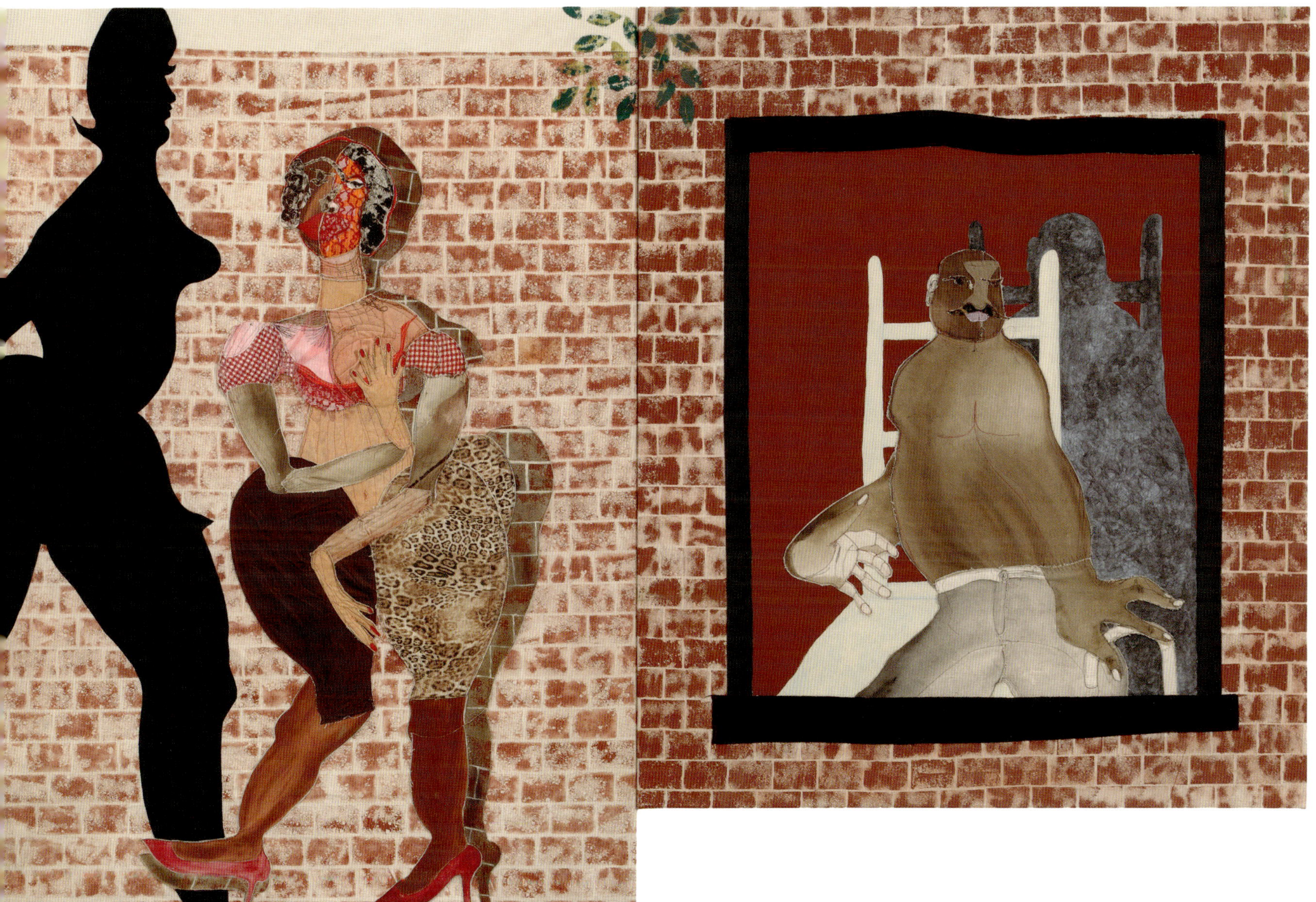

Vaughn Spann
*Juneteenth on the grass (after lunch)*, 2022
Oil on canvas
78 × 130 × 1 ½ in. (198.1 × 330.2 × 3.8 cm)

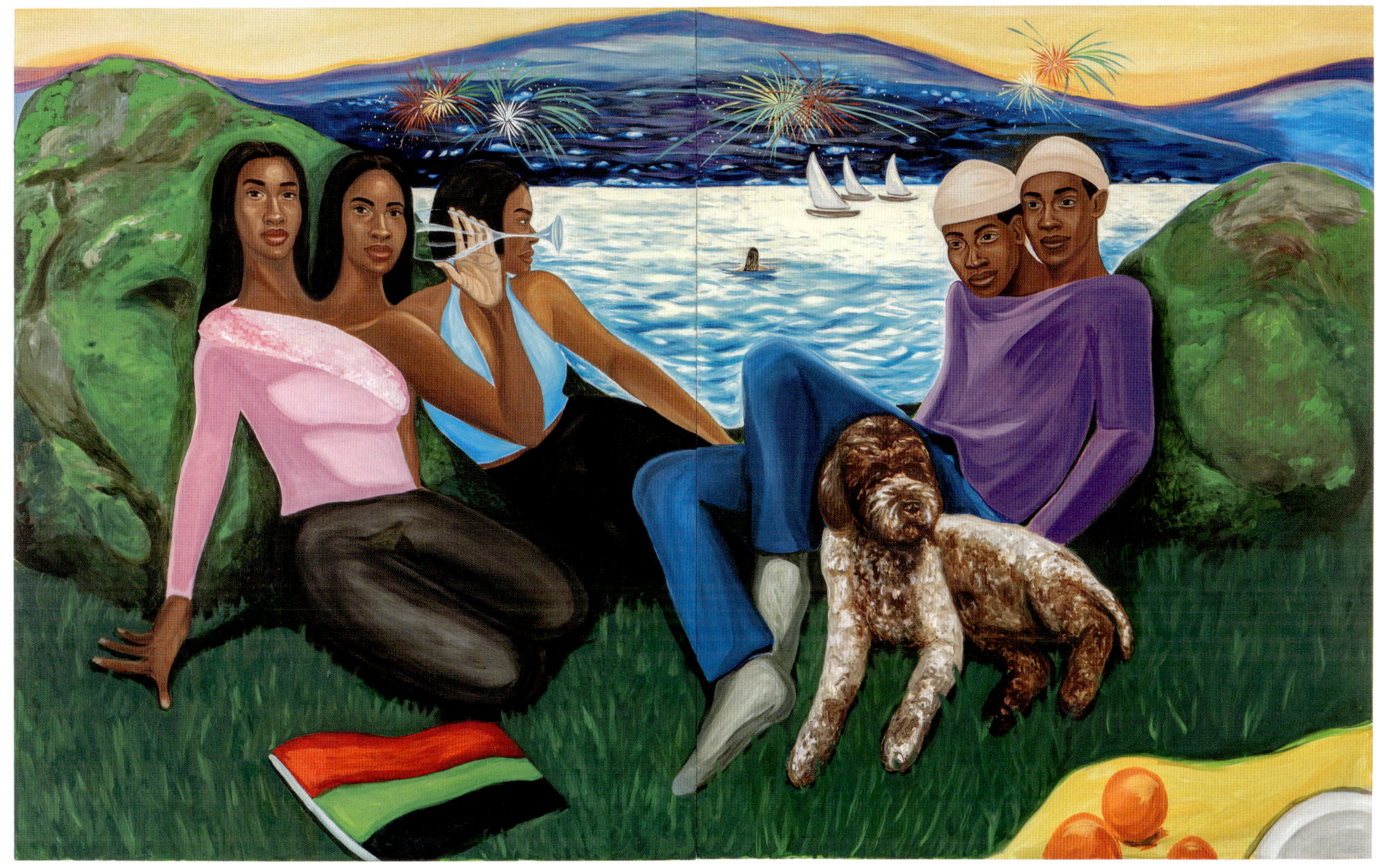

Mickalene Thomas
*Le Déjeuner sur l'herbe les Trois Femme Noires d'aprés Picasso*, 2022
Rhinestones and acrylic paint on canvas mounted on wood panel
96 × 120 in. (243.8 × 304.8 cm)

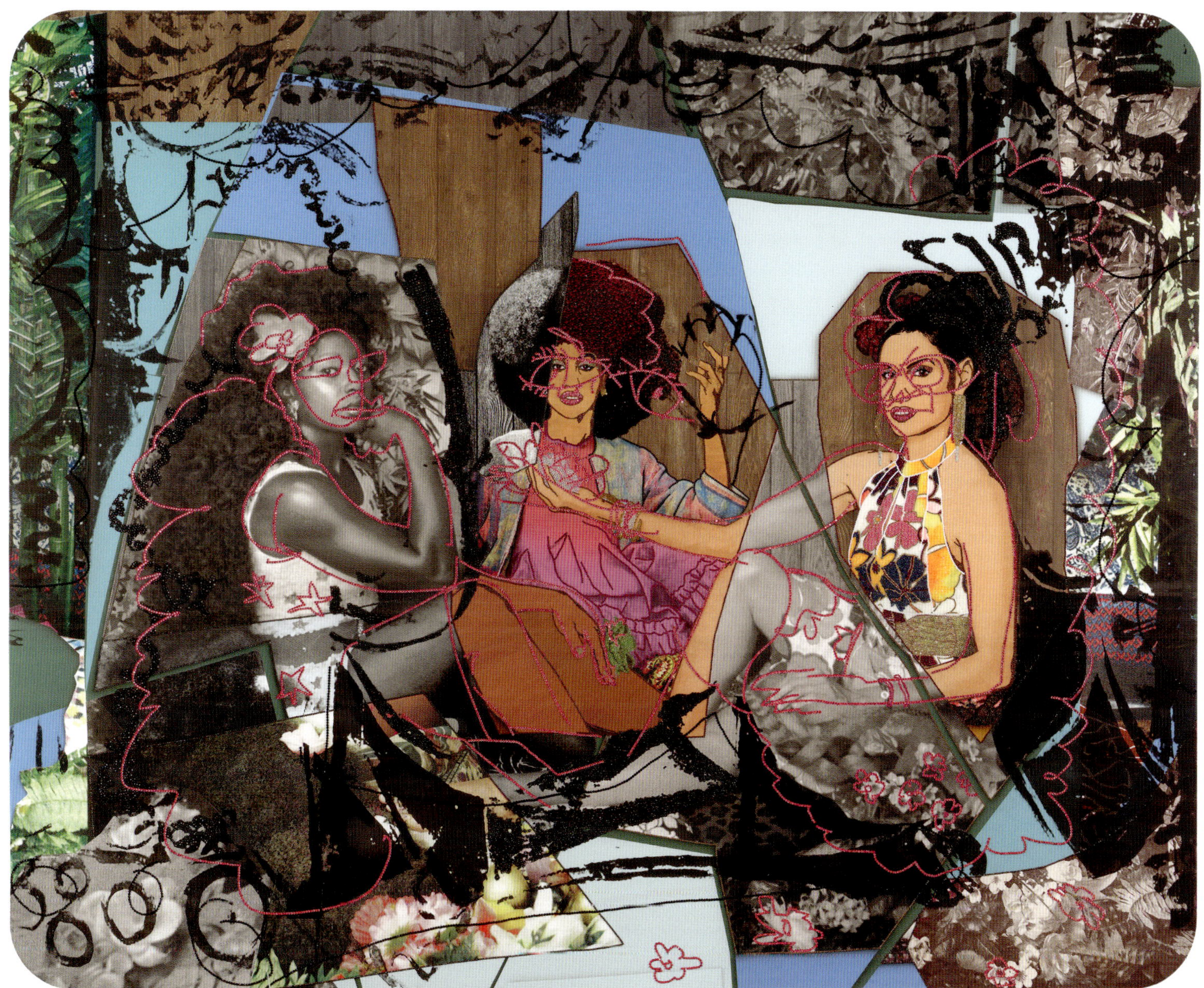

Salman Toor
*The Garden*, 2020
Oil on panel
30 × 24 in. (76.2 × 61 cm)

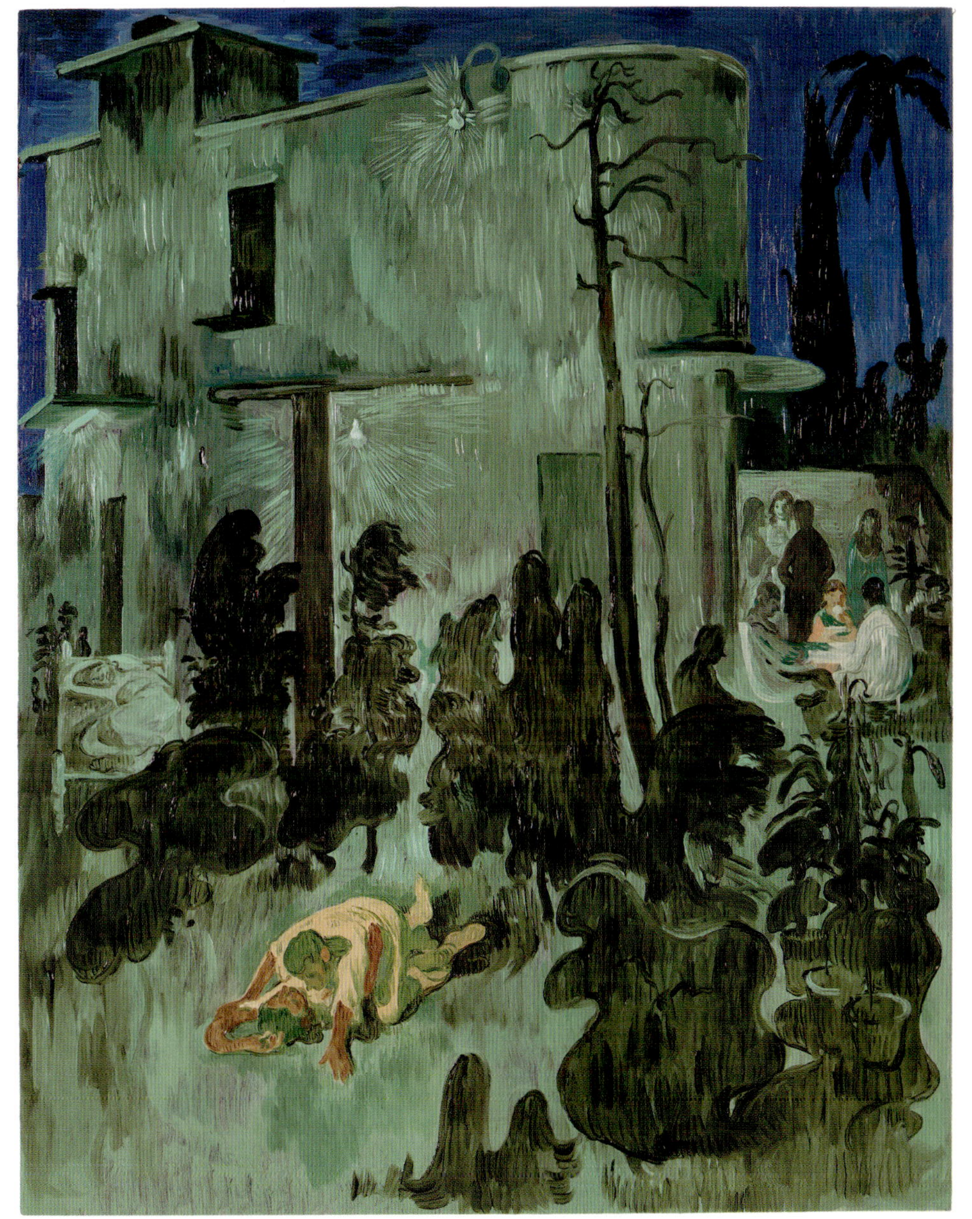

John Wesley
*Chocolate Major*, 2002
Acrylic on canvas
63 × 53 × 2 in. (160 × 134.6 × 5 cm)

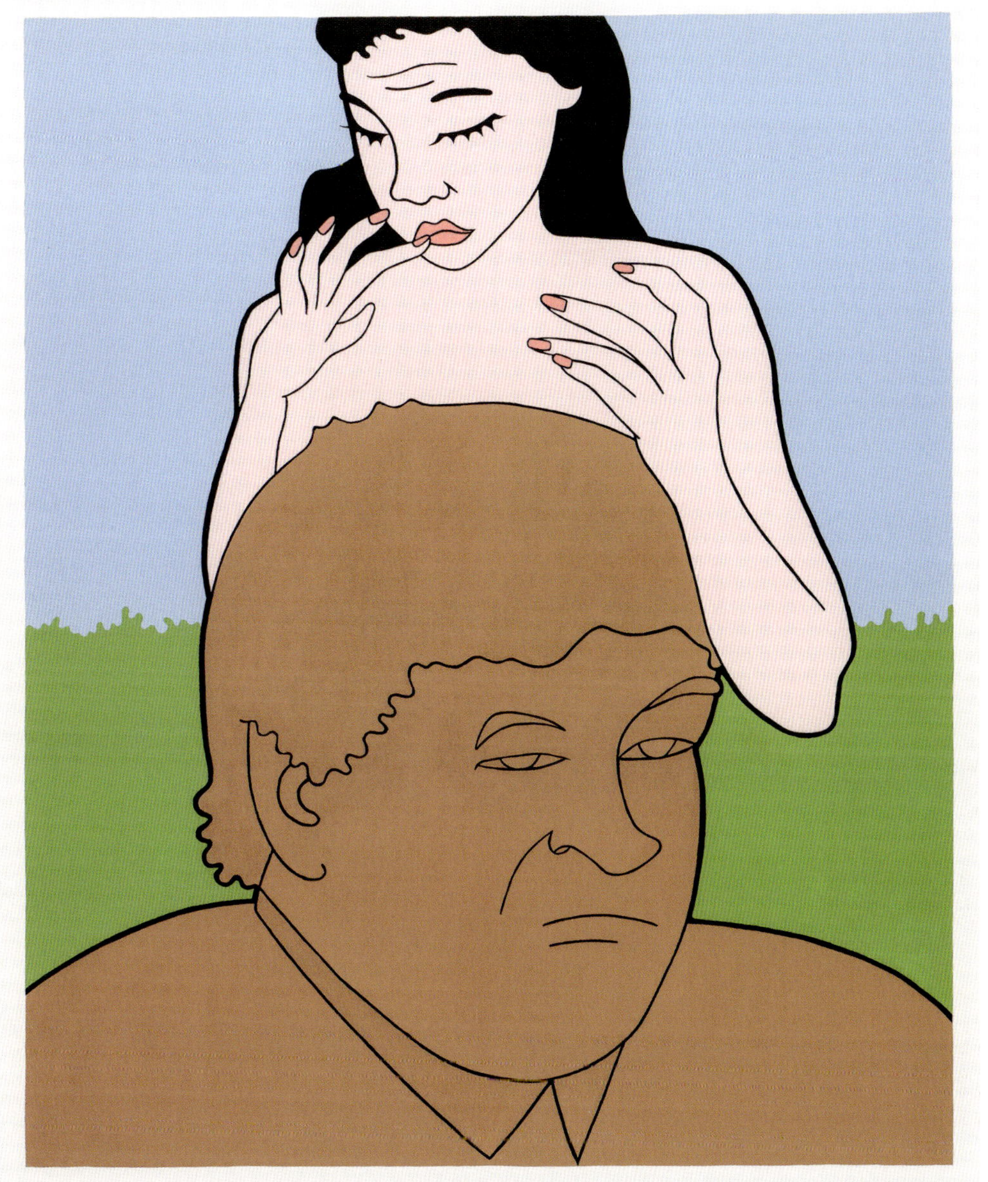

Kehinde Wiley
*Lunch with Inettia, Lucemy and Soukenya*, 2022
Oil on paper
Unframed: 48 × 72 in. (121.9 × 182.9 cm)

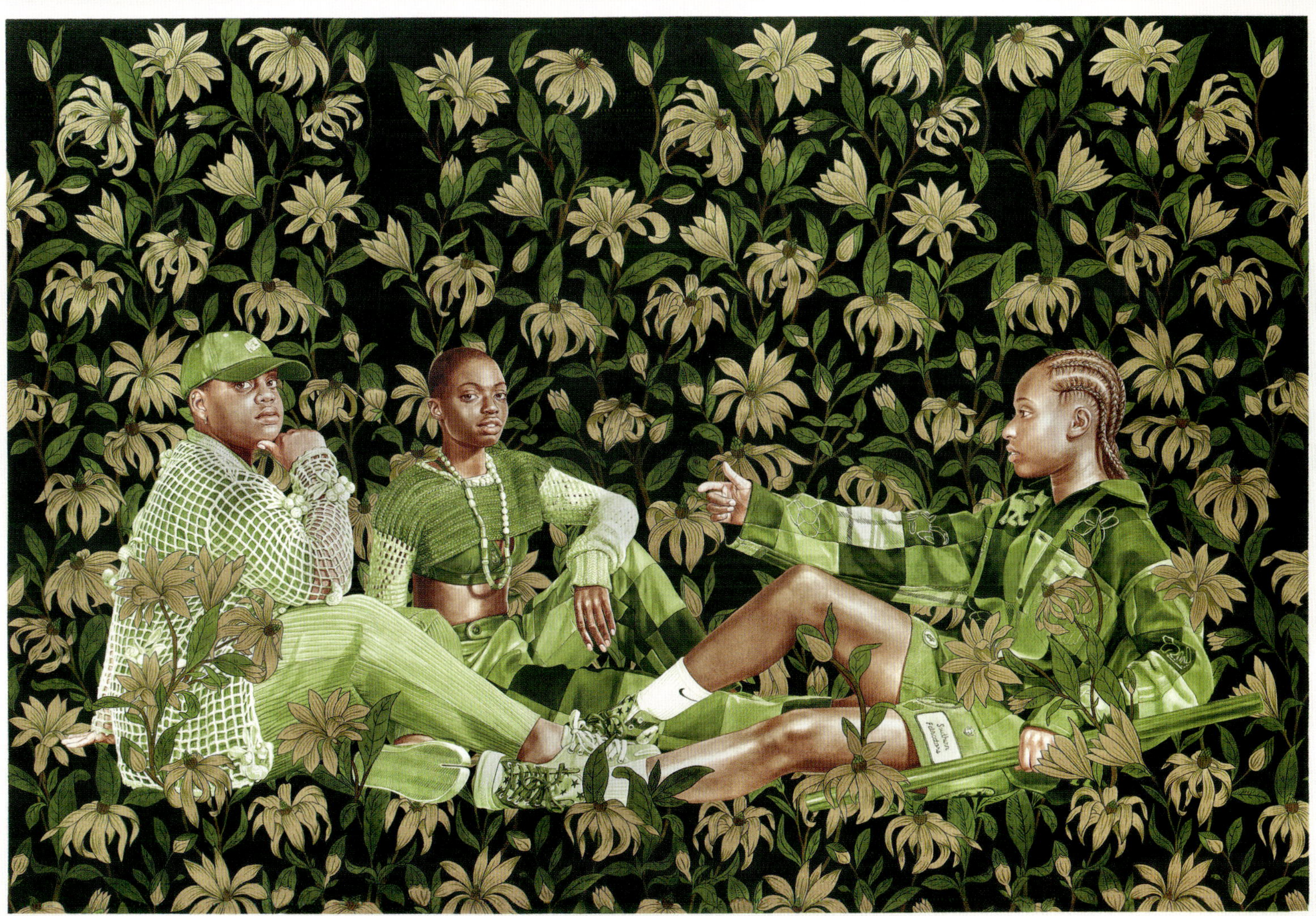

# PLATES II

Fernando Botero
*Le Déjeuner sur l'herbe*, 1969
Oil on canvas
70 ⅞ × 74 ⅞ in. (180 × 190.3 cm)

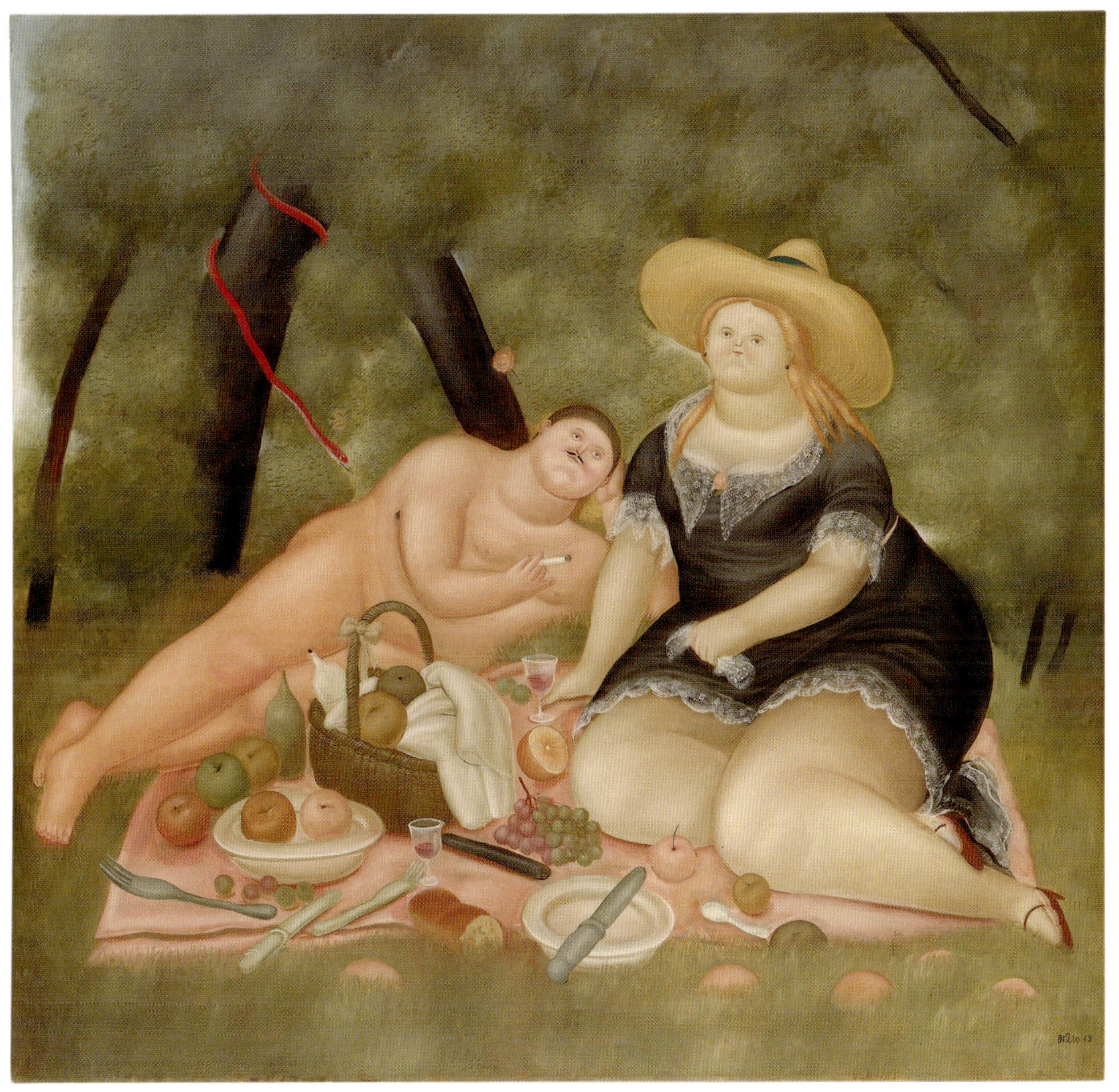

Renee Cox
*Cousins at Pussy Pond*, 2001
Archival digital chromogenic print mounted
on aluminum panel
48 × 60 in. (121.9 × 152.4 cm)

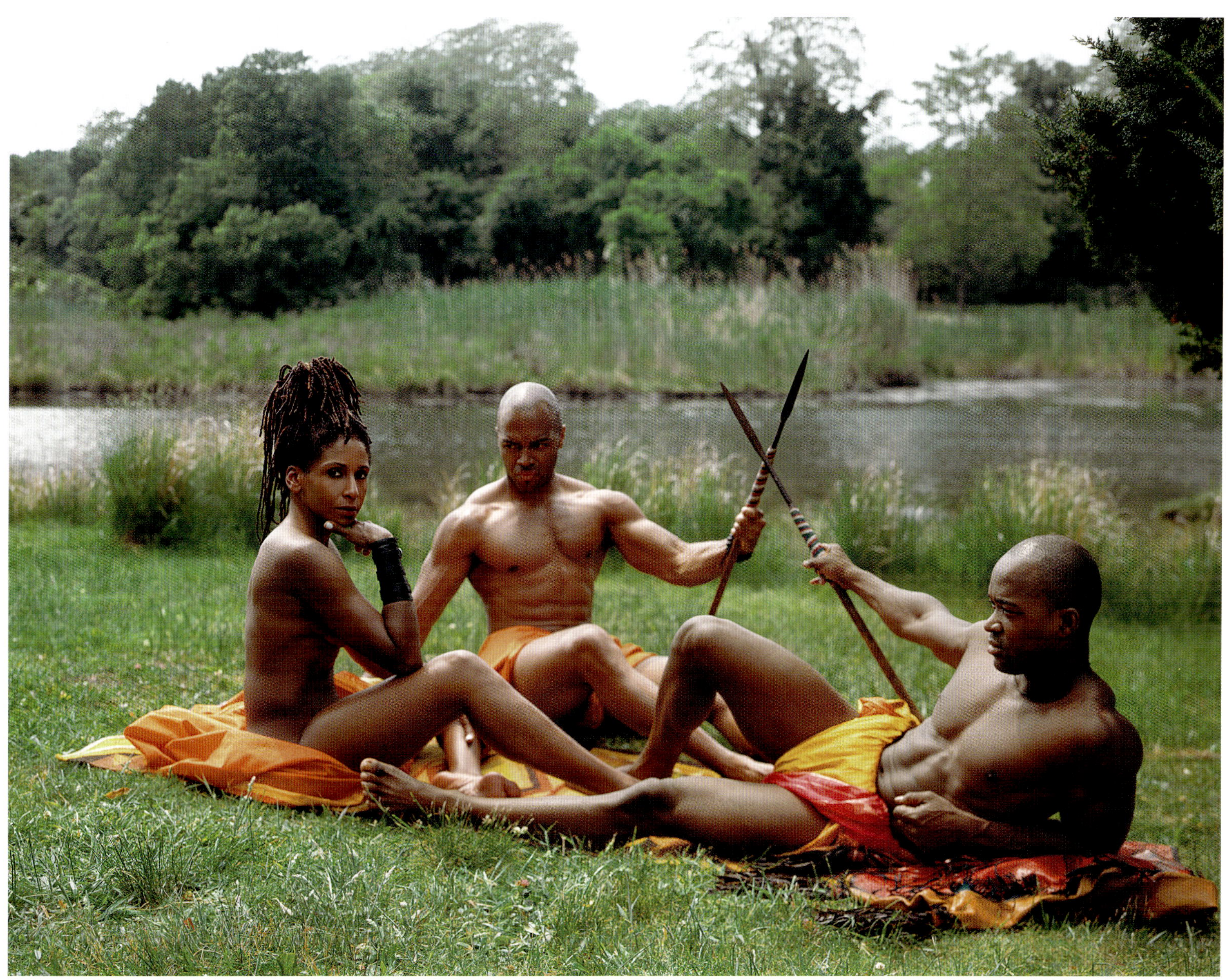

Tacita Dean
*The Story of Beard*, 1992–93
Billboard sited in Manchester, Belfast
(destroyed), and London

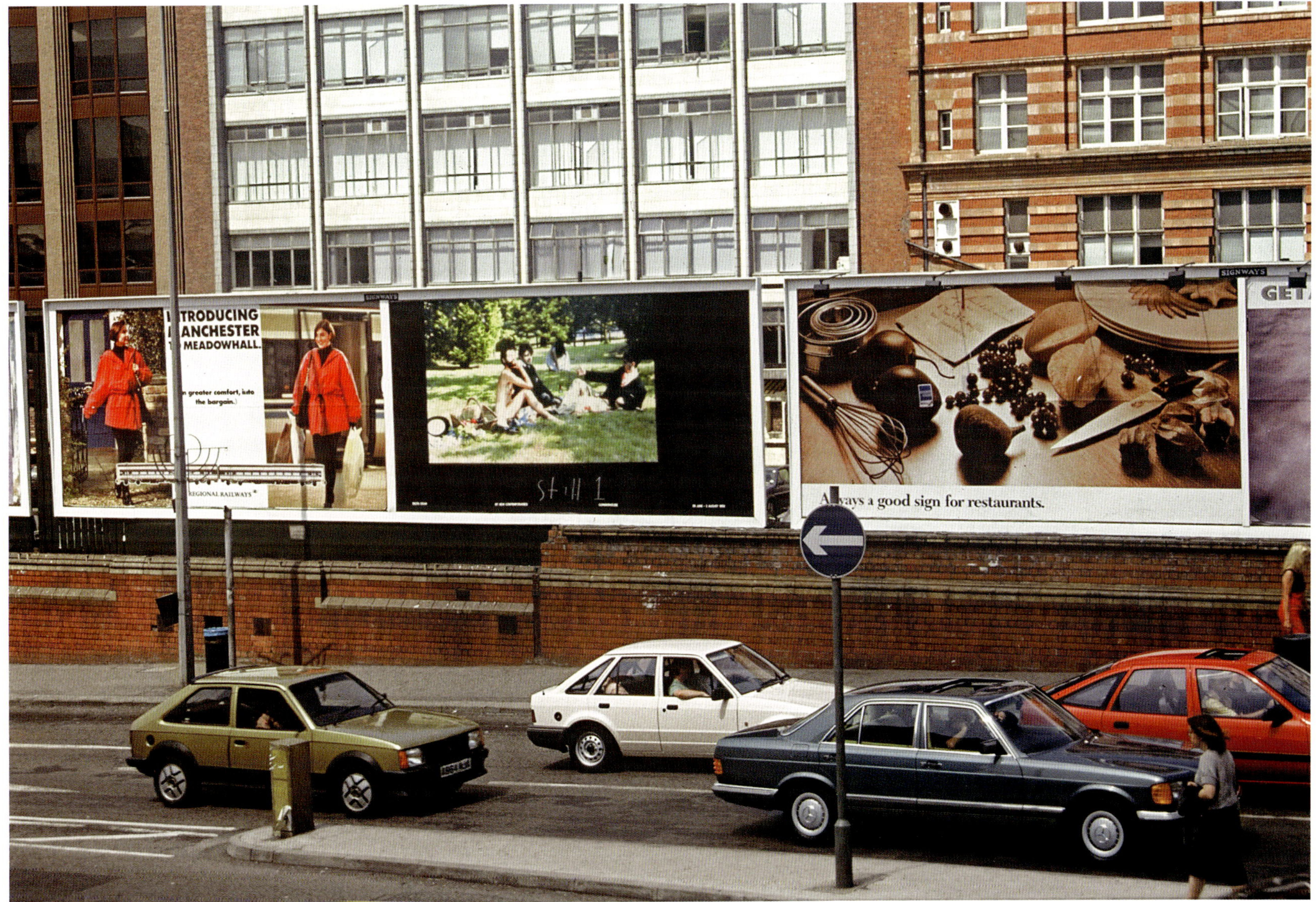
TRODUCING
ANCHESTER
MEADOWHALL.
greater comfort, into the bargain.
REGIONAL RAILWAYS
SIGNWAYS
Still 1
A ways a good sign for restaurants.
SIGNWAYS
GET

Beauford Delaney
*The Picnic*, 1940
Oil on canvas
25 × 30 in. (63.5 × 76.2 cm)

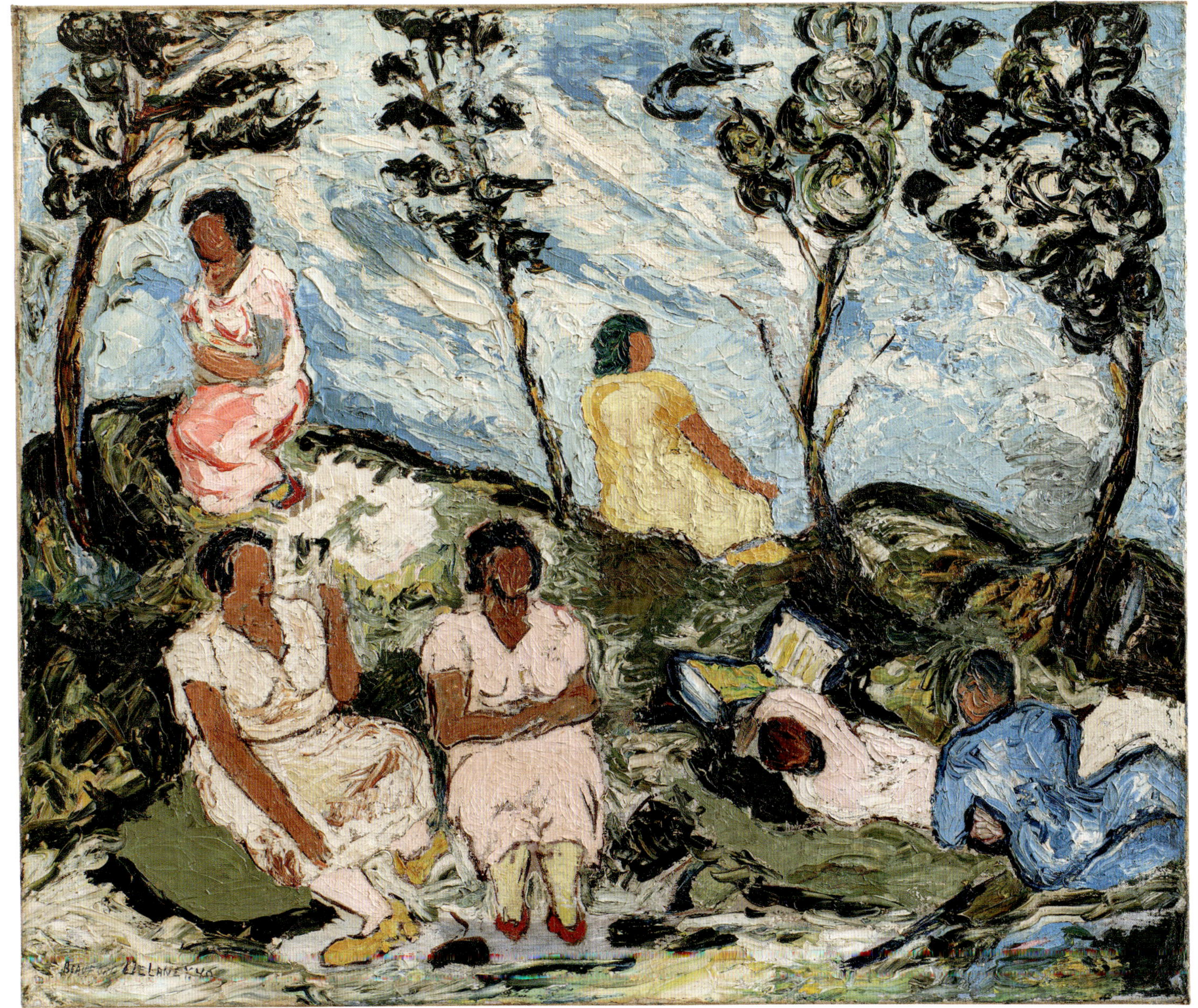

Umar Rashid
*Le dejeuner sur l'herbe a été interrompu par des chefs de guerre (After Manet). [The luncheon on the grass was interrupted by warlords]. Or, the historical origin of Kolonial Fried Chicken.*, 2022
Acrylic and ink on canvas
72 × 84 × 1 ½ in. (182.9 × 213.4 × 3.8 cm)

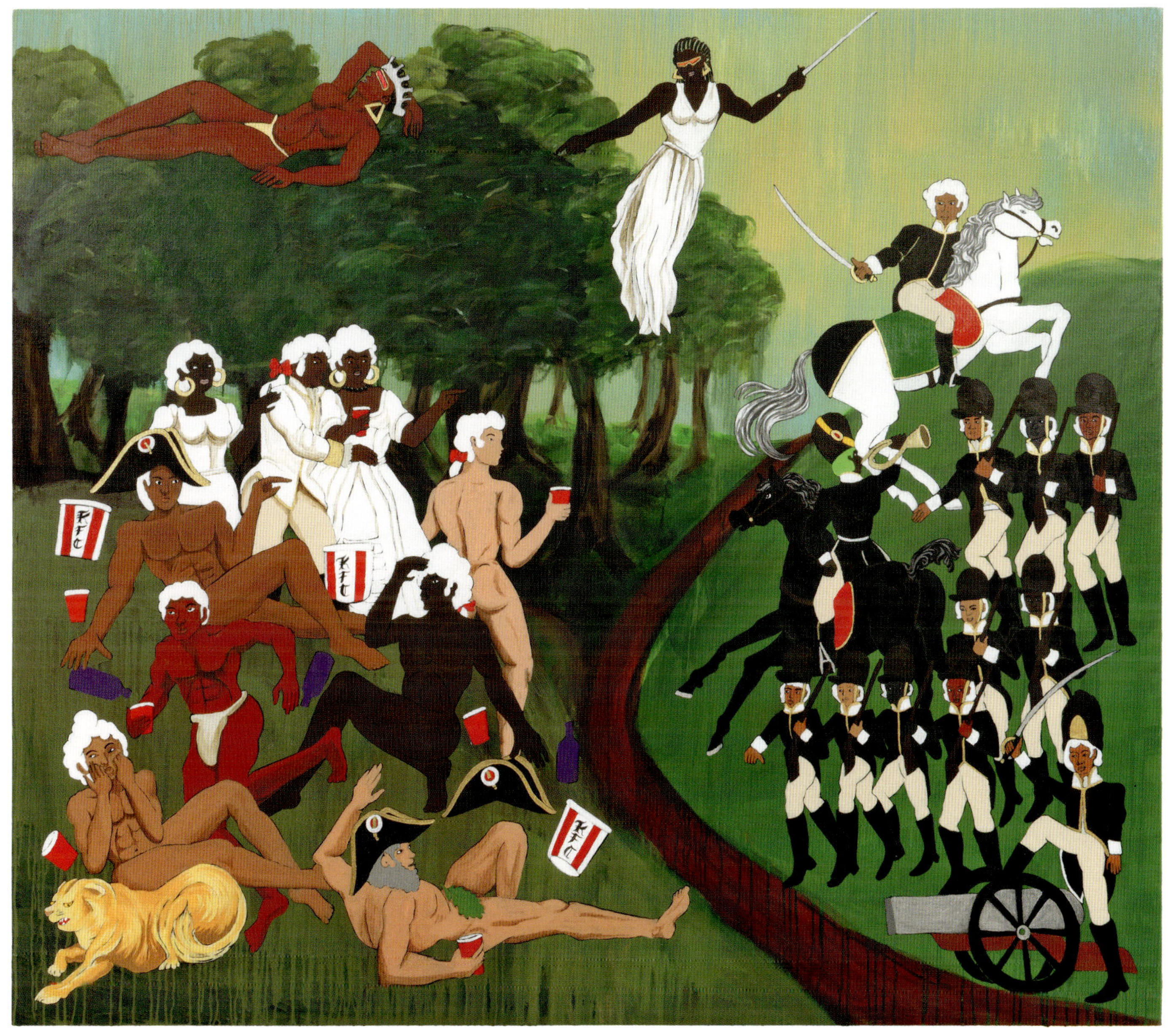
KFC
KFC
KFC

Faith Ringgold
*The French Collection Part I, #3: The Picnic at Giverny*, 1991
Acrylic on canvas with pieced fabric border
73 ½ × 90 ½ in. (186.7 × 229.9 cm)

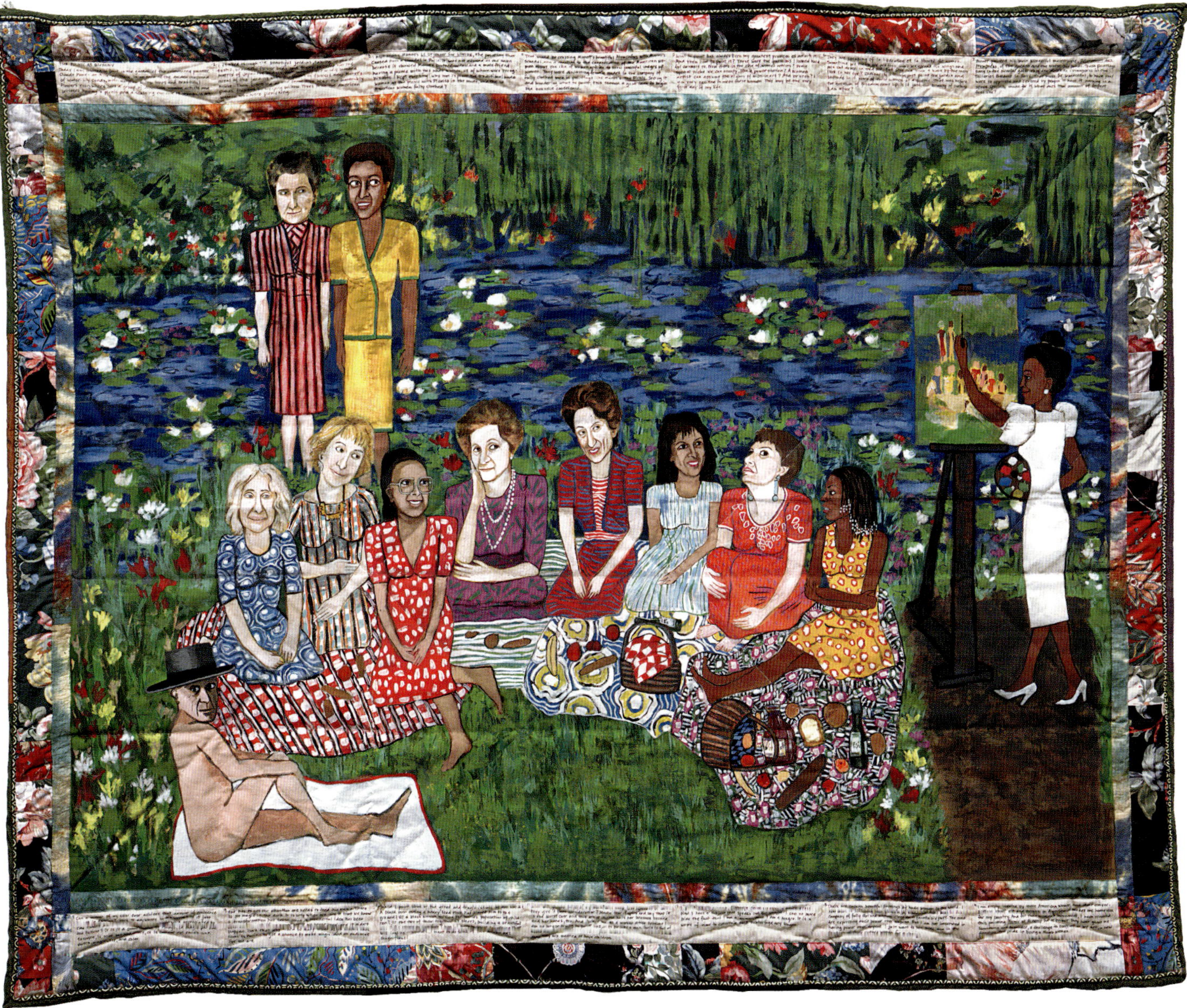

Jacolby Satterwhite
*Black Luncheon*, 2020
Animated neon and hand-painted enamel
on 3D-printed resin
84 × 88 × 12 in. (213.4 × 223.5 × 30.5 cm)

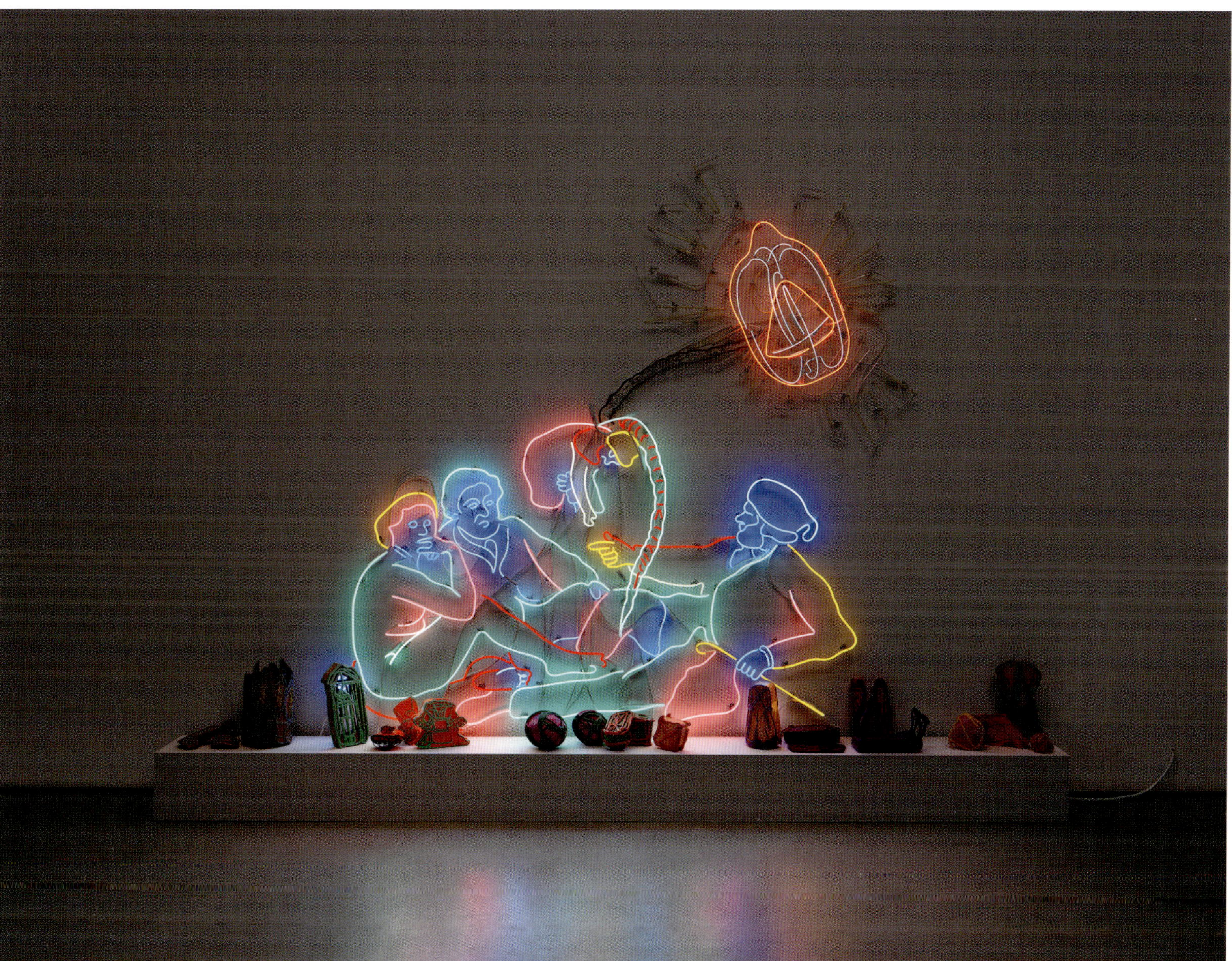

Raqib Shaw
*From Narcissus to Icarus after Déjeuner sur l'herbe*, 2017–18
Acrylic liner and enamel on birchwood
60 5⁄8 × 71 11⁄16 in. (154 × 182 cm)

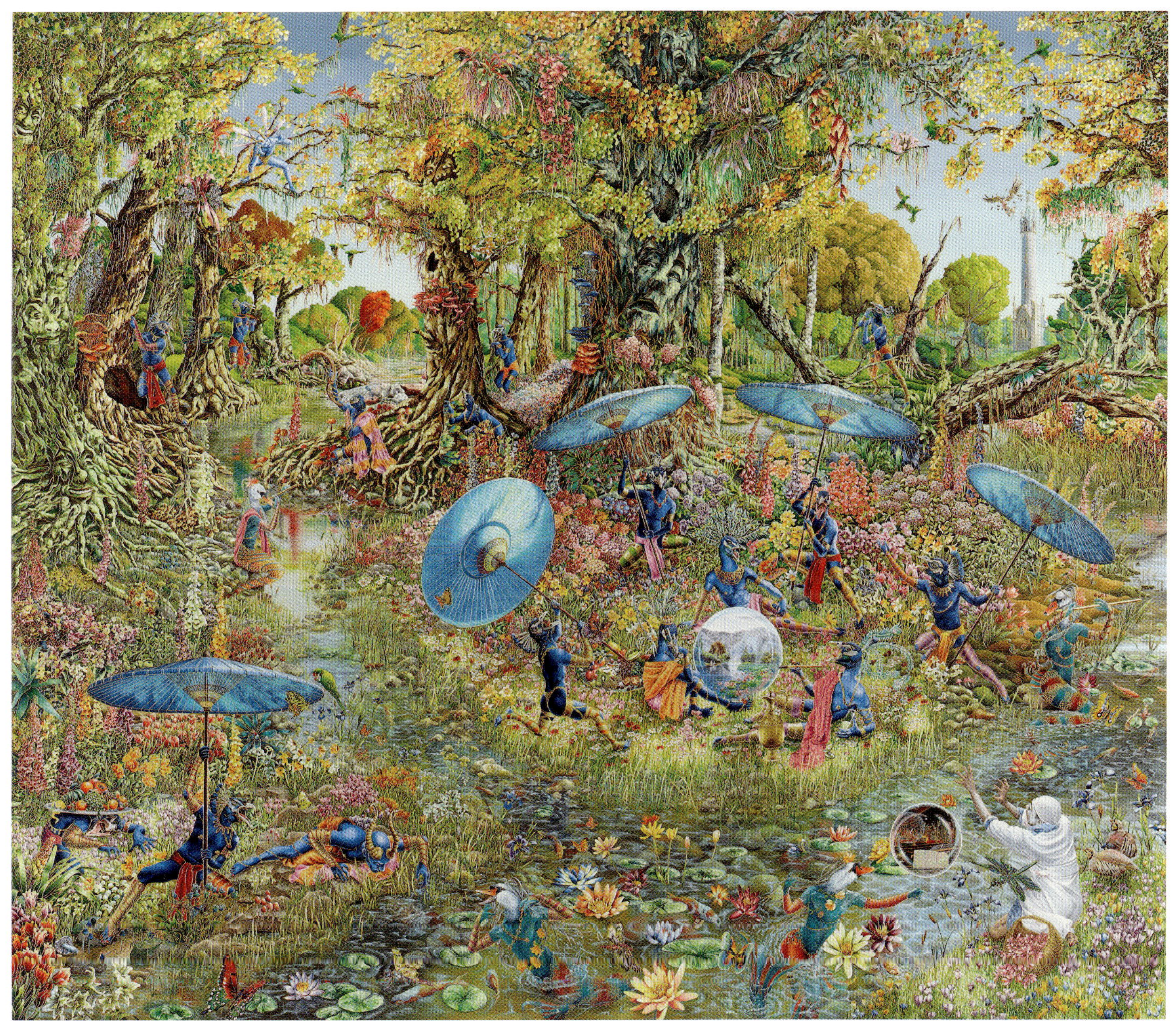

Kyungmi Shin
*and the sweet upside-down cake*
*(Lunch on the grass)*, 2022
Acrylic on archival pigment print
with UV laminate
56 ⅛ × 71 ⅞ in. (142.6 × 182.6 cm)

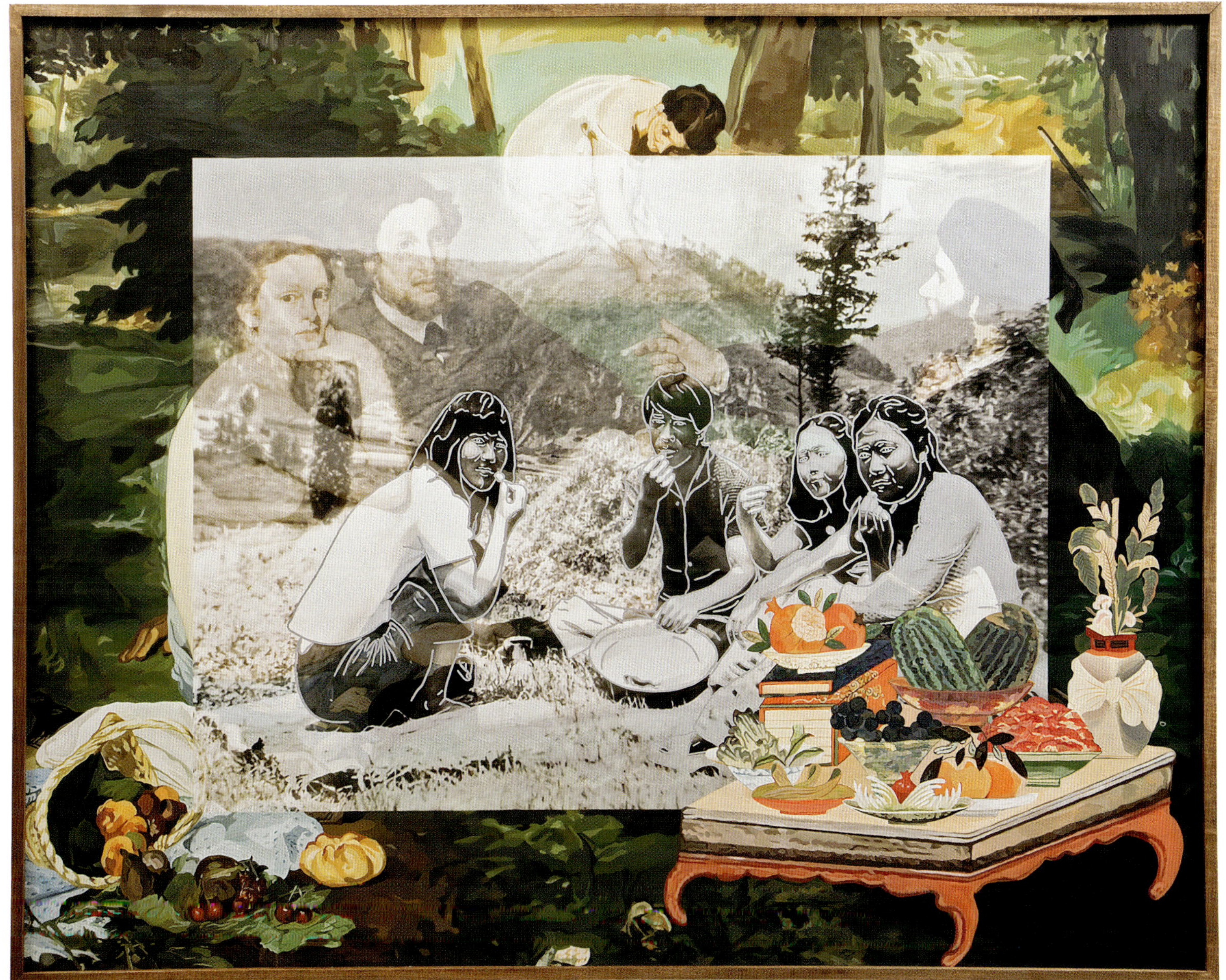

Bob Thompson
*Untitled (After Manet)*, 1961
Oil on board
3 ⅞ × 5 ⅞ in. (9.8 × 14.9 cm)

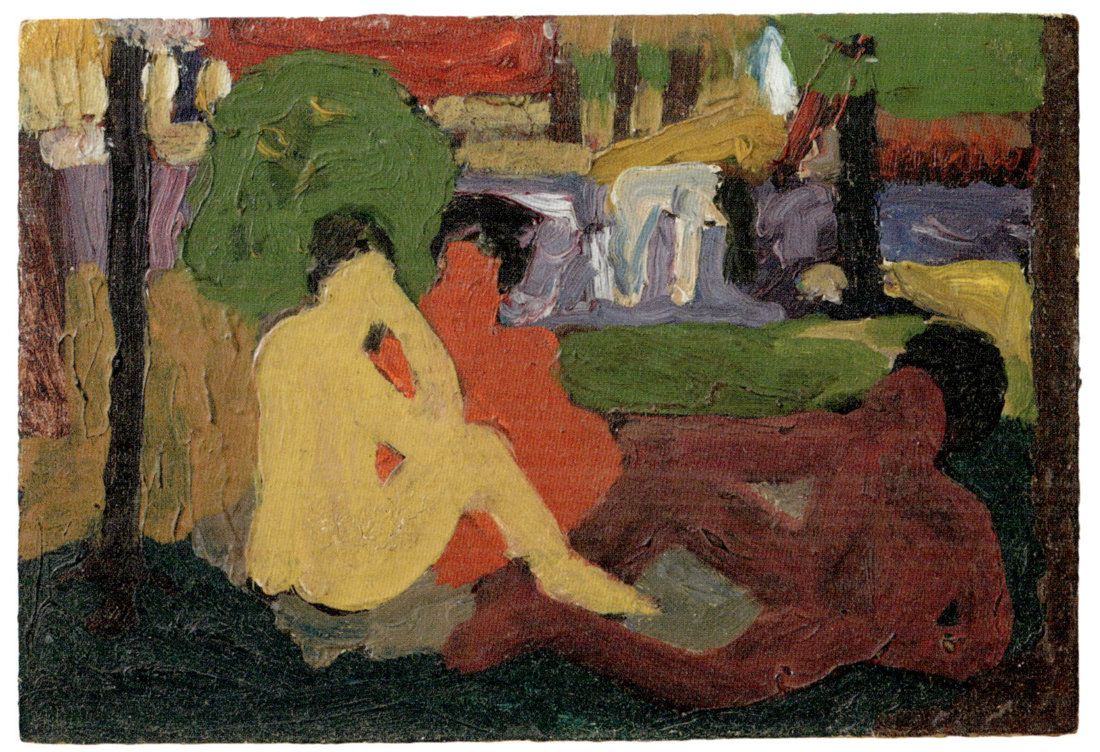

Kara Walker
*Picknicky*, 2022
Ink and cut paper on paper
76 ¾ × 74 ¼ in. (194.9 × 188.6 cm)

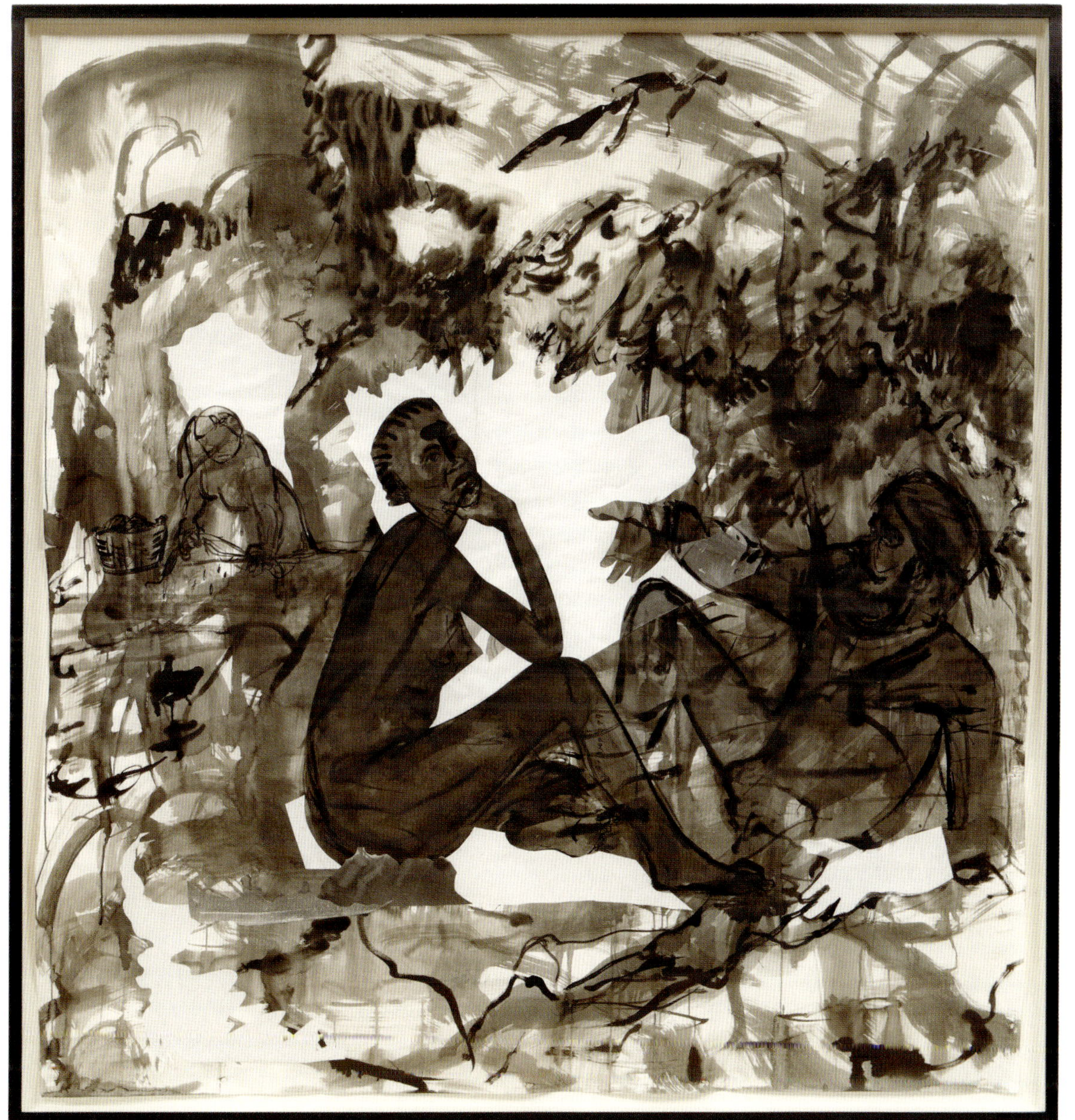

# Nina Chanel Abney

Combining representation and abstraction, Nina Chanel Abney's paintings capture the frenetic pace of contemporary culture. Broaching subjects as diverse as race, celebrity, religion, politics, sex, and art history, her works embrace disjointed narratives in lieu of linear storytelling. Through a bracing use of color and unapologetic scale, Abney's canvases propose a new type of history painting, one grounded in the barrage of everyday events and funneled through the velocity of the Internet. Abney was born in Chicago in 1982 and currently lives and works in New York.

ARUNA D'SOUZA

Manet's original painting presented a pretty stark power dynamic—two bourgeois men who relax and sort of survey their domain and a naked woman who gazes coolly out of the canvas but is, nonetheless, the object of the viewer's gaze. *Outdoor Dining #1* really upends that power dynamic in the way those three central figures relate to each other. There's also a real play with the question of binaristic gender itself. Can you talk about that?

NINA CHANEL ABNEY

In responding to Manet's original painting, I opted to eliminate the presumed dynamic often assigned to gender and rendered three figures interacting without a hierarchy. In *Outdoor Dining #1*, the scenario depicted leaves any narrative in the hands of the viewer based on how they identify the figures. I love a playful, sometimes sarcastic exploration of the alleged gender and racial binaries. My use of shapes, symbols, and colors is strategically placed in an attempt to push the viewer to question and recognize their own tendencies and biases.

D'SOUZA

Richard Powell gave a lecture recently at the National Gallery of Art and spoke of your radical use of the color brown—it's not quite a "naturalist" signifier of skin tone; it's more like a collage element. It seems to function both as a joyful celebration of difference and a way of questioning ideas of race. Could you talk a bit about that aspect of your work?

ABNEY

In all of my paintings, I work toward techniques that simplify figures to their barest elements, leaving each with the minimum required to be recognizable or legible to the viewer. These elements become symbols that build a visual language and a library of references for me to play with. This language can be used conceptually and compositionally. I think about the signifiers of race and gender, and the stratifications of both, in terms of skin tone and gender presentations. With skin tone, in particular, I often question the presumptions of the viewer through my treatment of various iterations of brown, thus probing the interchangeable meanings assigned to skin tone.

D'SOUZA

Your work has long engaged certain iconic figures in art history—Stuart Davis, for example, and Henri Matisse. Have you had Manet in mind before? What does this painting mean to you in your understanding of modernist art?

ABNEY

My understanding of modernist art is that of art that rejects conservative values, art that is experimental and innovative with form leaning toward abstraction. Though Manet is often cited as a founding father of modernism, and was considered pretty radical in his time, in a contemporary context I still look at Manet's work as rather conservative, so never really had Manet in mind before when reaching for inspiration. When formulating my own artist voice, I was looking to completely reject any realistic depiction of subjects, and in my eyes Manet is a realistic painter. Any current referencing of his work has been for contrast, a way to reimagine the stories that his paintings tell, the scenes that he depicts. I pulled from Manet's beautiful landscapes, scenes, and epic compositions to make a painting that centers Black queer people, creating a new narrative in which I feel seen.

D'SOUZA

Manet's painting to me is all about *pleasure*—the pleasure of the figures in the landscape, the pleasure of the viewer. And your reinterpretation seems all about pleasure, too. What or whose pleasures did you try to evoke?

ABNEY

I, too, wanted to evoke the pleasure of the figures depicted. I also wanted to evoke the pleasure of freedom. The freedom to enjoy the mundane, to engage in everyday activities without being gendered, racialized, or scrutinized because of these signifiers of identity. The freedom to just be. At the time of the pandemic when I created this work, I felt I was given a rare opportunity to quiet the noise and lean into the most simple pleasures. When I look at art, I want to wonder, I want to be seduced into the artist's world, simultaneously finding and creating my own place within what is presented to me. For the viewer, I hope to probe the pleasure of imagination and discovery.

D'SOUZA

I love the red and white stripes and blue blocks of color—very Fourth of July. It feels like you've taken a quintessentially French painting and turned it into a very American one, albeit with a very strong proposition about how "American" is defined. Can you tell me about that?

ABNEY

When creating my take on Manet's painting, I aimed to be on the opposite end. What better way to contrast this Manet's work, painted in what I perceived to be an elegant, even romantic manner, than to depict a Fourth of July picnic, which at times can be outright absurd. Also, I was humorously looking at the history and French origins of the picnic and what it has evolved to be. Perhaps for Manet, depicting two male figures with a nude female figure was pushing boundaries. For me, within the current times I am living in, during which Black and queer people seem to be constantly under attack, it was important to depict a scene that in the future could potentially be seen as pushing boundaries as well.

## Diane Arbus

Diane Arbus is one of the most original and influential photographers of the twentieth century. Her depictions of couples, children, female impersonators, nudists, New York City pedestrians, suburban families, circus performers, and celebrities, among others, span the breadth of the postwar American social sphere and constitute a diverse and singularly compelling portrait of humanity. Arbus was born in New York in 1923, and she died in the same city in 1971.

Nudist camps was a terrific subject for me....

They seem to wear more clothes than other people. I mean the men wear shoes and socks when they go down to the lake and they have their cigarettes tucked into their socks. And the women wear earrings, hats, bracelets, watches, high heels. Sometimes you'll see someone with nothing on but a bandaid.

After a while you begin to wonder. I mean there'll be an empty pop bottle or a rusty bobby pin underfoot, the lake bottom oozes mud in a particularly nasty way, the outhouse smells, the woods look mangy. It gets to seem as if way back in the Garden of Eden after the Fall, Adam and Eve had begged the Lord to forgive them and He, in his boundless exasperation had said, "All right, then. Stay. Stay in the Garden. Get civilized. Procreate. Muck it up." And they did.

—Diane Arbus, 1971

from *Diane Arbus: An Aperture Monograph*, edited by Doon Arbus and Marvin Israel (Millerton, NY: Aperture, 1972), pp. 4–5; "edited from tape recordings of a series of classes Diane Arbus gave in 1971 as well as from some interviews and some of her writings."

# Vanessa Beecroft

Born in Genoa, Italy, in 1969, Vanessa Beecroft has been showing internationally since 1993. Her performances, photographs, paintings, and sculptures often highlight the tensions between nakedness and clothing, constraint and freedom, the collective and the individual, and human strength and weakness. She was one of the first artists to collaborate with fashion brands, starting in the 1990s. Beecroft lives and works in Los Angeles.

Inspired by both *Le Déjeuner sur l'herbe* and Paul McCarthy's *The Garden*, Vanessa Beecroft created a photographic tableau of the artists and staff of Deitch Projects for the September 2000 issue of *Harper's Bazaar*.

The then-director of photography at *Harper's Bazaar*, Cary Leitzes, was tasked with commissioning a photograph to accompany a story on Deitch Projects. We decided to make a "Deitch Project" out of it, asking Vanessa Beecroft, the artist with whom we opened the gallery, to create a performance work in photographic form. Vanessa had been inspired by my 1992 *Post Human* exhibition, which featured Paul McCarthy's astonishing work *The Garden* (1991–92). Her concept was to create an expanded version of *Le Déjeuner sur l'herbe* in a set inspired by McCarthy's *The Garden*. All the artists who had presented projects with the gallery were invited to pose, along with the gallery directors. Several of the artists declined to participate, but the work became a wonderful document of the early history of the gallery. It remains in the art historical record as a fascinating fusion of the history of Deitch Projects and the artistic vision of Vanessa Beecroft.

—Jeffrey Deitch

# Cecily Brown

Cecily Brown's paintings shift effortlessly between figuration and abstraction, across canvases that both suggest and obscure human and animal forms. Ranging from wild bacchanalia to intimate portraits, and even historical battle scenes, Brown's work is in dialogue with many of painting's historical masters while positioning itself as a unique and firmly contemporary revision of the medium. Born in London in 1969, Brown moved to New York in the 1990s, where she still lives and works. In 2023, she received her first full-fledged museum survey in New York at the Metropolitan Museum of Art.

MARINA MOLARSKY-BECK
What is your relationship to Manet?

CECILY BROWN
Manet is one of my favorite painters, but I'd never worked from him in a direct way until now.

I always wanted to be a figurative artist, and I think being a figurative artist is the hardest thing of all: to be able to paint the figure in a new or interesting way. I'm constantly striving to be more figurative. When I work from an existing image, it can actually take care of a lot of problems for me—the main one being finding the composition in the first place.

I started trying to draw the *Déjeuner sur l'herbe* still life. And I found it *the* hardest single bit of copying that I have ever attempted. The whole jumble of forms has a menacing underlying quality. You've got your lovely bright spring day, but if you put your head down in the grass, you're going to see nature at war. And in Manet's time the objects would have been read as clues telling a story: revealing a narrative.

I jumped at the chance [to participate] not just because I've always loved Manet's paintings, but also because one of my favorite bands when I was about thirteen was Bow Wow Wow, and their famous album cover [with the song] "Go Wild in the Country" is based on the *Déjeuner sur l'herbe*. In fact, I knew that album cover before I knew the painting. [The lead singer Annabella Lwin] was only fourteen at the time the picture was taken.

The story goes that she didn't know she was going to pose nude that day. They drove to a park outside London—which I recently found out was the park in my hometown. So, while they were taking this picture, I could easily have been on the other side of the pond getting high.

Apparently, they got there, and [the band manager] Malcolm McLaren said, "All right, Annabella, get your kit off," and she's like, "What are you talking about? My mum will kill me!" And he shows her the reproduction of *Déjeuner sur l'herbe*. You can just imagine him saying hurry up, and like that they do the picture. I looked equally at Manet and the record cover while working on my *Luncheon on the Grass* paintings.

There were just so many things that drew me to it and made it an exciting project. I'm actually still stewing over it. That's the great thing about working from [a] painting like this—I'm definitely not done with it. I'm still making paintings that relate to it and now that I've done these, probably always will.

MOLARSKY-BECK
How were you were thinking about the gender and sexual politics of the painting?

BROWN
One of the reasons I make such a big deal of the Bow Wow Wow cover is that I was so interested in all those politics around it. It's unbelievably loaded and layered.

The still life within the Manet is weighted formally by the butter dish. Butter is a lubricant. I emphasized the dish—not only as this wonderful slab of yellow enclosed by a space frame that works really well as a formal device, but also because I think you assume that there's going to be sex involved at some point. We know a bit about the female protagonist (or heroine) of the Manet, Victorine Meurent, who was also a painter. So here's the painter as model, the painter as sexual being.

So, of course, I was thinking about the fact that Annabella Lwin was very young and manipulated, and especially in the large work, my Victorine character is very tough and looking you squarely in the eye. Wasn't the direct gaze of the woman part of the scandal in Manet's time? She's confronting the viewer.

Of course, if you're a woman painting a woman, her gaze looking out and engaging you is different from when a man paints it. It's not a self-portrait, but of course when you're painting a female nude or any nude, you're thinking, how does it feel to sit like that, where is my weight? You might even look at your own arm, for example, to see what your hand looks like in that position and work from your own body. And I become the nude, and the nude becomes me.

It's so layered, so complex, both psychologically and pictorially, which probably is why I'm still grappling with it.

This has really been a new starting point for me moving forward with figuration that the *Déjeuner sur l'herbe* paintings really helped with.

MOLARSKY-BECK

You often work on linen—how did you come to do so?

BROWN

I've worked on linen since really young. It's kind of a name-drop-y story. Malcolm Morley gave me a little piece of extra linen that he had—lead-primed linen—when I met him when I first came to New York. He just said, "oh, try this." And I never went back—I couldn't afford linen then, but as soon as I could afford it, specifically lead-primed linen. Painting on this lead-primed linen was like painting for the first time, because the paint just goes on completely differently.

This conversation has been edited and condensed.

# Caitlin Cherry

Caitlin Cherry, a painter of cyber-multitudes, draws on painting, sculpture, and installation in her multifaceted practice, coalescing into articulate and alluring representations of Black femininity. Filtering media through layers of digital manipulation, her work draws parallels between Black femme bodies, frequently commodified and positioned as sexual assets, and the seductiveness of art objects in the commercial gallery circuit. Resisting easy placement in the cultural marketplace of hot takes, these paintings decline respectability politics in favor of a nuanced and unabashedly sexy assessment of online drama, distortion, and desire. Born in Chicago in 1987, Cherry lives and works in Richmond, Virginia, and Mérida, Yucatán, Mexico.

ARUNA D'SOUZA

Your painting seems to say out loud what Manet's only implied: Manet seems to tease the audience by suggesting that this group had just or would soon have a little orgy in the woods. (Why else would the women be undressed or half dressed?) But you cut to the chase: your work is all about different forms of pleasure—bodily pleasure and optical pleasure, above all. Can you talk about how those forms of pleasure intersect in your work?

CAITLIN CHERRY

I used the prompt of Manet in this painting to create a more overtly sexual scene, and that is not typical in my work, though I often paint images of the "sexy" female figure. There are a lot of sexual acts and images collaged together in the composition, and I felt like this is probably what Manet wanted to paint but could not bring himself to do. Pleasure is incredibly personal and political, particularly for Black women, and we are often shamed for seeking it out. Therefore, I find it rare, outside of the realms of pornography and music, though even those realms are compromised by male consumption, that I see Black women able to manifest or demand pleasure on their own terms and not for male attention or approval. My work attempts to keep it a closed loop of female gazing and pleasure-seeking. There is my pleasure in producing the work, observing these women, representing them in a way that makes them dignified while also indulging in their sexual gluttony.

D'SOUZA

The painting is really clearly formally related to Manet's painting—you've got that patch of light in the center and a sort of pyramidal central grouping of figures. Manet's space wasn't altogether conventional—the perspective is messed up between foreground and background—but you seem to blow apart the picture surface entirely. Can you talk about this aspect of your work?

CHERRY

I appreciate how Manet's painting is composed from collaged elements, like a group of vignettes that constitute the scenario instead of Manet posing his subjects outdoors and painting from life. There is a female figure in the background much larger than she should be in terms of perspective realism, and the main group of picnickers in the foreground are awkwardly interacting at best. My work also utilizes collage to generate compositions in paintings, though there are more obvious delineations of where my vignettes start and begin. My brand of collage comes from this era of technological tools I use to generate painting references, and I overemphasize a feeling of too many open browser windows with stacked JPEGs on a computer desktop. I bring my tools of construction of my paintings to the forefront of my practice, and they assist in providing meaning and context for my figures.

D'SOUZA

One of the reasons I love this response to Manet is that he was already thinking about painting at this moment of technological change in the image world—in his case, photography and even newspapers. Your work, too, is all about how Black women negotiate desire, subjectivity, power, money, etc., through the lens of social media and digital technology. Can you talk about your thinking in relation to race, gender, and technology?

CHERRY

Certainly as painters in this day and age, we continue to negotiate our relevance through and against photography, and both sides play in the spaces between our disciplines constantly. As someone who consumes most of my media and news on the Internet through social media, I investigate how photography has changed to suit the design of these platforms, how social media has even influenced how cameras should be constructed and formatted. In my artwork, I capture images taken from social media of Black celebrities and consider that formatting of that image. Therefore, I will use particular dimensions of canvas, or a particular iconic "Instagram" square format, to express a similarity to these digital experiences. I like the awkward cropping we need to do to the images we post every day to fit into these social media platforms. I also like how we see them through our increasingly taller phones with higher-resolution screens or even absorb the information through the endlessly long and tall linear scroll down. My art practice considers how Black femininity is networked, because we as a culture are often reduced to our representations, and in this age these representations live online, and therefore our online content is linked and flattened as a kind of singular powerful entity known as "Black Culture" in the minds of others.

# Joe Coleman

Joe Coleman is a world-renowned artist known for his meticulously detailed paintings. He has exhibited for more than four decades throughout the world, including solo museum exhibitions at the Wadsworth Atheneum Museum of Art in Hartford, Connecticut, Palais de Tokyo in Paris, and the Kunst-Werke Institute for Contemporary Art in Berlin. Born in 1955 in Norwalk, Connecticut, Coleman lives and works in New York.

ALEXANDRA M. THOMAS

How did you decide on this approach as a response to Manet?

JOE COLEMAN

I decided to sit down on grass and have lunch with the painter Édouard Manet. So, the painting is a portrait of the painter himself gazing at me while I painted it. But gazing at the viewer when exhibited. The portrait is inspired by Manet's self-portraits as well as the photographs of Manet taken by Gaspard-Félix Tournachon, known by the pseudonym "Nadar." The painting is about influence, appropriation, reference, and art history presented as a carnival house of mirrors.

THOMAS

What are some of the prominent art historical references?

COLEMAN

The painting is also about birth, controversy, and scandal. Manet's most infamous and groundbreaking painting, *Le Déjeuner sur l'herbe* is seen on the right side of the seated Manet. It is giving birth to an unlikely horde of more recent avant-garde artists including Jean-Michel Basquiat, Pablo Picasso, Roy Lichtenstein, and George Grosz.

THOMAS

Can you tell me more about some of the background scenes? What does the text say, and what's happening in the background?

COLEMAN

On Manet's left, we see that *Luncheon on the Grass* is actually born of an earlier work from 1510 by Giorgione or possibly Titian called *The Pastoral Concert*, which in turn is siring a host of art radicals, too. Keith Haring, Francis Bacon, and Philip Guston all seem comfortable cavorting in the Renaissance.

THOMAS

What is the scene above Manet's head?

COLEMAN

Above Manet's head appears Marcantonio Raimondi's engraving *The Judgment of Paris* from around 1510–20. It is yet another child bearer to *The Luncheon on the Grass*, bringing forth more mutinous artists from Jim Nutt to Jean Dubuffet, while KAWS's *Companion* floats above, unable to look down.

This delirious kaleidoscope drips down on both sides of the painted portrait. On the left, the model for the nude picnicker from *The Luncheon on the Grass*, Victorine-Louise Meurent, is now legless, seated in a wheelchair in the pose she had for another iconic and scandalous Manet painting, *Olympia* (1863). In my painting, she has spawned the Diane Arbus photograph *Masked woman in a wheelchair, Pa. 1970*. However, because I painted this work at the height of the COVID-19 pandemic, the Arbus Halloween mask is replaced by a face mask and shield associated with the pandemic.

THOMAS

So there is an abundance of art histories referenced, but contemporary issues as well. Are there other ways that current issues are explored alongside the history of art?

COLEMAN

On the opposite side, we see Manet's *The Head of Christ* (1864), with Christ also wearing a COVID mask but with the words "I can't breathe" (mantra of the Black Lives Matter movement). The phrase originates from the last words of Eric Garner, an unarmed black man who was killed by police in 2014. The Christ head looks down at a reclining man in the pose of the Manet painting *Young Woman Reclining in Spanish Costume* (1867). Though the reclining man's head is the crying child from David Alfaro Siqueiros's *Echo of a Scream* (1937), there can be no doubt who the reclining man is when you read the text above: "Go hide in your bunker racist president" (Protest sign 6/3/20).

THOMAS

I am interested in hearing more about your use of language in the work.

COLEMAN

The text to the left of Manet's head is a quote by Willem de Kooning: "I feel like Manet who said, 'Yes, I am influenced by everybody. But every time I put my hands in my pockets, I find someone else's fingers there.'" The subject of de Kooning's *Woman 1* (1950–52) is now working at *A Bar at the Folies-Bergère* from the 1882 painting by Manet. The visual mirrors can be found to echo in the painting's text.

One can continue to get lost in this painted house of mirrors, but at some point the viewer may realize that, as the title suggests, we are having lunch on cannabis with a fabled mythological progenitor who also bears an unmistakable physical resemblance to the artist who painted it.

THOMAS

How does this work relate to your general practice?

COLEMAN

The process that I used in the making of this painting is much the same as with all of my works. The sizes vary as greatly as the subject matter. I do no preliminary sketches, and I paint with a jeweler's loupe and minute brushes, even when working on larger pieces. An enormous amount of research goes into each work, and since there are no preliminary sketches, the painting unfolds or reveals itself to me roughly one square inch at a time. This allows me to discover things as I am painting and react to those discoveries as I am painting. Since this painting was inspired by Jeffrey Deitch's concept for the show, it allowed me to rediscover the French Impressionists and specifically Édouard Manet. I had always felt more of a kinship with the moody, emotionally charged work of the Expressionists and felt often that the Impressionist painters in general were, in my mind, more decorative painters. Through the creation of this work, I came to realize and appreciate the serious risks Manet took and the profound effect he had on many of the radical artists that have inspired me. I found a new admiration for this artist who, after all, may not be so different from myself.

# Robert Colescott

Over a nearly six-decade painting career, Robert Colescott was a proud instigator who fearlessly tackled subjects of social and racial inequality, class structure, sex, and the human condition through his uniquely rhythmic and often manic style of figuration. Colescott's intense interest in critiquing painting's failure to accurately represent the Black experience is manifested in a lifetime of work that offers a revisionist art historical narrative and has subsequently influenced an entire generation of artists. Born in 1925 in Oakland, California, Colescott died in 2009.

## Robert Colescott's *Sunday Afternoon with Joaquin Murietta*
by Lowery Stokes Sims

Robert Colescott was a vision whenever he visited New York in the 1980s. A California native and resident of Arizona, he cultivated his cultural identity in western-style attire—a fringed jacket, a silver-and-turquoise belt buckle, and bracelet and cowboy boots—and even in his art. A number of his paintings from the 1970s depict wagon train camps, gold seekers in the company of black cooks, and even anthropomorphic cacti mimicking the plein air fornications of cowboys and cowgirls. Of particular interest to this discussion are his paintings and drawings of cowgirls executed between 1976 and 1980, which contextualize our comprehension of the Black female figure who stars in his 1979 painting *Sunday Afternoon with Joaquin Murietta*, Colescott's adroit appropriation and parody of Édouard Manet's *Déjeuner sur l'herbe* of 1863.

In 1976 and 1977, with *Tin Gal*, *Cactus Gal*, and *Two by Four*, Colescott created characters who are seen outfitted in western regalia: gun belts, guns and holsters, hats, and boots. It is intriguing that Colescott chose tin, cactus, and wood personifications as avatars for these assertive women rather than fully formed human figures. He mischievously stenciled comments in the compositions that subtly swipe at that female assertiveness: "fearless avenger," "Invincible her only fear is coming unscrewed," "A Prickly Affair," and "Avenger Gals of the Old West." Nonetheless, these avatars have a degree of self-assurance and agency that their real-life counterparts would have had to have in the hypermasculine cultures of *cow-person-dom*. They are a far cry from the hapless women in two of Colescott's earlier western paintings—*Cowboys and Indians* and *Pancho Villa* (both 1971)—who faint in shock, or fend off the sexual advances of rambunctious men.

Colescott directly takes on the prototypical cowgirls promoted by Hollywood and the media in the 1950s and 1960s, which gentrified and whitewashed the history and personalities of the American West. There was Dale Evans, the wholesome housewife companion to Roy Rogers in their television show, which ran between 1951 and 1957.[1] The quintessentially wholesome American woman, Doris Day, starred in the 1963 film *Annie Get Your Gun*,[2] which was based on the life of sharpshooter Annie Oakley, who traveled with Buffalo Bill's Wild West show in the late nineteenth and early twentieth centuries.[3] Their storylines promoted the premise that independent women of the postwar, prefeminist era would ultimately accede to the authority of men.

Although they were created after *Sunday Afternoon with Joaquin Murietta*, Colescott's 1980 series of drawings in colored pencil and graphite, *Girl of the Golden West*, should be considered here. They reference the 1938 western movie musical (based on the 1905 original play by David Belasco, which also provided the plot for Giacomo Puccini's 1910 opera, *La Fanciulla del West*).[4] Colescott subtitles them as specific locales: *Arizona*, *California*, *Dakota*, *Oregon*, *Texas*, *Utah*, and *Wyoming*. These cowgirls pose provocatively, tote guns (the one in *California* also grits her teeth on a knife, and in *Arizona* she has an arrow shot through her hat), or barhop (*Girl of the Golden West*). Flirtatious, buxom, and self-aware, they, too, expose Colescott's ambivalence toward and attraction to women, Black and white—recognizable attitudes of, and conundrums faced by, the so-called Mad Men generation of American males.

This makes the woman in *Sunday Afternoon with Joaquin Murietta* all the more striking. As noted at the outset, compositionally the painting is a spot-on parody of Manet's *Déjeuner sur l'herbe*. As is his wont, Colescott has code-switched the signifiers of the original painting without losing its initial shock value. The principal female figure is now a red-haired Black woman who sports red lipstick. She is now espied in a glen in California in the company of the legendary bandito and Robin Hood figure Joaquin Murietta and one of his comrades.[5] This Girl of the Golden West (who in the original play, incidentally, is a frontier woman who falls in love with a bandit) meets the mythic Mexican who disrupted the gold economy of nineteenth-century California.

Colescott's heroine regards us, as unintimidated and unafraid as does her counterpart in the Manet. There is none of the ambivalent commentary as Colescott presents another Girl of the Golden West—the Black woman, who along with other Black individuals were integral players in the "ecology and economy of the Americas."[6] She also seems to cast a knowing glance at Colescott himself, confronting him with the conundrums and demons with which he is dealing. Her embellished red boots may highlight her nudity, but she seems totally at ease in the company of Joaquin Murietta and one of his comrades, who approximate the poses and positions of the two male figures in Manet's *Déjeuner*. Colescott has almost faithfully reproduced the pose of the woman in the middle ground of the Manet, who is wading—semi-dishabille—in the water. The woman's discarded clothing and remains of a pastoral feast—seen at the lower left of the Manet—are replaced by some of Colescott's favorite motifs: a pink garter belt and bra, a knife and a gun, and a basket, what he once described as the "popular trash, studio sweepings, or works that didn't pass art history."[7]

Colescott's appropriation of Manet achieves his abiding goal to "interject blacks into art history."[8] To achieve that, he found it useful to tweak familiar art historical masterpieces just enough so that the original would be recognized. And then, by switching the usual visual codes, he shocks viewers into questioning their habitual presumptions about culture, race, gender, and identity. Here he additionally demolishes the usual narrative of western lore in America, expanding the cast of characters who would impact the course of that history.

1 *Britannica*, s.v. "Dale Evans," accessed May 4, 2023, https://www.britannica.com/biography/Dale-Evans.

2 Wikipedia, s.v. "*Annie Get Your Gun* (Doris Day and Robert Goulet album)," accessed May 3, 2023, https://en.wikipedia.org/wiki/Annie_Get_Your_Gun_(Doris_Day_and_Robert_Goulet_album).

3 Wikipedia, s.v. "*Annie Get Your Gun* (musical)," accessed May 4, 2023, https://en.wikipedia.org/wiki/Annie_Get_Your_Gun_(musical).

4 Wikipedia, s.v. "*The Girl of the Golden West* (1938 film)," accessed May 3, 2023, https://en.wikipedia.org/wiki/The_Girl_of_the_Golden_West_(1938_film).

5 Wikipedia, s.v. "Joaquin Murrieta," accessed May 4, 2023, https://en.wikipedia.org/wiki/Joaquin_Murrieta.

6 Janice Rhoshalle Littlejohn, "Exploring the Hidden History of Black Cowboys and Cowgirls," Shondaland, March 17, 2022, accessed March 6, 2023, https://www.shondaland.com/live/travel-food/a39455814/exploring-the-hidden-history-of-black-cowboys-and-cowgirls/.

7 Robert Colescott, artist's statement, in Marcia Tucker, *Not Just for Laughs: The Art of Subversion*, exh.cat. (New York: New Museum, 1981), p. 29.

8 See "Robert Colescott—Reenvisioning History Painting," Artdex, accessed May 5, 2023, https://www.artdex.com/robert-colescott-reenvisioning-history-painting/#:~:text=To%20quote%20Colescott%20himself%2C%20the,main%20figures%20in%20those%20paintings.

# Somaya Critchlow

Somaya Critchlow was born in 1993 in London. While the women Critchlow depicts are fictional, they draw inspiration from pop culture clichés, her own photographs, and studies from life. Critchlow's subjects are both intriguing and unsettling; they seduce viewers into a world that at times references art historical and literary precedents. While Critchlow's handling of paint merges representation and abstraction, her imagery endlessly questions the complexities associated with image making, the model, and perception. The artist lives and works in London.

ALEXANDRA M. THOMAS

*Mr. Peanut! (The Picnic)* is a unique and surprising response to Manet's *Luncheon on the Grass*. How did you decide to paint this scene, and what does it mean?

SOMAYA CRITCHLOW

I tried to respond to the Manet work with what is already running through my own works. Mr. Peanut is a motif that has recurred a few times in a few paintings. It was a painting that I wanted to do anyway, and I thought it fit well with Manet's *Luncheon on the Grass*: the absurdity of a figure in a certain setting. I'm not sure what it means. I try not to overdetermine meaning onto a painting. It's just being intrigued by the idea and going for it.

THOMAS

How does the painting illustrate notions of race, sexuality, and consumption?

CRITCHLOW

If I were to perhaps answer that objectively, having now made the painting, there is the symbolism of Mr. Peanut as a colonial mascot for mass-produced goods, something I actually learned after having made a few Mr. Peanut paintings. I paint Black women because I am a Black woman; I look at the autonomy of being Black and how it fits into the imagery. I like to take things that have a sinister undertone to them and work through them. There's a bit of dark humor. It gets you to look at things from different perspectives. There is perhaps shock but also intrigue.

THOMAS

In form and content, how does this work relate to your practice in general?

CRITCHLOW

It fits into my practice because I mostly paint figures. Mr. Peanut is not an object or a person; he is a stand-in for something. The works are like psychological portraits, more so than portraits of a specific person. It's a character that I've used in paintings before, and I continue to use.

THOMAS

What does *Mr. Peanut!* add to the discourse on modern and contemporary painting?

CRITCHLOW

When Manet made *Luncheon on the Grass*, it was a total disruption at the time. Painting is often cyclical. My opinions are always changing, but I know that painting has been around for so much longer than I have, so it'd be a shame not to look at and engage with earlier painting. It's how we got here; it's who we are. Historic paintings can take you to a different time and place.

# Celeste Dupuy-Spencer

Born in New York in 1979, Celeste Dupuy-Spencer is a painter based in Los Angeles. The artist moves between styles and genres of painting to capture the profoundly layered and wildly varied American contemporary moment, its historical trajectories and prevailing structures of power. At times both troubling and endearing, her characters' idiosyncrasies are as complex as the United States themselves. Painted with seemingly rushed and raucous brushstrokes, her works leave the viewer with a sense of existential grappling.

ARUNA D'SOUZA
Celeste, you've done something pretty radical by transforming Manet's image of homosociality—the relationship between men that takes place through the instrumentalization of women's bodies, whether it's going to a strip club with the boys or having a picnic in the woods, where men remain fully clothed, and women are naked—and turned it into something else. There are no women here, just men—the two guys from *Déjeuner* in the foreground, and people from multiple eras in the background. Can you tell me who they are?

CELESTE DUPUY-SPENCER
That's right, I decided to extend the group of men through time. And once a story of these men extends through time as a frame with which to look at society, the women lose any last sliver of meaning—if they ever had one. Anyway, I'm not terribly interested in any particular distinct relationships, so these men aren't anyone. I wanted to make a response to Manet's painting by zooming out on the world-building function of these idealized homosocial relationships, which, for all time, is the primary myth on which our civilization was built. They are less painted as men than they are indications of time. I want the viewer to, by means of the men, draw the line from the world of *Luncheon* to the landscape of today's world.

D'SOUZA
As a follow-up, can you tell me why you decided to make this picture of an all-boys party? What was it about Manet's painting, or even painting in general, that pushed you in that direction?

DUPUY-SPENCER
Manet was a painter of modern times, and what we are supposed to see when looking at his works is the world in which he was existing. He was famously a commentator, so I used his painting as a way to think into the broader European Victorian past, a prompt that sends my mind to images marking the total restructuring of society, of wealth, industry, the strange hybridization of Christian doctrines and modern secular STEM and... alcoholism would be my best guess. Culture had turned en masse toward championing the freedom to become this brand-new kind of person by toppling and/or demonizing the garish and feminine, mostly decorative kings on earth as well as in heaven, to erect governments of men. It makes me think of Verdi's *Requiem*, which denounces the church's hold over humanity, which it kept paralyzed in terror, and portrays heaven's hosts as horrifyingly frivolous courtmen who, when forced to acknowledge a human, do so with smug contempt (an arrow Verdi kept trained on the monarchy's pompous decorative soldiers), before he ends it with a desperate cry for freedom. As the facades of the bloodlines fell, fraternities reigned high and philosophers drew crowds. And above all, still more industry, colonization, wealth versus labor, workhouses, capital, categorization, resource grabs. Bottomless entertainment and a constant stinking mass of dehumanizing poverty.

Looking back to the Manet painting, it's striking how natural and fully embodied these relaxed men are, as it is only through the trappings of male friendship that wealth can be multiplied endlessly. So, easily they reinforce their relationships with one another, the same as it always was, and the women provide the setting or the main event, the same as it always was. Her only function is to bind the men together. It's an all boys party in Manet's painting as well.

The title of my painting is *Ode to Enjoyments*. I'm locating the beginnings of the Industrial Revolution as the moment when this impulse, natural or unnatural, clicked into overdrive, and the Western society we inhabit today was shaped by a scramble to the top in order to attain "enjoyment" or pleasure. The entire world was bent to this end, and it was divided up in two categories: "resources" and "men."

I removed the women because I'm not interested in pretending that they have a chance in hell of even existing as people in this setting. I can squint and see she's always been allegorical since the beginning of time—she's dead. And if I were to bring her from Manet's painting to mine, she would only serve to encourage our sympathy for the men, maybe by reshaping the painting into a portrait of innocent men who are longing for sexual freedom and a return to nature. That's also the danger of looking at the these men as though they are reminiscent of lads at a strip club without women—the danger turning them into sympathetic figures. I wanted them to be generations of the same relationship, not simply men, but a line drawn from Manet's *Luncheon* to today, in a natural progression, which ends with them picnicking not in the forest but on the pulverized earth on the edge of a mine.

D'SOUZA

I've been trying to figure out what I'm seeing in the background—it looks a bit like a strip mine, if I'm not mistaken. Could you talk about that element of the landscape and what it meant to transform Manet's limpid little pool of water into this hill?

DUPUY-SPENCER

Yeah, it's a strip mine. I painted it as a replacement for the women, not the pool. I transfigured her to her function. It felt more direct. And more humane.

But my other reason for putting a mine in place of the trees and water is the absolute brutality of the mine on the landscape. It's just shorthand for "exploit to death." But I needed it to be familiar, something that anchors the painting in the real world.

D'SOUZA

I am noticing some really subtle but unmistakable nods to Manet's palette: the particular blues of the water pooling on the ledges of the hill, the splashes of yellow, the very precise greens and grays (not to mention black) that you employ in the foreground. Can you talk about Manet as a painter, and what this process meant to you? Your work is rooted in such a deep interest in art history; I'd imagine Manet has always been someone you've thought about.

DUPUY-SPENCER

I mean. He's Manet. I fucking love Manet.

## Dominique Fung

The second-generation Chinese Canadian painter Dominique Fung refigures art history to give her subjects real agency. Fung was born in 1987 in Ottawa, Canada, and her early artistic passions were influenced by Vermeer, Manet, Rembrandt, and Goya, but her sense of Chinese art history was largely informed by vessels and objects that she saw at home and on display at the Metropolitan Museum of Art in New York. These objects "made me question my place in the world and how I felt in terms of my displacement from my origins," explains the artist. In Fung's paintings, the decorative language on which Orientalism relies is more than just ornamental; these ancient vessels and sculptures are animate protagonists in their own right. Fung lives and works in Brooklyn, New York.

VIOLA ANGIOLINI

Dominique, can you tell us about your composition and your interest in addressing the still life that appears in the foreground of Manet's *Luncheon on the Grass*?

DOMINIQUE FUNG

My work references overlooked or forgotten historical East Asian objects, from deities and funerary objects to utilitarian objects. My interest in them has personal significance, and additionally, they are symbolically and formally interesting as subjects to paint. Naturally, I gravitated toward the objects, the still life, and the symbology of Manet's *Le Déjeuner sur l'herbe* painting. The still lifes in *Le Déjeuner sur l'herbe* are used as a secondary element, as poetic symbols to express themes of sexuality and the natural world.

The still life in the lower left corner of *Le Déjeuner sur l'herbe* consists of a basket of fruit, a round loaf of bread, and the woman's clothes. The fruit, which includes apples, pears, and grapes, is ripe and abundant, suggesting abundance and fertility. The bread, a symbol of sustenance, also suggests the importance of nature and the physical world. The woman's clothes, which are casually discarded, suggest both her sexuality and her vulnerability.

Instead of the still life being a secondary source of symbology, I am interested in the still life as the foreground, front and center of the painting. I included similar food items as a nod to the original painting but placed in the center focal point; a grill with skewers, a snack box, tea, and watermelon is what I would have brought to the picnic. I am inserting myself with ordinary foods that signify my cultural identity and using the food arrangement as imbued foods of desire to express body as subject and object.

ANGIOLINI

Could you elaborate more on this concept of bodies as subjects and objects?

FUNG

The binaries of men and women are highlighted through clothes and the discarding of clothing. Manet highlights the world of the men in this period, which is symbolically represented by the formal attire, the picnic basket, and the bread. The woman is represented by her nudity, discarded clothes, and the fruit. I believe Manet makes this contrast to suggest the tension between the traditional and the contemporary, the respectable and the scandalous. I wanted to remove some of these binaries and barriers or break this apart as much as possible. Intentionally removing the fully nude body, I am attempting to subvert the rational mind, leaving more space to accept new realities or question old ones. Because I only painted limbs, the viewer is uncertain whose limbs are in the picture. Who is respectable, and who is scandalous? In Manet's painting, the expression of the nude figure shows she is aware of the audience's gaze. In contrast, I intentionally painted the portrait of my figure looking elsewhere, enjoying a cigarette; the figure is simultaneously being consumed by the viewer or consuming themselves in a state of unconcern.

ANGIOLINI

Gravity and humor are often able to coexist in your works. How do you achieve this?

FUNG

A balance of lightness (humor) and heaviness (gravity) is something I strive to achieve in each of my works. The hallmarks of some of the best comedies and storytelling [are that they] all have great pacing and a balance of this heaviness and lightness layered on top of abstract thinking, emotional intelligence, social intelligence, and critical thinking. The same can be applied to image making.

ANGIOLINI

Your work subverts Western interpretations of the East through the lens of traditional European painting. What is your relationship with Manet and other European masters, whose palettes and atmospheres are often evoked by your paintings?

FUNG

I use color palettes from traditional European paintings and have equally utilized compositions and other formal elements from Asian paintings. I am interested in light, luminosity, and shadow, and paintings from sixteenth and seventeenth century Europe do this well. Whereas three-dimensionality was not a central element for image making in Asia, there was a focus on line, composition, and the poetry of image making that I have borrowed in my art practice.

The emphasis on the scale in *Le Déjeuner sur l'herbe* was in reaction to religious and historical paintings. I used the exact size parameters to experience the same surface scale as Manet did in 1863. I wanted to experience the same surface and composition parameters Manet had to contend with.

# Alain Jacquet and Sophie Matisse

Born in Boston in 1965, Sophie Matisse began her studies at the Massachusetts College of Art and Design, but dropped out after her first year and relocated to Paris to attend the École des Beaux-Arts, where her great-grandfather Henri Matisse had studied. There, she met the artist Alain Jacquet, whom she married in 1992. As an artist, Matisse became known for her series *Be Back in 5 Minutes*, in which she re-created recognizable works from art history but left out the people. She has been living and working in New York since 1996.

Born in 1939 in Neuilly-sur-Seine, France, Alain Jacquet emerged as a contemporary artist during a remarkable boom in image reproduction techniques. He tirelessly analyzed the ways in which representation informs the viewer's gaze. From his first abstract canvases to his mechanically generated paintings via silkscreen printing or computer, he continuously experimented with techniques throughout his career, yielding an impressive oeuvre of various forms and media. Guided by diverse principles, Jacquet demonstrated an incredible capacity for ingenuity with the examination of the liminal space between abstraction and figuration; the "latent image" within both collective and individual memory; and the appropriation of images from contemporary popular culture and iconic works showcased in museums. He died in 2008 in New York.

VIOLA ANGIOLINI
Sophie, could you explain for us Alain's "Mechanical Art" process?

SOPHIE MATISSE
Alain's process included photographically reproducing his subject matter and applying a photo screen. In the beginning, these works were primarily produced using a silkscreen technique. This photomechanical process Alain used as early as 1964, when he made his iconic *Déjeuner sur l'herbe*, shifting his painting technique from manual to mechanical. It was at that time that Alain coined the term "mec art," to refer to art made mechanically. This approach consumed him as he explored all different genres of photo screens used for various works he produced from that point forward. In fact, Alain always seemed especially proud to announce that his painting had been made by a robot when discussing his large space and planets paintings from the 1990s. I think he loved the idea that a work of art didn't have to be made by hand to be taken seriously—his Duchampian influence.

After all, the actual "art" happens in the mind of the viewer.

ANGIOLINI

Why do you think he chose this particular painting by Manet?

MATISSE

For Alain, Manet's *Déjeuner* presented itself as an interesting work to address photographically by means of silkscreen. He wanted to supercharge the photographic appearance and give it a more cinematic appearance. He cut his palette from six to three colors and, like Manet, chose his actors carefully. Manet picked his favorite model, along with some close relatives; Alain chose his friends as the real elements that make up the business of art; the Artist (Mario Schifano, an Italian artist), the Gallerist (Jeannine de Goldschmidt of Galerie J), and the Art Critic and Theorist (Pierre Restany), and, of course, the Spectator (Jacqueline Lafon), seen on the other side of the pool.

ANGIOLINI

Your work *Be Right Back* (2003) is just as much a response to Manet's *Déjeuner* as it is an homage to the paintings by your late husband, Alain. Can you tell us more about it?

MATISSE

Alain and I started dating at about the same time as his twenty-fifth anniversary of the making of his *Déjeuner sur l'herbe*. The exhibition took place at Marianne and Pierre Nahon's Galerie Beaubourg in Paris in 1989. This painting of Alain's led to so many other works such as *Portrait of a Man* (1964), *Limite entre le béton et l'eau* (1965), and *Portrait de Jeannine* (1965). Alain's *Déjeuner sure l'herbe* was the most written about of almost all his works. It really became so much part of our life together, and this is why I wanted to include it in my *Be Back in 5 Minutes*. Almost all of the paintings I made for that series I painted in the studio we shared in New York, where our daughter, Gaïa, was raised.

ANGIOLINI

You come from a family of important artists. How do you think your work is influenced by their legacy?

MATISSE

Growing up, there were two major forces to be reckoned with artistically and emotionally. The first, of course, was my great-grandfather Henri Matisse. The second was Marcel Duchamp, who was my step-grandfather [married to the ex-wife of Matisse's son Pierre]. As I was only three years old when he died, I always thought of him as my grandmother Teeny's other half that still somehow magically existed, but just not physically. As things turned out, I can't say I started my life with much self-confidence, and the overbearing black-and-white images of a stern-looking old man (HM), who was apparently one of the most influential artists of our time, didn't exactly help. But Marcel was also in the picture, along with Teeny. He came across as a much lighter presence, far more forgiving. As I got older, I became more and more conscious of the importance of these two artists. Their close proximity never stopped me from making my own paintings, but I can't say it was ever "easy," no matter how well I could pretend otherwise. I think, ultimately, they gave me far more positives than negatives. For instance, I went to Paris and attended the fine arts school there—just as Matisse had done. It was very meaningful for me to learn the classic French painting techniques. I also got very lucky and had a great professor, Pierre Carron. With Matisse in the back of my mind, I do think I paid extra attention to light and line in my work. With Marcel also in the back of my mind, I felt a liberation from all the heavy weight of Matisse. Marcel's ethereal presence felt like one of those first warm spring days when you can go outside without a coat on and actually relax! There was an "unseriousness" that I associated with Marcel that really was a great help for me growing up and clearly had an influence on much of my work. And then I married a very famous artist! What was I thinking?! But Alain was like a mix of both Matisse and Duchamp in many ways; even Teeny felt the same way.

# Kurt Kauper

Kurt Kauper was born in 1966 and raised in a suburb of Boston. He received his BFA from Boston University in 1988 and his MFA from UCLA in 1995. Kauper's paintings of historical and imagined people elide simple categorization. In contrast to his clear and precise articulations of form, Kauper's content is characterized by indeterminacy, unintentionality, ambiguity, fluidity, destabilization, strangeness, uselessness, and the neutral. Kauper has lived in New York City since 1999.

ALEXANDRA M. THOMAS
What is your relationship with Manet?

KURT KAUPER
Before Jeffrey Deitch invited me to participate in this show, *Le Déjeuner* was one of those icons of art history I didn't question. After, I printed out a high-res image and looked at it long and hard over a period of months. I ended up being fascinated by it and by the dominant interpretations of the painting, which I generally don't find convincing. For example, I don't find his paintings all that flat. There's flatness throughout the history of painting—in Titian, Chardin, Goya, and many others. Manet's flatness doesn't seem to me any more unusual and no more a prediction of modernism than anybody else's. That seems like a convenient art historical fiction.

THOMAS
How were you thinking about the gender dynamics here?

KAUPER
I don't experience the male figures in Manet's painting to have any agency. They gesture to nobody, they're flat, they merge into the ground. After seeing the painting, you forget them. The female figure, on the other hand, is fully volumetric; she has weight and occupies space. She fully and confidently engages the viewer. She has agency in spite of the fact that on the surface, she shouldn't: a naked, ostensibly passive object of desire.

Her agency upends all the hierarchies of power we expect in painting: because the location of meaning (at least for me) in the painting is in the relationship between her gaze and the viewer's—outside of the painting and partially independent of the artist's intent. Meaning is generated in the mutual act of looking that requires the viewer to be there. There's a radical equality in that. While Jacques-Louis David's late paintings also include a figure staring intently out at the viewer and predate Manet, they're still within the classical model, which is an authoritative mode. They're never able to be so fully about mutuality and intersubjective equality.

I thought that if I tried to include a female figure, my painting would obviously fail compared to Manet's. I didn't want to make the inevitable failure any more obvious.

And I prefer painting men: I'm a man; I was raised in a working-class, Irish Catholic town, where men were (are) expected to behave in specific ways I've never felt inclined to. Men are expected to be violent, an expectation that comes from both other men and women. Even if indirectly, my paintings get at those things.

One last thing: I've always loved the strangeness of Fra Angelico's *The Beheading of Saints Cosmas and Damian*. I couldn't decide how to move forward with my painting based on *Le Déjeuner*, and I thought to combine both paintings. The sword-bearer in Fra Angelico's painting turned into a bat bearer in mine. And the reclining figure is also inspired, less directly, by that painting.

THOMAS
Can you tell us about the still life elements?

KAUPER
I've always been fascinated by clearly delineated objects in paintings, things that insist on their presence even when it seems like they should be marginal: the specifically chipped rock at the bottom edge of a Van der Goes painting or

the discernible fibers of fabric in a Christopher Williams photo.

I think it has to do with the way an object like that can deflect attempts to experience the painting discursively—as if each formal and iconographic choice were a clearly defined linguistic link leading to determinate content. That seems like a kind of tyranny of meaning to me. I prefer experiences with works of art that derail or baffle discursive meaning—Barthes used the phrase "off-the-mark enigmatic." (The whole sentence: "Therefore: derailment, bifurcation, rerouting—very strong impression of the uncanny, of mooniness, of the off-the-mark enigmatic: an opening in the direction of an undefined something else." It just occurred to me that that's a spot-on description of *Le Déjeuner*.)

I hope objects like the cooler in my painting deflect viewers from an impulse to construct a clear narrative and might prompt them to think of any number of other things—maybe the catalogues that might contain a photo of it or their parents' garage that it could be stored in.

THOMAS

What prompted the nighttime setting?

KAUPER

The night scene was prompted by a series of other paintings I'm working on that take place at night—I don't have a determinate narrative reason. Maybe I just like the feeling of night scenes, the disparity between the clarity of light and rendering in the figures as opposed to the nocturnal landscape? I love elements in paintings that insist on individual iconographic presence and don't need to conform to any kind of unity. That's something I came to love about Manet: that he seems to completely disregard unity—physical, narrative, or otherwise.

# Karen Kilimnik

Drawing a correspondence between Romantic painting tradition and contemporary culture, Karen Kilimnik's work unites high and low. Whether originating from the glitz of glamour fantasies or the Romantic quest for the sublime, Kilimnik's imagery belongs to fairy tales, the historical past, and our present alike. After working predominantly with mise-en-scènes, drawings, and photographs, Kilimnik became, since the early 1990s, one of the leading proponents of the resurgence of figurative painting. Like her early mise-en-scènes, her paintings present historical facts and references as theater. Beauty and romanticism are viewed through playful observations. Kilimnik lives and works in Philadelphia, where she was born in 1955.

# Cindy Ji Hye Kim

Working across drawing, painting, and sculpture, Cindy Ji Hye Kim explores the anatomy of images. The artist often works in the monochromatic grisaille palette, a preliminary underpainting scheme designed to disappear when painted over with color. Kim likens the grayscale painting process as a metaphor in her work: her subjects are rendered as fading away into the unconscious, situated in fleeting scenes of memory, dreams, and myths. Using figurative representation as a visual instrument for depicting both truth and fiction, Kim creates a poetic tension between what is remembered and forgotten. Born in 1990 in Incheon, South Korea, Kim lives and works in New York.

MARINA MOLARSKY-BECK
What is your relationship to Manet?

CINDY JI HYE KIM
Before starting the mural project, I had more of an intellectual appreciation for Manet's paintings and less of an emotional connection, the kind of connection I have with works by Goya, Velázquez, or Titian. I've always felt a level of impenetrability in Manet: people in his paintings seemed cold, indifferent, and callous. After spending time looking at *The Luncheon on the Grass* in preparation for the mural, I've found within Manet's painting a new kind of dynamism rooted not in pathos but in form.

MOLARSKY-BECK
How did you develop the concept for your mural?

KIM
Back in 2018, I made a mural based on Bruegel's painting *The Blind Leading the Blind* as part of a solo exhibition at Interstate Projects in Brooklyn. I traced the image on a black wall with graphite, and I omitted all six figures from the painting as a way of thinking about presence and negation. I was interested in seeing my own marks occupying the erased space of Bruegel's bodies. When I was asked to participate in the exhibition at Jeffrey Deitch, I wanted to exercise the same gesture—of my hand occupying a void—on Manet's painting, as my own contemporary response to *The Luncheon on the Grass*.

MOLARSKY-BECK
What does erasure mean to you?

KIM
When making art, I find it critical to take myself out of my work: it's extremely difficult, but it creates a productive tension between my ego and the materials I work with. And I don't mean self-denial when I say self-negation, because there is a lot of confrontation and an eventual acceptance in this somewhat masochistic process of art making. I'm most moved by works of art that possess a mysterious mixture of anonymity and singularity, in which I can feel the ghostly presence of its maker. This is exactly what I find in Manet's painting and what I aimed to achieve in my mural.

MOLARSKY-BECK
How did you achieve the spectral effect?

KIM
Using a projector, I traced the image of Manet's painting directly onto a black wall with graphite. Graphite is one of the main materials I use in my practice; I make paint with raw graphite powder and use graphite pencils. The best way I can describe graphite is that it has a wonderful combination of shyness and aggression. I find it to be a versatile medium, and by applying it on a black wall, it shines and fades in unexpected places.

MOLARSKY-BECK
What was it like translating Manet's scene into grayscale?

KIM
When tracing the image in grisaille, I was able to understand the tonal anatomy of the painting; it became apparent where the most contrast was

located in the composition and how Manet organized his darkest darks and the lightest lights in his picture. It was interesting to see the building blocks of *The Luncheon on the Grass*—thinking about the hidden and structural layers of a painting is what I find most exciting about working in grisaille in my own practice.

MOLARSKY-BECK

Were you thinking about gender and visibility, with the central female nude becoming a void?

KIM

When I was looking at Manet's *Luncheon*, I felt that the flesh tones of all four of the figures created a powerful dynamism within the painting. It's a picture that keeps unfolding: the arm of the bathing figure in the background extends toward the hand of the male figure in the foreground, whose slightly curved index finger echoes the slightly raised toe of the female nude.

Our eyes jump back up to the bathing figure at the top, but now the line of her slouched back slides down to the two faces on the left, and the side of the female nude pulls our gaze back to the center of the painting, and we start looking at the picture once again. For me, omitting these bodies that are so integral to the visual experience of the painting was a way to insert myself into Manet's delicately composed picture, almost as an act of debasement. I guess you could see that as a feminine gesture.

# Jeff Koons

Jeff Koons is one of the most prominent artists working today. Born in 1955 in York, Pennsylvania, he has shown his work in galleries, museums, and cultural institutions throughout the world since his first solo exhibition in 1980. Koons is widely known for transforming everyday images and objects into works of art that engage the viewer. He has created works that explore themes of self-acceptance, empowerment, and transcendence. Koons is known for his bold paintings and sculptures, including *Rabbit*, *Michael Jackson and Bubbles*, and *Balloon Dog*. The smooth, mirror-finished surfaces of his iconic stainless steel sculptures reflect and affirm viewers and their environments.

JEFFREY DEITCH

Over the years, you have often talked about your interest in Manet. Along with Picasso and Duchamp, I get the impression that Manet is an artist who has especially inspired you. What has drawn you to his work? Your engagement probably goes back when you were an art student.

JEFF KOONS

Exactly, Jeffrey. That's when it started for me. I grew up in Pennsylvania, and I had an aunt who lived in Philadelphia who occasionally would take me to the Philadelphia Museum [of Art]. I really did not visit art museums often, but I took art lessons as a child. My parents were very supportive that way. Then, on my first day of college, my art professor brought up an image of Manet's *Olympia*. He put it on the screen and started to speak about the painting: how the woman in Olympia being in a certain position was referencing Goya's work; how the black cat in the right corner would have certain connotations in nineteenth-century Paris; and how the bouquet of flowers that is being presented to this woman had certain implications of somebody courting her and her being a courtesan. So, all of a sudden, through Manet's work, I had an understanding of the power of art, how effortlessly it connects you to all the human disciplines. Prior to this art history lesson and learning this through Manet's *Olympia*, I had no understanding of what art could be. Drawing and painting were activities I always did my whole life but were something that probably would have created anxiety because of performing some skills. It wasn't anything that connected me to something outside myself, something that really gave me a sense that I could transcend. From Manet's work, I picked up that I could have a dialogue with philosophy, sociology, psychology, physics. This was revealed to me by looking at *Olympia*.

DEITCH

It's fascinating that the memory of your first art history class is so vivid.

KOONS

My teacher was Bo Davis. You know, it hasn't changed from that moment, Jeffrey. There is pre–Manet's *Olympia*, and pre–this art history lesson, and there's after. There's not a day that I don't wake up and have a sense of understanding that I can transcend and find things much greater than the self in the external world. Art is this device that can continue to provide this interest in this interaction.

DEITCH

When we were organizing our exhibition, I knew that you had created a *Gazing Ball* painting with *Le Déjeuner sur l'herbe*, and I was not surprised to find out that, from the series, this was the work you had kept for your own collection. I want to ask you about your engagement with Manet's *Le Déjeuner sur l'herbe*.

KOONS

I always enjoyed this aspect of Manet being part of the "avant-garde" and wanting to be part of something, the desire of being part of a group that was actually trying to achieve something, trying to define their era and their existence. I think I didn't realize it at the time of that first art lesson, but underneath the sensual quality of the work, it was the connectivity that Manet found in art, in other artists' work and referencing other artists, that attracted me. I learned from that first lesson that in the *Olympia* Manet's referencing Goya, but in *Luncheon on the Grass*, of course, he's referencing the Raimondi print, which is based on Raphael's *The Judgment of Paris*. He's referencing what they thought was Giorgione, but now they attribute to Titian, *The Pastoral Concert*, a painting that's in the Louvre. We also know his love of Velázquez. This inner connectivity, this love of being part of something greater than the self, this humanism in the surface of Manet's work is what really attracts me. It's also its sensual desire to be part of life and life's energy and biology. It's not trying to fight that, but instead is giving into that desire, appreciating it and celebrating it.

DEITCH

I'd like to ask you specifically about how, in the *Gazing Ball* painting series, the gazing ball connects the viewer in a deeper way to the painting.

KOONS

Like I was just mentioning, it's about enjoying this connectivity of the individual, finding something greater than the self. This is really the basis of love. This is the basis of all transcendence. In the *Gazing Ball* paintings, I'm giving it up to the artists who I chose to put within this certain group of work. They are people within the canon of art history who have affected me. It's rather subjective how I've chosen these different works. Manet is a central one. When you place a gazing ball in front of these images, for me, it's like a supercharger. It's similar to wrapping up a car and having headers on it and putting a double-barrel, you know, a carburetor, manifold, and everything. It supercharges the paintings. These paintings are fantastic in their own right—I mean, these are masterpieces of art history. But the gazing ball brings out a sense of generosity about them. They reflect in 360 degrees—or almost, other than their very base. They affirm you, the viewer. They're celebrating the work because it's also being reflected. The gazing ball becomes this rabbit hole to enter the painting. When you do so, that's when you can be in contact with the celebration that Manet is giving to other people within his work and what he's giving it up to in life.

Another interesting thing about the gazing ball is its form, the sphere, which is the most important shape that we have within the universe. Our whole understanding of science and the universe really comes from the understanding of the sphere. The universe is made up of all these billions of spheres. Our understanding of our positioning and of our mind rewards our body, and our bodies reward our mind. It goes in both directions. The gazing ball also heightens our knowledge of where we are at any given moment within space. It informs the meaning you have of where you are, of your environment, at that moment.

For me, the gazing balls are these rabbit holes you can enter and be in dialogue with

Manet. It's the closest thing I have to be able to do that.

DEITCH

Jeff, one of the great art experiences I've had in the past decade was that gazing ball tour you gave me of the environs of York, Pennsylvania. You knew all these gazing balls that existed in the area. You were driving very fast through these winding roads around rural Pennsylvania, pointing at the gazing balls…

KOONS

There really is a sense of that type of generosity when you look at one. It's just joyous, you know. It's reflective, and by being reflective, it's connecting you to celestial events, to the sun and the stars. So, reflectivity starts with this type of connection to the environment, to this inner life and external world, and, of course, with art.

DEITCH

Your *Luncheon on the Grass Gazing Ball* painting is a fusion of your aesthetic with Manet's. It's fascinating how you achieved that.

## Ella Kruglyanskaya

Born in 1978 in Riga, Latvia, Ella Kruglyanskaya paints and draws bold images that subvert the canonized representation of women in traditions of Western painting and visual culture. The female protagonists in her work, rendered in an assertive and graphic gesture, confront their audience with an unabashed femininity that infuses gendered tropes with a brash comedic approach to representation. The artist lives and works in New York City.

VIOLA ANGIOLINI

Your painting *The Rug and the Blinds (Red)* (2022) responds to *Le Déjeuner sur l'herbe* in a way that is the furthest possible from being literal. Yet, it successfully echoes some of the critical aspects that Manet's painting problematizes. One example is his interest in recontextualizing and contradicting a fixed set of inherited ways to depict the figure. How did your interest and approach to painting the figure come about in your practice?

ELLA KRUGLYANSKAYA

And I worried that even that was too literal! I thought I painted "the elephant in the room," that being the naked lady in the middle of it all. But yes, I can see also that there could be a more literal approach of interpreting this source. Mainly I see myself sharing this interest in "recontextualizing and contradicting a fixed set of inherited ways to depict the figure." That's really well put, and the task at hand is different for different generations; it's a moving target.

ANGIOLINI

In a previous conversation, we talked about how there is often a "what can I get away with" attitude in Manet's paintings. What interests you about Manet's deliberate economy of brushstrokes?

KRUGLYANSKAYA

We are now used to all sorts of approaches to painting; the entire history of painting is up for grabs in terms of what and how to paint. Manet's approach must have been shocking to the average bourgeois on several levels. One, on the level of painterly technique, they expected a certain type of refinement, or "proper effort," from their painters. Manet's brushwork, in contrast, does not seem concerned with that. It is like an insult, a concern instead with an economy of painterly gesture. A kind of a "less is more" or a desire to get more out of less. This direct approach of painting things "as they are" in the world, things like problematic class, labor, gender, and erotic relations.

ANGIOLINI

This also makes me think of your equalizing approach to painting and drawing. How do these two mediums coexist in your practice?

KRUGLYANSKAYA

Yes, this "getting away with" is directly related to my approach to "drawing" within painting. Drawing is the foundation, the raw material, of my practice, as it is for many. Having gone through some rather traditional academic training, I was brought up with certain notions of what drawing was and how painting was distinct from it. It had something to do with line versus brushstroke, paper versus canvas, and a kind of "shortcut" that drawing provided, the speed of the drawing line itself being much faster than that of a painted brushstroke that appeared as a line. Wow, I sound like a nerd. In some way, I see myself taking this shortcut as a nod to Manet's attitude toward artistic "labor," a kind of rejection of a bourgeois notion that time and effort result in a more "valuable" thing. The painting of the drawing has other layers of meaning, of course.

ANGIOLINI

The provocative nature of *Le Déjeuner sur l'herbe* is something impossible to dismiss. Its infamous initial reception makes it amply clear that the painting appeared to be crossing the line of what would have represented "bad taste" for the cultural and social standards of the time. Your work plays with this aspect of Manet's iconic painting by alluding to a famous, indecent idiom. Can you elaborate on how you incorporate language, especially puns, in your work?

KRUGLYANSKAYA

"Bad taste" is much more in "good taste" in our day and age, in part perhaps due to Manet's transgressive genius. The mix and match of high and low has become the default stance. We are very self-aware, and no one is insulted; everyone's "in" on the joke, and we can all "enjoy" our belonging. Despite all that, there is still that initial delight in discovering how the puzzle fits (or slightly mis-fits) together.... I am a relative newcomer to the English language (I didn't start speaking English 'til age seventeen), and that point in learning a new language where you start "getting" the humor—the puns, the idioms, the idiosyncrasies. I never really got over that. Every time I discover a pun or make my own, there's a tiny burst of excitement.

# Liu Xiaodong

Liu Xiaodong is a painter of modern life, whose large-scale works serve as a kind of history painting for the emerging world. Liu locates the human dimension to such global issues as population displacement, environmental crisis, and economic upheaval, but through carefully orchestrated compositions; he walks the line between artifice and reality. A leading figure among the Chinese Neo-Realist painters to emerge in the 1990s, Liu lives and works in Beijing but has undertaken projects in Tibet, Japan, Italy, the United Kingdom, Cuba, Austria, and, closer to home, in Jincheng, in the northeastern province of Liaoning, China, where he was born in 1963.

VIOLA ANGIOLINI

Your paintings chronicle history as it unfolds through ordinary people's everyday life, whether they find themselves in politically charged situations or go about their daily routine. *Newcomers in the Village—Response to Manet* (2021) seems to depart from most of your work, since you purposefully created its composition to echo that of

Manet's *Le Déjeuner sur l'herbe*. At the same time, the sociological content remains at its core. Can you talk about the conception of this work and the themes it addresses?

LIU XIAODONG

Manet's *Le Déjeuner sur l'herbe*, as I understand it, depicts the new social form of France in the nineteenth century, the new relationship between men and women, as well as the relationship between man and God. I thought that I could describe today's Chinese social form by making use of Manet's composition.

ANGIOLINI

One of the aspects that makes Manet's painting so enigmatic is the illusion of having been painted en plein air, and only a closer inspection reveals that the composition was studied in the studio and the landscape added as a "backdrop." Your work takes this ambiguity further by restaging *Le Déjeuner*'s composition and painting it outdoors. You also complicated the scene by adding more figures—the two bystanders on the left and the child in the background. How did you construct this composition?

LIU

I mostly copied Manet's composition. I only added two bystanders holding shovels, and instead of the woman bending over like in Manet's work, I painted a mother teaching her son to walk. In my youth's memories, if a man wears women's clothes or a woman wears too revealing clothes, he will be put in prison or even shot. In the discourse system of socialist societies, all the decadent signs of capitalism should be buried away. For this reason, I painted two people who are prepared to bury these new things with their shovels, but they are also sexually aroused by what they see. By drawing a little child who walks toward us, I wanted to say that he has two options in life, become the one who buries or to be buried himself. I wish this figure to remind the audience of the past, present, and future of Chinese society.

ANGIOLINI

In preparation for your paintings, you often travel to immerse yourself in the environment and the community you are interested in representing. What is your relationship with the models for *Newcomers in the Village*?

LIU

The main characters of this work are personal friends of mine; only the two persons holding shovels and the woman with the kid are locals.

ANGIOLINI

How did you prepare your sitters?

LIU

I usually only give some advice on what clothes to wear and whether or not they should hold any prop in their hands. Then sometimes major last-minute changes happen when I have them sitting in front of me.

ANGIOLINI

And how did you choose the setting for this painting? Your works often reveal an interest in the divide between urban and rural environments.

LIU

As usual, I had a general idea of the area I wanted to paint in this work, and then when I arrived there, I visited the surroundings and chose what I thought was the most appropriate setting for this work.

ANGIOLINI

In 2020, while in New York for several months, you realized a series of watercolors, including the one titled *Coming across a scene like this one cannot but think of Manet's Le Déjeuner sur l'herbe 2020.06.12*. The reference to Manet's painting in this work comes about through a completely different process than in the work you made for our *Luncheon on the Grass* exhibition. Can you talk about this work and the circumstances in which you made it?

LIU

In 2020, I stayed in New York for nine months, witnessing both the empty city of the first pandemic wave and the BLM movement. At that time, I felt that African Americans began to occupy a central position in public discourse and other aspects of society. Art museums and galleries were also keener to exhibit more diverse art. So when I was walking in the park and saw a group of white people surrounding this Black guy, I decided I wanted to paint it. With the help of Manet's *Le Déjeuner sur l'herbe*, I wanted to hint at the social reality of the United States.

ANGIOLINI

Something else I find particularly interesting about this watercolor is the way it plays with visual memory. How interested are you in this aspect and incorporating art historical references in your paintings?

LIU

Of course, it's always interesting when art imitates life or vice versa; it brings a wry smile to people's faces.

# TALA MADANI

Born in 1981 in Tehran, Iran, Tala Madani makes paintings and animations whose indelible images bring together wide-ranging modes of critique, prompting reflection on gender, political authority, and questions of who and what get represented in art. In Madani's work, slapstick humor is inseparable from violence, and creation is synonymous with destruction, reflecting a complex and gut-level vision of contemporary power imbalances of all kinds. Her approach to figuration combines the radical morphology of a modernist with a contemporary sense of sequencing, movement, and speed.

ARUNA D'SOUZA

I laughed-screamed when I saw your reinterpretation of Manet's *Le Déjeuner*—it is both gorgeously and lushly painted, as well as being utterly and hilariously puerile and even a bit brutal. Is that a pickled penis in there or a stool sample floating in urine? And how could it possibly be painted with brushstrokes so juicy that I want to lick the surface?! What did you see in *Le Dejeuner* that made you make this painting?

TALA MADANI

Well, it wasn't the painting *Le Déjeuner* that inspired that possibility but more the proposition of using that painting as an anchor for making something today.

D'SOUZA

Your work so often takes us through a back door into pathos and sometimes even violence. I'm so often drawn in by your technique, by your way with color and brushwork, and then have to stop and ask myself what exactly I'm looking at. Can you talk about this strategy, and what motivates it?

MADANI

Well, for me it's actually very shocking that today's brushworks or color or technique can be described as moving, given the history of painting that we've experienced. What I mean is that if they don't work it's very obvious, but when they do work they have to be at the service of the idea, so to enjoy them in isolation on a formal level, looking at a contemporary work, I think is probably impossible. What you might be alluding to is a presumed disconnect between what is socially perceived as pathological or problematic and a formal treatment of the subject that is sympathetic. Your question was about motivation. I'm probably interested in creating relationships and proximity between subjects that seem far away from each other.

D'SOUZA

Your work engages with the history of "fine art," but at the same time really draws upon lots of other visual forms, including cartoons—in that way, you're a perfect person to riff on Manet, who was notorious for doing the same back in the 1860s and 1870s. And your technique here really seems to evoke Manet's own—I'm thinking specifically about the way he paints the liquor bottles in another of his iconic works, *A Bar at the Folies-Bergère*. Can you talk about what you drew upon in terms of technique and approach to mixing high and low?

MADANI

I feel like no one is a perfect person to riff on Manet. Mixing high and low is always a good conversation, but who is to say what should be low and what should be high, or even if we should accept the values passed down to us through any art history? So, to question those perceived hierarchies and challenge them is useful.

# Paul McCarthy

Paul McCarthy is widely considered to be one of the most influential and groundbreaking contemporary American artists. Born in 1945 and raised in Salt Lake City, Utah, he first established a multifaceted artistic practice that sought to break the limitations of painting by using unorthodox materials such as bodily fluids and food. He has since become known for visceral, often hauntingly humorous work in a variety of mediums—from performance, photography, film, and video to sculpture, drawing, and painting. He lives and works in Los Angeles.

ALEXANDRA M. THOMAS

My first question is about the relationship between the sculptural installation and the set of prints. Can you walk me through your approach to the different mediums and how they interact in the work?

PAUL MCCARTHY

There are two different sets of photographs. The first, larger photograph was taken during the filming of one of the CSSC (*Coach Stage Stage Coach*) performance days in 2017. This scene went on for about twenty minutes. Prior to that, when I was writing the CSSC script, I made drawings of that scene. I decided I needed a mock-up of it, and so I made this small sculpture. There ended up being a series of them, about two or three. And the sculpture, the one that's in the exhibition, was the first; it's a little diorama. The second diorama sculpture that I made, based on the drawings and the script, was more finished, in a forest with a stream. I had it photographed. So the exhibition has the sculpture (the first diorama), the CSSC performance photograph, and a selection of five photographs of the second diorama.

THOMAS

Great. Thank you for the clarification. Can you talk about some of the characters and their stories? What is the narrative of the work?

MCCARTHY

In the film, there are six individuals in a stagecoach traveling across the West. There is an older man, whom I play, named Ronald Raygun. And although she is not in this photograph, his wife, Nancy, is traveling in the coach as well. And Mary Magdalene, but we're not really sure what her name is; she says she is Mary Magdalene, but it could very well be a joke. There's another character who is not in the photograph, Jesus Christ, who could also be joking about his name. And then you have Adam and Eve, two young innocents. Adam is a dentist; Eve is an actress who says she lives in Silver Lake and works in commercials, so it's obvious that it's not a period piece. So, you have Adam and Eve, Ronald and Nancy Raygun, Mary Magdalene, and Jesus Christ all traveling together in a stagecoach. The older, experienced characters begin to pick on and abuse the innocent, younger passengers, Adam and Eve.

THOMAS
And how does this relate to Manet's *Luncheon on the Grass*?

MCCARTHY
At some point in 2017, while we were working on the scene, I wanted it to be reminiscent of *Luncheon on the Grass*. It's noticeable in the composition: Eve is bending over in the background; Mary Magdalene and Ronald are straddling Adam. Mary is nude, while both male characters remain fully clothed.

THOMAS
How does your work in general relate to Western historical painting?

MCCARTHY
Art is often in discussion with itself. I've always been interested in this painting, along with several other paintings from that same period. I don't remember which came first, the decision to do a picnic or the decision to remake the scene from *Luncheon on the Grass*, but the scenario fit. Works of art are always in my brain. It's referring, remaking, and reshifting to a newer context. It is a way of layering something and creating meaning.

## Sam McKinniss

Born in Northfield, Minnesota, in 1985, Sam McKinniss is an artist living and working in New York City and Kent, Connecticut. Subjects for his figurative paintings are often sourced from popular culture, professional sports, the entertainment industry, and the Internet. In a 2019 *Artforum* cover story devoted to McKinniss's art, the novelist and critic Gary Indiana writes, "McKinniss's recent paintings suggest a deft, saturnine, facetiously sincere autobiography of taste and tastelessness that reveals less about the artist than the spectator, though in this case, the artist is spectator, too. These paintings...are really unlikely things, samples from the blazing horror vacui we inhabit as alleged global citizens, ergo very familiar, but suffused with pathos, even suffering, as well as with flash and comic incongruity."

MARINA MOLARSKY-BECK
Can you tell me about the genesis of this work?

SAM MCKINNISS
Before Jeffrey approached me, I had made two

or three other paintings from *Cruel Intentions*. I had done a big group scene that I showed with Michael Ovitz in 2021 and before that I made another version of the kiss between Sarah Michelle Gellar and Selma Blair. It was a much smaller, a more intimate, picture and much less labored.

That was still hanging out in my mind when Jeffrey said, Make a version of *Le Déjeuner sur l'herbe* for our time. They are on a picnic when [Gellar and Blair] are doing the scene in Central Park. So, I thought that might be a natural tie-in where I could bring imagery that I've been focused on and match that to the nineteenth-century Manet version.

My next thought was, I won't try to push a nude bather into that Central Park scene. I'll just do a second painting that will involve Ryan Phillippe entering or exiting a shower. There's already a bather worked into the moving picture, *Cruel Intentions*—the material already exists. My practice is just finding and appropriating things that already look like art: imagery that exists that has already impressed itself onto the culture's imagination. And the only thing left for me to do is accept that and invite it into my working oeuvre.

My friend Gary Indiana referred to it as inbuilt cultural power. It saves me a lot of time and effort. I mean, I spend time finding those things or re-collecting these materials. But what I did not know was that these paintings would cause their own moment.

[McKinniss shows me a copy of *People* magazine featuring the stars of *Cruel Intentions*, Selma Blair, Sarah Michelle Gellar, and Ryan Phillippe, posing with his painting at Jeffrey Deitch.]

The public response to this has been larger than typically anticipated. And it's exciting for me when my work rolls on a track that's already in circuit within entertainment media and then comes back around and something new happens.

MOLARSKY-BECK

*Cruel Intentions* has found a large queer audience, despite its ostensible content.

MCKINNISS

I think I knew that if I used this material, it would be a way for me to wink at queer viewers. You're right, it's there, and I'm attracted to it for the same reasons that any other queer viewer is titillated by Ryan Phillippe being nude or a lesbian kiss. At the time when the movie was out, it was exciting and a little bit shocking, because there wasn't so much queerness in popular entertainment.

MOLARSKY-BECK

That's obviously not the only appeal of the movie.

MCKINNISS

But it is a big appeal. The queer flirtiness or exhibitionism. That was exciting, as a young person. That wasn't really as ubiquitous as it is now. And it wasn't as comfortable for young people to talk about or address or explain same-sex attraction. It was still harshly taboo.

With Manet, there's a level of exhibitionism inside that painting. Then it went to a bourgeois reception, and that was shocking. It's impossible for *Cruel Intentions* to shock us now. But the material still carries the residue of the shock that it created in 1999. That was my response to Manet's ambition. My way of responding was to recall 1999, even though that's also expired, the same way Manet's ambition to shock us has expired. Because the politics have updated and styles have updated.

MOLARSKY-BECK

What's your relationship to Manet?

MCKINNISS

He was really useful to me when I was studying art. I think what impresses me about Manet is the boldness of his outline.

Scholarship suggests that he was using photography to aid the creation of his paintings. That has always intrigued me as someone who uses photography pretty exclusively now to derive compositions for my art.

I was really young when I went to Paris for the first time to go to Musée d'Orsay to see *The Luncheon on the Grass* and *Olympia*, but also the *Peonies*. The *Peonies* proved something to me that I've always tried to contemplate later, after seeing them, which gets back to inbuilt cultural power. It's a floral still life; it adheres strictly to a genre, and yet there's so much life and so much power, so much electricity. If I could use a cliché, it's hip to be square. Why is it so hip to be square? Why does that work? Why does that relay so much electricity, so much verve? That's a question I think about all the time.

MOLARSKY-BECK
Especially now, everything circulates as an image at the end of the day.

MCKINNISS
And the circulation is never-ending. But one thing that the painting does, even if it's just for the time it takes to visit an art show, and for me privately, for as long as it takes to execute the painting—that circulation stops. That circuit stops for a little bit. Or it pauses, briefly. It gets off the track, gets off the circuit, and becomes something else, after it stops being a JPEG.

MOLARSKY-BECK
It's a different kind of viewing experience.

MCKINNISS
Just through being aware of your body next to a human-scale object. When I get to live with that JPEG for a little while—while I'm working with the paint—my memory, my brain, my lived experience relates to it. I have the opportunity to consider the image differently, almost as a symbol. Some other narrative starts to take shape—the memory of viewing the thing that I'm painting the first time that I saw it starts to meld with the memory of my entire life. I can locate depth. And that's rewarding, when I have the opportunity to remember my own life and consider it in a very careful and private way, with whatever piece of the public imagination that I'm using to get there. The only other process by which I can reconsider my own lived experience is psychoanalysis.

# Jill Mulleady

Jill Mulleady was born in 1980 in Montevideo, Uruguay. She is based between Los Angeles and Paris. She works primarily in painting and often intervenes in the spaces where she exhibits, staging the paintings with readymades, sculptures, and architectural installations, exploring themes of memory, transformation, and the power of history. In her work, references to historical painting are put into communication with images taken from both popular culture and personal life, creating an anachronistic feeling of merged and frictional temporalities. Her practice shifts between close observations of everyday reality and highly elaborated imaginary worlds. These paintings can be seen as allegories for the contemporary experience of the image as interface: not just a picture but a means of mobilizing attention, bodies, and affects within an increasingly virtualized social space.

MARINA MOLARSKY-BECK
Could you tell me a bit about your relationship to Manet?

JILL MULLEADY

Manet is one of my favorite painters, in the way that I consider him probably the first modern painter. I did my essay on "The Painter of Modern Life" when I did my MA at Chelsea College [of Arts in London]—based on Baudelaire's text that has the same title. There's a current that thinks that being a modern is destroying everything that was done previously—and finding a total new form, having zero attachment to history. I love that idea when it resonates, like punk. But this is kind of another take on the idea of modernism. When I paint, I'm more into developing a language that already exists and injecting it with *l'air du temps.* I see painting as a conversation, not only with the present times but with its history, too.

And then well, I had my daughter when I finished school, and I called her "Olympia." Like Manet's painting.

When you see [Manet's] work and see his brushstrokes, they still look fresh. He managed to capture the moment, and it's alive. Painting can be a capsule of time; that's when the miracle happens. A lot of contemporary things look good on the screen, and then, when you see them in real life, in the flesh, they are dead. They have no force, no energy.

*Le Déjeuner* has been reproduced and redigested so much in pop culture—I'm interested in Manet himself. He had intense relationships with each of his models. One was his wife, Suzanne. Then there's the wonderful painter Berthe Morisot. The one in *Le Déjeuner* is Victorine Meurent. I actually focused more on the idea of choosing a model. I looked for someone that I thought Manet could use as a model in present times.

So the first thing I had to do was to find the right model. The model of my painting is Nicole-Antonia Spagnola. She's a singer in two punk bands, called Purity and P22. She's also a great artist and a friend.

MOLARSKY-BECK

I was curious if you were thinking of the gender dynamic of the man in the background being naked.

MULLEADY

The composition in *Le Déjeuner* is sort of centripetal: everything goes to the center. And so, in this painting, I did the opposite and inverted the composition: there's this triangle that is centrifugal. It starts with this gesture of a woman eating strawberries. It comes from a reference of Manet's painting *The Street Singer*, where this same model, Victorine Meurent, is eating cherries while holding a guitar.

In the original, there's this triangular composition, where everything goes to the center, and it ends up with herself naked and all the men dressed. So this is the opposite. She's dressed, and then it ends up with the man naked in the background.

MOLARSKY-BECK

I know your work is often discussed as being Surrealist, and I was curious how you think about that?

MULLEADY

I grew up in Buenos Aires in Argentina. When I started painting, people around me were immediately trying to pin me down: "Oh, this is Surrealism," or "It's magic realism." I immediately tried to detach myself from that. I respect Leonora Carrington and Leonor Fini, and I think they're amazing painters. But if I have to look at an artist of those times, I'm more interested in Méret Oppenheim.

She was the first woman to be in the collection of MoMA. They bought [*Object (Breakfast in Fur)* (1936)]. And Americans labeled her immediately as a Surrealist. She reacted to that. She stopped producing what was expected from her. The core idea of Surrealism is actually to go against labels. Like once you pin it, it vanishes. When there's a label, it's because it already exists in the functional world, and Surrealism was trying to find things that were in a sort of dysfunctional relationship to the world. Pushing the limits of what's in the shadows, going to the edge of things, and triggering its meaning.

# Ariana Papademetropoulos

Born in Los Angeles in 1990, Ariana Papademetropoulos received her BFA from the California Institute of the Arts in 2012 and has studied at the Universität der Künste Berlin. She is known primarily as a painter, but her visual practice also encompasses sculpture and film. Papademetropoulos's work explores a variety of themes ranging from mythology and femininity to archetypes of Jungian psychology. Art historical references from medieval or Renaissance periods often appear in her paintings; Papademetropoulos reinterprets traditional iconography and symbolism as she incorporates them into her own contemporary narratives. Rooted in hyperrealism and illusion, Papademetropoulos's paintings collapse realities into surreal tableaux, portals to fantastical scenes.

JEFFREY DEITCH

Can you tell us about your painting and its title *It Becomes Blurry in That Moment*?

ARIANA PAPADEMETROPOULOS

Manet's *Luncheon on the Grass* was originally called *The Bath* or *The Bather*, so I wanted to focus on the bather in the background. I also thought of what a picnic is. It is bringing domesticity to the natural exterior world. So I thought it would be interesting to do the inverse of that, which is to bring nature into an interior space. I usually work intuitively, where I'll paint something and then I'll figure out exactly what is going on afterward. But the other night I was talking about the painting *Luncheon on the Grass* with Jill Mulleady and Celeste [Dupuy-Spencer], who are also in this show, and we were discussing why this painting is still so relevant and what draws us into it. What we thought is that the painting holds energy because there is a mystery to it, it asks an eternal question. There are the two guys in the painting who are looking away, and then there is the main figure, who is making eye contact with the person viewing it. That detail transcends the painting and creates this moment where the viewer is a part of this conversation. And what Jill said is that "it becomes blurry in that moment." I didn't have a title at that point, so I was like "that is exactly what I'm trying to do with my paintings!" I'm trying to create images that can be mysterious enough to draw you in and go beyond being a painting where the viewer can be a part of that conversation.

DEITCH

How do you compose a work, and where does it come from? Are you looking at found images, altering them? Tell us about your technique.

PAPADEMETROPOULOS

I collect a lot of books, and the background image for this painting is from an interior design book that Paul Anka had, and the waterfall is from a vintage postcard. I thought of the couch as a bath, pulling you in as if it was a portal. It was important to me to compose an image where the natural world is blending into domesticity, the inverse of the picnic.

DEITCH

Are you thinking at all, in addition to the Manet, to Duchamp's *Étant donnés* (1946–66), which has a waterfall as the focal point?

PAPADEMETROPOULOS

I actually didn't think about that! But I have painted waterfalls as mirror images of hair, so that's a theme in my work. The hair, waterfall, and curtains all blend in with one another, a merging of worlds.

# Naudline Pierre

Naudline Pierre's work situates personal mythology and transcendent intimacy alongside canonical narratives of devotion. Her work is distinctly narrative in nature, and it continues the art historical tradition of portraying encounters between the earthly and the otherworldly. She draws from sacred architecture and fantastical scenes of mythic and celestial beings—as well as Renaissance modes of working such as forced perspective and flattened space—to conjure a futuristic, atmospheric world in which all-female characters play out scenes of caretaking, confrontation, entanglement, and engulfment. Born in 1989 in Leominster, Massachusetts, Pierre lives and works in Brooklyn, New York.

ALEXANDRA M. THOMAS

*In Our Midst* is a celestial painting. How did you arrive at this work in responding to Manet's *Le Déjeuner sur l'herbe*?

NAUDLINE PIERRE

My goal was to use the original composition of *Le Déjeuner sur l'herbe* to create something new in a way that makes sense to me and the characters I engage with in my work. I was interested in using the structure of the painting, particularly the triangular shapes of the overlapping legs in the center of Manet's composition. Touch is important to the images that I make, so I saw the tangled legs as an opportunity to express that. Beyond the three figures, you can see flames reaching toward each other, creating an arched effect—much like a forest canopy. Those flames were inspired by the trees in the original composition and add a sense of contrast, while also creating a focal point at a dark body of water reflecting light from the stars above. The winged being at the top right hovers above the three figures in the foreground, not fully part of the conversation but still important to the overall image.

THOMAS

What is your relationship to the Western genre of modern painting? How does your intervention expand our understanding of painting and its possibilities?

PIERRE

I'm not here to reinvent anything. That's too much responsibility for me. I'm here to make the images that I want to see. The language of my paintings is all about the freedom of possibility. I can make anything I want; I can imagine anything I want.

THOMAS

Who are the figures in this painting, and how do they relate to each other?

PIERRE

The pale green figure is my protagonist. She is a staple of everything I make and exists in an alternate world. Although she is a recurring figure, her appearance is fluid, depending on the colors I choose. She's usually surrounded by other celestial beings in a place that feels otherworldly. These characters reveal themselves to me in the act of painting, and I allow them to guide some of the decisions I make in the compositions. In this particular painting, these figures are resting. It's a soft moment with a few points of contact, two of them being the green figure's hand on the purple scaled figure's knee and ankle—both emphasized by jagged bursts of light. We've caught these characters in a private moment, and they are aware of our gaze. A large part of my practice is about allowing myself to be okay with not knowing. I can't say that I know everything about these figures, but I do know that they know that they are being observed.

THOMAS

How does *In Our Midst* expand upon other conceptual and aesthetic threads in your practice as a whole?

PIERRE

*In Our Midst* is certainly a continuation of the

themes that already exist in my practice. As is the case in all my work, the scene takes place in an unknown world populated by otherworldly beings. Each painting I make takes me deeper into this other place. In every work I make, my characters are continuing their quest to explore freedom, agency, and self-possession, adding to the story that's been unfolding and will continue to unfold.

THOMAS
What part of the painting felt the most urgent and exciting to represent?

PIERRE
The way the bodies gather at the center of the image and the sightlines created in that gathering.

THOMAS
My eyes are drawn to the magenta feathers/scales/covering (can you clarify?) on the figure with dark lipstick and curly hair. Who is she?

PIERRE
She is a winged figure whose body is covered in scales, a guardian taking care of the central figure. She is close to the characters in the composition, who I imagine to be engaged in an intimate conversation. Maybe they're speaking in hushed tones—I don't really know. At any rate, she's present and knows her power.

## Christina Quarles

Christina Quarles is a Los Angeles–based artist whose practice works to dismantle assumptions and ingrained beliefs surrounding identity and the human figure. Born in Chicago in 1985 and raised by her mother in Los Angeles, Quarles took art classes from an early age, developing a solid foundation for a lifelong practice. Today, she still sees her work, be it ink on paper or paint on canvas, as being rooted in gestural drawing. Seeking a vehicle for expressing feelings and experiences that language alone cannot articulate, she conveys in her work the experience of living within a body, rather than depictions of looking at the human figure.

VIOLA ANGIOLINI
When Jeffrey and I approached you with the idea of the exhibition, you showed us one of your recent works, *We Knew So Little Then/I Know Even Less Now…* (2019), and proudly told us that your partner had nicknamed it your "Olympia" in reference to Manet's famous painting. What is your relationship with art history? Do you often find yourself looking at historical artists, or is this more of an internalized dialogue that transpires through your work?

CHRISTINA QUARLES
I'm inspired by images that trickle down, from art history or other sources, and become a part of my everyday world. I spent many years studying art and art history, but it's not usually a direct or immediate reference in my work. I'm more interested in the third, or fourth, iterations of images, as in when a piece of art history is redeployed in pop culture or social media or made culturally ubiquitous in some way. I look for patterns that have a sort of visual punning to further this sense of being fused in multiple locations. For example, an image of a flower that was once found in art history originally came from nature, and that particular image might now be mass-produced. Or in another one of my works, *Bless Tha Nightn'gale* (2019), I rendered a stained-glass window that mimicked a quilt I encountered in a meme, which was taken from Disney's original *Pinocchio* (1940).

My compositions are also determined as I work through a painting—it's not something that's decided beforehand. I'm always looking at the decisions that I make in my paintings and narrating them back to myself through observation. The narrative and logic behind the work unfold as I progress and examine my decisions, which are sometimes unconscious, and yet, a well-known historical composition can emerge, like in *We Knew So Little Then/I Know Even Less Now…* (2019).

My wife, Alyssa, made that reference after the fact, which was an interesting connection. This was not a conscious decision, but compositions that I've studied or looked at for a long time become entrenched in my own vocabulary. In my work, decision-making is an ongoing process, based on looking at what I've done in the past or all of the decisions I've made up to this point. Rather than having a goal at the outset of making a painting, I allow close observation and study to become a part of the work's history. There is always a back-and-forth between my intention and what is actually in front of me.

ANGIOLINI

I see your panting *Yer Apart of Everything* (2022) as a response to the invisible tensions that Manet orchestrates in *Le Déjeuner*: the contrast of the nudity of the female figure against the fully clothed men sitting next to her; her gaze stares back at the viewer, breaking the fourth wall. How do you interpret the power dynamics of this scene? Do you see the female protagonist being more vulnerable or empowered?

QUARLES

Having been very familiar with this painting, and scholarly work around it, I challenged myself to try and look at it as if I didn't know all of those things—the idea was to meet the gaze of the woman in the foreground.

What I found especially interesting was the composition of the feet and legs in *Le Déjeuner*. There's a threading, or entanglement, happening with the various figures' legs; like the moment when a shoe faces a bare foot or the way in which reclined positions mirror one another. And there's a moment in my painting, with interlocking toes, almost overemphasizing the footsie that's happening in Manet's piece.

Because my paintings are more about an embodied or internalized experience of looking at one's external environment, I tend not to render a gaze that confronts the viewer. I'm very careful in my avoidance of direct eye contact in my figuration, because this action, of looking out, externalizes the figures' experience.

Referencing *Le Déjeuner* became an interesting exercise for me, since that gaze is such a significant part of Manet's painting. It's sort of the main point of tension, where power shifts. This is why Alyssa dubbed my other work my "Olympia," because in addition to the front figure's pose, there's also more eye contact than in most of my other paintings. It brings a long discussion into question—what the power relationship is in my work, or in figurative painting in general, and whether that confrontational gaze immediately renders power.

My work has always dealt with more of an inward gaze, confrontation, or observation. It's about a personal sense of looking out, in relation to the self and one's social environment, rather than an interaction with another person. So the question was, how do I maintain that perspective, while thinking about this painting with a very direct gaze?

ANGIOLINI

How did you construct the composition?

QUARLES

What was unusual about the specific process in *Yer Apart of Everything* was working back from an existing image, which was the opposite of what I typically do. Normally, when I make a piece, it's based on gesture and building a composition from memory. I'm interested in natural occurrences that fall short of, or exceed, what I intend to do. This zigzagging leads to an unexpected place, and because I'm not working from sketches, the painting is not trying to be anything other than what it becomes.

In keeping with my usual process, I wanted there to be a rough composition that began with laying down my figures. I laid a cluster of figures to the left, an isolated figure to the right, and I really wanted that female figure in the background—which I feel gets talked about less—to be compositionally central.

I tried blurring my eyes and looking at the painting to play with forms of light and dark. I wanted to render an L shape, with a spot of light, a sort of "sunspot," in the center, which referenced that clothed woman in the background. She's compositionally central, she's a bright light, and then the nude female is this brighter color, referencing that sense of mirroring in Manet's composition. I also knew that I wanted to create a patterned plane based on the shady grove, but I turned the actual picnic blanket into this folding of the landscape, so that the perspective shifts downward in my work, rather than out.

ANGIOLINI
And could you elaborate on your technique?

QUARLES
My technique in this work was similar to my usual process. I lay down gestural lines first, allowing intended marks and drips or bleeds that happen by chance to form the figures. Then, I'll photograph my work and bring it into Adobe Illustrator to work out the patterns and planes. Though it is a digital medium, there is still that same interaction between intention and accident. Often an unintended glitch in my digital drawing will lead to a new direction for the composition.

Although I referenced an existing image in *Yer Apart of Everything*, I allowed the work to emerge through process. Those drips are still present, and my sense of improvisation and working from memory remained.

ANGIOLINI
What inspired the title?

QUARLES
I was interested in playing with a pun; being "a part of" and "apart from" something. I interpreted the power dynamic in terms of a sense of isolation versus connection, thinking about figures as being pulled apart, but also bringing the environment back into the foreground. The landscape and the figures are embedded into one another, while the grouping on the left and the figure on the right are being pulled apart.

As I thought about this compositional tension, I also considered the fact that art exists within the historical context of when it was made, but is constantly being recontextualized by ongoing interaction with the viewer, across time. Despite its influence, Western art history can feel exclusionary in terms of who gets to learn about it and the voices that have been memorialized up until recent years. In this way, art history can feel apart from the larger culture's experience of looking. I think art history becomes a part of our present visual culture when it's reinterpreted by new audiences, perspectives, and voices.

## Walter Robinson

Born in 1950 in Wilmington, Delaware, Walter Robinson is a New York–based painter and art critic. As an art writer, Robinson was founding editor of *Artnet Magazine* (1996–2012) and of *Art-Rite* (1973–77), and he also wrote on art for *Art in America*, Artspace.com, the *East Village Eye*, and the *Observer*. Robinson has been called a "neo-Pop" painter, as well as a member of the 1980s "Pictures Generation." *Walter Robinson: Paintings and Other Indulgences*, a retrospective exhibition of ninety works dating from 1979 to 2012, opened in 2014 at the University Galleries at Illinois State University in Normal and subsequently traveled to Moore College of Art & Design in Philadelphia; its final appearance was at Jeffrey Deitch in New York in 2016.

VIOLA ANGIOLINI
What is the inspiration behind *Affronter sur l'herbe* (2022)?

WALTER ROBINSON
Just a bit of whimsy, really, the coincidence that *Le Déjeuner* (1863) was painted at the same time

as the American Civil War (1861–65). Manet was fairly radical politically as well as artistically and made several works addressing current political events, notably his series devoted to *The Execution of Emperor Maximilian* (1867–69) and *The "Kearsarge" at Boulogne* (1864), his rendering of a Civil War sea battle that took place off the coast of France. I suppose *Affronter* reflects contemporary sexual politics, taking Manet's passive bather from the background and foregrounding her as an active and even dangerous agent. The notion that female nudity can be a weapon is a timeless motif.

ANGIOLINI

In a 2016 *New Yorker* article, Peter Schjeldahl described you as a "Manet of hot babes and a Morandi of McDonald's French fries and Budweiser beer cans"—a quote that has since reappeared in virtually any writing about your work, this one included. What is your relationship with Manet?

ROBINSON

Manet paintings second-guess their own content. They draw attention to their own conventions. Jokes do that, and Manet made jokes—dressing Meurent as a toreador, and having her wave at the bull a pink, what, negligee? Many Impressionists played with the pose. Morisot's 1869 *Two Sisters*, which could well be the same model painted twice, is an example, as is Gauguin's slightly Renoiresque 1870 *Study of a Nude*, a decidedly nonclassical painting of his naked housekeeper sitting on a bed doing some sewing. These insights come to me via the art historian Charles Stuckey and inspired my 1980s series of nudes of my then wife, including the first-ever painting in Western art history of a nude flossing her teeth.

ANGIOLINI

Your figures are often inspired by models from mail-order catalogs, pulp-fiction paperback covers, and magazine clippings, and more recently, you have been using AI to construct your subjects. Can you tell us more about your process for this painting?

ROBINSON

This painting is sourced from a pulp paperback cover and is not AI generated. But AI suits me particularly well and is proving to be a great resource. Postmodernist representation in general is obsessed with templates, clichés, and the circulation of signs, and its kinship with what we call AI seems all too obvious. Programs like ChatGPT and Midjourney draw on the vast dataset of texts and images found on social media, determine the conventions by which they operate, and almost magically formulate new variations.

If I might quote one of my own Instagram posts: AI paintings are very much Conceptual Art, notably Sol LeWitt—start with a command, a text, a description—but instead of "A wall divided horizontally and vertically into four equal parts. Within each part, three of the four kinds of lines are superimposed." (*Wall Drawing 11*, 1969), go with "old-fashioned basket of apples / a basket of apples sits on a table / rumpled white tablecloth"—in this instance the AI command is prompted by the new T. J. Clark book *If These Apples Should Fall: Cézanne and the Present*. Ordinarily making an artwork begins with such a mental idea, or command to the self. With AI, the command is written out and delivered to a program, which can produce almost infinite alternatives based on the prompt. Glitches are frequent enough—an apple with three stems, say—which is the computer's own kind of creativity.

# Giangiacomo Rossetti

Born in Milan in 1989, Giangiacomo Rossetti is a painter based in New York. His works outline the implications of feverishly looking at, studying, and absorbing painting, while retracing the imprint it makes consciously and subconsciously on his production. Rossetti makes use of style and painterly tropes to filter the compositional strategies in his own work. This impulse, uniquely woven through the fabric of Western art history, entangles subjects taken directly from the artist's personal life and surrounding orbit.

VIOLA ANGIOLINI
Often in your work, even if you're portraying people in a mundane setting, there is a fantastical element....

GIANGIACOMO ROSSETTI
I'm not really searching for that, but I was excited when I noticed the two men walking in the background of the photograph. The painting is called *New Year* (2023), because it was during Rosh Hashanah that the photographical reference material was taken. Young Jewish men were wandering through Prospect Park looking for other people of Jewish descent to blow the shofar. They had approached me and the friends I wanted to portray in the painting, and after they walked away, I took some pictures of them. I didn't notice the two men until I came back to the studio. In one image, the two figures are perfectly framed, crossing the line that separates the shadows and the sun on the lawn. That discovery gave another element to the painting—the two men are at the center of the perspective. So the view goes behind the subject of my friends. It's a known way of structuring a painting: your eyes are drawn toward something that is behind the subject, so that the subject exists in between the viewer and something else as if suspended.

ANGIOLINI
It's interesting how this coincidence made your composition evoke even more Manet's *Le Déjeuner*, with the female figure bathing in the back.

ROSSETTI
Yes, exactly.

There is something holy in the composition. The child holding the bread in her hands, the mother holding the baby, and the two men in the background...there is a sense of mystery. Even the way the light shines through the painting. But, you know, all these were elements that just happened to be there and I didn't ask for, but I happily welcomed in the work.

I was thinking about all these elements, so it didn't even occur to me how close my painting was to the one of Manet. Someone else—maybe you?—had to tell me.

ANGIOLINI
Can you talk about your relationship with Manet? I'm also thinking about *Injured Jockey* (2021–22), the painting you contributed to our *Luncheon on the Grass* exhibition, which was made before this one. That work was inspired by the composition of a painting by Edgar Degas, a contemporary of Manet.

ROSSETTI
Although I myself adopt Manet's approach; sampling different things and just placing them in dialogue without being academically correct but for the purpose of its own discourse, I deviate from his clarity. Everything is very intentional, while Degas's is very contradictory, incomplete, which I find more congenial. The tight relationship between the two is a known fact. At the time, I painted *Le Jockey blessé* as a way to declare my failure in undertaking such a big task as directly relating to Manet and *Le Dejeuner sur l'herbe*, with his sharp, irreverent nature and all his political baggage.

I guess Manet's painting and the challenge of relating to it unknowingly kept lingering in my head to then very unintentionally resurface in *New Year* and pleasantly surprised me.

# David Salle

David Salle helped define the postmodern sensibility by combining figuration with an extremely varied pictorial language. Solo exhibitions of his work have been held at museums and galleries worldwide, and his paintings are in the collections of major museums here and abroad. Salle is also a regular contributor to the *New York Review of Books* and a member of the American Academy of Arts and Letters. Born in 1952 in Norman, Oklahoma, he lives and works in East Hampton, New York.

ALEXANDRA M. THOMAS

Please narrate how *Tree of Life (After Manet)* is influenced by Manet's *Le Déjeuner sur l'herbe*. Is this in homage, a reimagining, or an intervention?

DAVID SALLE

I would say none of the above, strictly speaking. It's an interesting question: what's left? Manet is more like an aroma or a rumor. No, that's not it, either. There is some shared DNA, but it's on different, more subterranean terms.

THOMAS

Who are the characters in this painting and how do they relate to each other?

SALLE

They are social types. They relate to each other by virtue of being in the same painting—that's their fate. They comprise notes on a chord, played with deliberation.

THOMAS

What are social types? And why are you drawn to painting them?

SALLE

"Social types" is the world viewed through the satirist's lens—characters whose behavior and appearance are one, the basis for a lot of what we call comedy. They are not real people—they're cartoons. But they remind us of real people. These particular characters are also from an era distinct from our own—they are at a distance. They're interesting to paint because of the pictorial encoding of the theatricality and the exaggeration; I was thinking of Goya.

THOMAS

At the foreground of the painting, there are objects such as the fruit basket and blue cloth that are present in Manet's *Déjeuner sur l'herbe*, but there also seems to be a mannequin missing its arms and legs and a blue-and-yellow ladder. What do these objects symbolize, and how do they relate to the narrative of the painting?

SALLE

They are mostly images of things that once were perhaps accessible and now are not. The ladder is there in case one of the characters wants to climb down (or up).

THOMAS

How does *Tree of Life (After Manet)* relate to your art practice in general?

SALLE

It's part of a series that I've been occupied with for the last several years. . . .

THOMAS

Can you tell me more about the series?

SALLE

I have been calling it *Tree of Life*. I've adapted a centuries-old convention of the central image of a tree flanked by examples of humanity. The paintings are about using relationships between people—essentially a literary subject—as a subject for painting. There's an element of vaudeville—the type you see in Beckett. My painting has often had this quality—it's just more noticeable now.

THOMAS
What does Manet mean to you?

SALLE
Manet is just the tops in every regard. Goya is more protean, with a more powerful imagination, but Manet is more like us. Or we are more like him. Not that we are *like* him. His achievement, the complexity of it, as well as the humanity; the bravery of his subject matter, the overall intellectual depth and awareness of his pictures not to mention the dazzling technical control and innovation, all played out over a relatively short working life, which is just astonishing. In the last two hundred years, there has been only one Manet.

THOMAS
And what are your thoughts on *Le Déjeuner sur l'herbe*? How did you decide on this painting as a response to it?

SALLE
The painting is actually too complex—where to begin? To *respond* to the painting is sort of like a child trying to make sense of the adult world. It was a hell of an assignment, at which one could only fail.

# Katja Seib

Born in 1989 in Düsseldorf, Germany, Katja Seib works figuratively, painting directly onto canvases of burlap using photographs on her phone. Through a combination of technologically mediated imagery, a fascination with surface pattern and texture, and a self-conscious glance back to the histories of her medium, Seib creates works that are simultaneously familiar and strange, combining a subtle interplay of texture and image with deft brushwork and a meticulous attention to detail. Seib graduated with an MFA from Kunstakademie Düsseldorf; she is now based in Los Angeles.

VIOLA ANGIOLINI
Can you tell us how you conceived your response to Manet's *Le Déjeuner sur l'herbe*?

KATJA SEIB
I've had really good feedback. Most people have appreciated that I chose to focus on the less obvious or concealed parts of Manet's painting. One of my friends observed that I had "used these elements as a back door to enter into the theme of this painting and created a new way to access it"; I think that my new narratives have allowed viewers to relate differently to Manet's work.

ANGIOLINI
In your painting, we find the main female figure, fully clothed, taking center stage. Can you talk about this twist?

SEIB
When Jeffrey asked me to participate in this group show and told me about the concept of making an exhibition in response to Manet's painting, I took a while to think about how I could create a painting that would correspond with my practice, as well as engage with the theme. I grew up seeing a lot of art, in particular painting. I became aware of this work early on in my childhood and of its unique importance in art history and consequently to contemporary painting. I first saw the painting in real life at the Musée d'Orsay many years ago. I remember observing how the bird and the frog were so skillfully rendered and made visible within the context of the whole composition; whereas, in photographic or printed reproductions, they are barely noticeable. I found this interesting, and I really connected with the animals, as nature is something I often explore within my work as both a subject and for its symbolic potency.

To begin with, I asked a friend of mine to model for me and photographed her closeup seated on a chair within an interior setting. I spent so much time indoors during COVID that my principal inspiration came from that experience of being inside. So in response, or as a reaction to the subject, I wanted to create a picnic inside with a fully dressed woman; this felt more contemporary to me and shifted the emphasis from a voyeuristic scene to one of a more psychological resonance. Manet's painting was shocking to the public in his time, and I knew that that effect was something that I wouldn't be able to re-create within the context, nor did I want to copy his intentions. I created a space that allowed me to find inspiration within his painting, but that still enabled me to feel like I was able to paint something that worked for me and my practice.

ANGIOLINI

In your paintings, you combine moments of domestic intimacy with allegorical meanings and mythological gravity. How do you create your compositions?

SEIB

I don't have a concrete idea of how the painting will look until it is completely finished; so much happens intuitively during the painting process. I usually start with a preexisting photo of someone or something. The photo is either staged, or it is not. It can be of someone who I know or it can be someone I met and photographed or even one I have found. Using the image as a starting point, I draw the photo directly onto the canvas and create a "room" that in turn stimulates more ideas to emerge during the actual painting process. I find inspiration from many different sources including European mythology, old master paintings, fairy tales, and so on.... The list is endless.

What I have found that emerges through this process is a natural attachment to the figure, and I begin to sense what else I can add to it or what else is needed to conduct an evocative atmosphere. I seek to incorporate moods, feelings, mystiques, and beyond, with symbolism and color; I choose and pick very carefully what color arrangements I use.

## Tschabalala Self

Tschabalala Self is an American artist born in 1990 in Harlem, New York. Self is a painter who works in various mediums and is exhibited internationally. She currently lives and works in the state of New York.

ARUNA D'SOUZA

Your painting is one of the more radical departures from Manet's original in this show. You still focus on the four figures—two men and two women—but you shift them from this bucolic little clearing in a forest to a street, against a background of brick walls. There's only one little sprig of leaves visible. Can you talk about why you wanted to do that?

TSCHABALALA SELF

When I think about Manet's *Luncheon on the Grass*, I think about a great departure in classical art, toward Impressionism. Manet, like many of his peers, rejected the concept of "timelessness" within his artistic practice and gave great value to the quotidian and everyday aspects of Parisian life. Similarly, in *12pm on 145th*, I am attempting to capture the hustle and bustle of a busy intersection of Harlem, near my childhood home. I wanted to place my figures within an environment more familiar to me, the metropolitan space of the street as opposed to Manet's pastoral bucolic, as a means to personalize my interpretation of the painting.

D'SOUZA

One of the elements that really connects your painting to Manet's is that you both focus on these really interesting and hard-to-read hand gestures—I can't stop looking at your figures' hands, in fact. Was that something you were interested in as you were thinking about *Le Déjeuner*?

SELF

Yes, entirely—the figure's hand was an entry point for me into *Le Déjeuner* and a starting point for my own work.

D'SOUZA

There's a lot of painting-within-a-painting going on here—the figure on the right could be someone sitting behind a window or a framed portrait, and the guy on the left has a T-shirt with a painting on it (or something that looks like a painting). These gestures, combined with the collage elements (the patterns on one of the women's clothing, for example), give the sense that art history is another of the materials you can use when you're putting your images together. Can you talk about your relationship to the history of art?

SELF

I look at art history, history in general, and my own personal history all as materials. I use these materials, their meaning and symbology—in this context being the meanings attributed to them rather than their inherent meanings—as building blocks for new narratives. I am greatly inspired by past artists and arts movements. I think it is extremely important for contemporary artists to have an understanding of art history, but not to become bogged down by the weight of this history, as such an attachment can prevent them from forging their own paths.

# Vaughn Spann

Vaughn Spann devotes his practice to abstraction and figuration as an investigation into space, time, and memory. He locates subjects from deeply personal spaces as he reconciles with his body within and out of the studio. With a deep admiration for formalism, he enjoys approaching paintings through the lens of color, line, and shape, but seemingly understands that one's subjectivity cannot simply be divorced from the studio. For him, a form is a striking means of generating content in ways that are compelling. His formal investigation permeates his paintings, symbolically reflecting his encounters with diverse people and places. Through his well-known stylistic separations, Spann continues to vigorously experiment with unconventional materials and expands on his personal and historical narratives. Born in Florida in 1992, he lives and works in New Jersey.

ALEXANDRA M. THOMAS

We can see they are celebrating Juneteenth, but other than that, who are these figures and what are their personalities, dreams, and narratives?

VAUGHN SPANN

I don't usually paint from life, but I try to embody characteristics or qualities of people I've met or close friends and family. These are contemporary Black folks. I'd imagine their dreams are to love, find peace, protect family, be treated with dignity, and enjoy a full life lived.

THOMAS

And the two-headed figures, what do they symbolize?

SPANN

I like what Picasso did with cubism...the way his fracturing of forms could present the viewer with different emotions or psychological states....Thinking about the figures more poetically, they are omnipresent. Self-aware and vigilant of their bodies in space....Fighting against any daily trauma together and not alone....

THOMAS

Their facial expressions are ambiguous: might this represent the ambivalence of celebrating Juneteenth while anti-Black racism continues today?

SPANN

I believe it's a lot to ask of Black artists to own the weight and burden of the world within their paintings when our counterparts aren't asked the same. In my paintings, figures are oftentimes relaxing, at peace, lounging. We need this duality because the issues that have plagued us historically aren't going to disappear, so how can one fight the fight but also protect our mental health? In my painting, this group of folks are just chilling and enjoying one's company....

THOMAS

Can you tell me more about why you chose to represent this scene in responding to Manet's *Luncheon on the Grass*?

SPANN

This work is a celebration of "the contemporary Black painter."...Paintings like Manet's and other artists of this time were celebrated for a world without representation and diversity.... In my work, I wanted to bring it back to our contemporary moment where Black people are active and visible....We are celebrating Juneteenth in a way that is owed to us....

THOMAS

Lastly, how does this work relate to your practice in general?

SPANN

My practice is diverse. I've always tried to just let the ideas flow and find ways to anchor themes in a relatable way....I think often "style" is limiting....I've been fighting to complicate that for myself for a while now.

## MICKALENE THOMAS

Mickalene Thomas is a multidisciplinary artist whose work has yielded instantly recognizable and widely celebrated aesthetic languages within contemporary visual culture. She is known for her elaborate paintings composed of rhinestones, acrylic, and enamel. Not only do her masterful mixed-media paintings, photographs, films, and installations command space; they occupy eloquently while dissecting the intersecting complexities of Black and female identity within the Western canon. Outside her core practice, Thomas is a Tony Award-nominated co-producer, curator, educator, and mentor to many emerging artists. Thomas was born in New Jersey in 1971 and lives and works in Brooklyn, New York.

ARUNA D'SOUZA

Mickalene, you've been engaging with Manet's *Le Déjeuner sur l'herbe* in your work for over a decade now, always replacing the grouping at the center of the original painting with Black women who you know and love. Can you talk about why this painting became a focus of some of your work?

MICKALENE THOMAS

Manet's *Le Déjeuner sur l'herbe* is an iconic work of Western art history, yet it exemplifies the limitations of historical Western painting in its portrayal of the female subject. *Le Déjeuner* is one of a few pieces I created in an attempt to recontextualize the work of painters such as Manet while also putting my personal story into the conversation. It dawned on me that I, too, like these female subjects in Western art, particularly Black female subjects, have been bound by such constraints, hence the reinvented versions of the works. Not only does this story resonate with me in terms of preconceived beliefs about Black women in the public eye, but it's also a reminder of how I'm regarded as a Black woman, and how I may contribute to this new historical debate by elucidating the "limitations" that are imposed upon us and the performances to which we are subjected.

D'SOUZA

The fact that you remove the clothed men from the composition and replace them with women who take on the originals' relaxed and (to my eye) privileged poses, and the fact that you present the woman who Manet originally painted naked with clothes on, seems to make a pretty profound statement about gender and power. Could you talk about that?

THOMAS

I draw a great deal of my inspiration from art history, and part of that motivation stems from a desire to claim and reinterpret these canonical ideas of beauty. The women in Manet's paintings are posed in a manner that is either secondary to the male subjects, and the presumed male viewer, or objectified and presented for the "male gaze." I wanted to place women, particularly Black women, in a position of agency and allow them to claim space, not only as subjects but as spectators in their own right. In presenting Manet's work through the perspective of the female, the male gaze is subverted and a different framework is created through which to converse with Manet's original.

The content of this work was very controversial and provocative during Manet's time; some might see the painting as anti-feminist. In my own interpretation, I felt it was important to depict Black women in leisure, joy, pleasure, and relaxation, similarly to the way Manet depicted the two men in his composition. I'm interested in the celebration of the beauty of Black women—way too often the stereotypes of our trauma are glorified and presented as an acceptable visual language. While the woman in *Le Déjeuner* is clearly presented as a spectacle, the men appear reclining and relaxed—a state in which Black women are so rarely depicted. I wanted to portray Black women enjoying the space and the freedom to luxuriate. That's the kind of conversation I want to press forward—a Black-female-centered conversation. There is a generation of artists, like myself and most contemporaneous artists, who responded to Manet's painting in their own time and may have had a similar desire to inject their own perspectives into the piece and into its artistic legacy.

I'm creating the context in which I want my work to be seen. Rather than being seen as a commentary or a departure, I aim to participate in these ongoing conversations, passed down and inherited through the art historical canon, and claim some ownership or participation in the work of artists such as Matisse, Manet, Bearden, Ringgold, Balthus, Courbet, Warhol, and Duchamp, among others.

D'SOUZA

You've reinterpreted Manet's painting several times, always with a difference in the types of materials you're using and the graphic treatment of the surface of the canvas. Can you talk a little bit about your choice of materials and technique here? It seems so emphatically different from the cool, understated, and very bourgeois look of Manet's original.

THOMAS

I use materials, such as textiles and fabrics, that hearken to certain eras and ideas in my personal history as well as the wider history of art, design, and culture. I use materials such as rhinestones, which are arguably the most salient part of this work, in a way that demands attention and deliberately takes up space. I want to portray Black female subjects and their inherent beauty unapologetically, so the use of materials and techniques such as rhinestones and enamel enables me to insert myself and my muses into the art historical discourse. In this reinterpretation, I overlaid Picasso's etching *Le Déjeuner sur l'herbe d'après Manet* based on similarities in the composition. Once I projected Picasso's image, I responded to the etched lines that I integrated and juxtaposed with my own depiction. It allowed me to consider the conversations of artists on multiple levels and obstruct the image slightly with the overlay of Picasso's, creating another dimension and dialogue with more than one artist at once.

## Salman Toor

Born in 1983 in Lahore, Pakistan, Salman Toor is a New York-based painter whose work addresses the anxieties and the comedy of identity. In many of his paintings, Toor creates subtly disarming depictions of familiar domestic environments in which often-marginalized bodies flourish in safety and comfort. In other pieces, the artist creates allegorical spaces of waiting, anticipation, and apprehension: border crossings into a world that may or may not be welcoming. In depicting the mundane and the memorable moments of his characters' lives, Toor reveals a deeply relatable existence, ultimately creating an opportunity for empathy through the language of painting.

ARUNA D'SOUZA

Salman, your painting *The Garden* is so moody—a moonlit scene, shrouded in secrecy, at some level. You seem to have unraveled two threads that are apparent in Manet's *Le Déjeuner*: the sort of frank eroticism of the nude woman who gazes confidently out from the forest clearing, her sexiness underlined by the fact that her companions are fully clothed; and the conviviality, the easy sociability, of the group with their relaxed poses and nonchalance. In *The Garden*, the sociability is located in the house and the eroticism in the coupling of the two figures outside it. Can you talk about what motivated your choices here?

SALMAN TOOR

I wasn't trying to shock in the way Manet gleefully does in *Le Déjeuner sur l'herbe* using a well-known artist and model, Victorine Meurent, hanging out naked by a stream with two bourgie men. These types of upper-middle-class men kept mistresses in Paris, a tolerated open secret in polite society, but artists never referred to it as overtly as this in a picture. My painting, *The Garden*, is a nostalgic imagined image of homes I grew up in or around, my grandmother's home, my aunts' or parents' home, spaces of safety and sometimes trauma. I was thinking of a family as a sheltering group that most queer people risk being banished from, or escape from, in order to be out or to be themselves in homophobic social systems. In the painting, there are aunts and uncles nestled in tea and laughter, trust and safety. And maybe they're a little bit like the society people Manet mocks in *Le Déjeuner sur l'herbe*, by slapping an image of Victorine Meurent's sexual agency in their faces. I think the family in *The Garden* might be a bit like Manet's respectable parents, like lawyers, or accountants, or doctors, and the proximity between the family and sex in this painting is exciting to me. The lovers own this narrative, they own this familiar home, this family—the lovers are not in the background; they are the protagonists. The family are the backdrop and simply a portion of the lovers' story.

The appearance of Victorine Meurent's nakedness in Manet's paintings must have been shocking at the time it was made. It signaled a shift in urban Western culture, questioning who deserves to be visible, who deserves to be a hero, who has the right to pursue happiness and power. That sounds pretty familiar right now!

D'SOUZA

There's always a great play between art historical past and present in your work, and here it is especially apparent on the level of brushwork and color. The palette, the energy of the mark making, the play of contrasting colors (orange and green in the naked couple), is reminiscent of Impressionist and Post-Impressionist painting—it's a bit like early Cézanne meets Van Gogh and Gauguin. But then the house in the background is modernist, all curved concrete walls. Can you talk about your play with time and history in your approach to painting?

TOOR

I use whatever visual language I feel like at the time. I often look at the romances of Watteau, the realism of Velázquez, and the gray area between the classical and the modern where Manet resides. I enjoy the concentric energy lines in late Van Gogh.

I'm not really good with color, so I use it sparingly in smaller areas of the painting and stick mostly to monochrome—so I'm kind of a tonal artist. I love looking at the past. Manet was certainly looking at the past when he painted *Le Déjeuner sur l'herbe*; the composition is a direct quotation from an earlier collaboration between Raphael and the engraver Marcantonio Raimondi in *The Judgment of Paris*. The past is now being revisited by a new generation of painters and thinkers through the prism of race and privilege and centered around a conversation about decolonization.

The question arises: do I feel bad that most painters from the past I look at were racists? Not really. They can't hurt me. I can take whatever I want from them. I enjoy for the new protagonists of my figurative painting to describe their relationship to power, to the grotesque, to dignity, and to look at the past without trauma—to own the future.

D'SOUZA

I'm haunted by the amoeba-like bushes that surround the lovers. They seem both protective and threatening, especially in the case of a few that seem to morph into people, like the man in profile near the terrace or the two possibly female figures on the other side of the tree from him. Can you talk about the idea of comfort and discomfort, of privacy and spectacle, of protection and threat that seems to be going on?

TOOR

There is a threat of violence in the proximity of the family and the queer couple. I wanted the trees to ooze the indifference of the natural world to this cultural taboo. I was thinking of a languorous freedom in the curves of the trees and danger in the shadows. The trees in the Manet painting are classical looking, though painted in a loose modern way. I wanted mine to be encroaching and sheltering forms.

## John Wesley

A unique voice in the canon of contemporary art, John Wesley is known for his precise and often deadpan painterly investigations of the American subconscious. Through a carefully refined visual vocabulary of clean lines, solid shapes, and repetition, Wesley imbued everyday scenes and quotidian subjects with humor and wry wit. Major retrospectives of Wesley's work have been mounted by MoMA PS1 (2000) and the Fondazione Prada (2009), and his work is held in public collections worldwide including the Art Institute of Chicago; Hirshhorn Museum and Sculpture Garden, Washington, DC; Kunstmuseum Basel; Museum of Modern Art, New York; Smithsonian American Art Museum, Washington, DC; and Whitney Museum of American Art, New York, among others. John Wesley was born in 1928 in Los Angeles and died in New York in 2022.

## Kehinde Wiley

Born in Los Angeles in 1977, Kehinde Wiley is an American artist best known for his portraits that render people of color in the traditional settings of old master paintings. Wiley's work brings art history face-to-face with contemporary culture, using the visual rhetoric of the heroic, the powerful, the majestic, and the sublime to celebrate Black and Brown people the artist has met throughout the world. Working in the mediums of painting, sculpture, and video, Wiley creates portraits that challenge and reorient art historical narratives, awakening complex issues that many would prefer to remain muted. He lives and works in Dakar, Senegal; Lagos, Nigeria; and New York.

Kehinde Wiley turned European art history upside down with his astonishing paintings in which contemporary African American young men replaced the figures in iconic old master and nineteenth-century compositions. Wiley later expanded his project to include women and other communities in the African diaspora.

Wiley's paintings subvert the lineage of historical painting and royal portraiture of European masters such as Peter Paul Rubens, Diego Velázquez, Sir Joshua Reynolds, Jean-Auguste-Dominique Ingres, Thomas Gainsborough, and Titian. Possibly the most iconic of Wiley's works is *Napoleon Leading the Army over the Alps* (2005), which is based on Jacques-Louis David's equestrian portrait from two centuries earlier. This towering work now confronts the visitors at the entrance of the Brooklyn Museum. Another known historical reference, Hans Holbein the Younger's sixteenth-century painting *The Dead Christ in the Tomb* (1521–22), inspired Wiley's commanding *Down* series. The series was exhibited in 2022–23 at the Musée d'Orsay. Wiley has since been especially inspired by *Le Déjeuner sur l'herbe* and other historic works in the collection of the museum.

For his response to Manet's *Le Déjeuner sur l'herbe*, Wiley cast three models, playing with a reversal of gender roles. *Lunch with Inettia, Lucemy and Soukenya* (2022) portrays the three figures on a background adapted from the green-and-brown textile pattern produced by William Cooke of Leeds in 1881. The background serves as an abstraction of Manet's landscape. From left to right, the models are Lucemy Perez, Soukeyna Diouf, and Dominique Reynolds. Perez is an LGBTQ activist and student at Trinity College in Connecticut, whose writing concerns topics of social justice and intersectionality. Diouf is a Senegalese-born, Los Angeles–based model and health care reform advocate, whose experience with treating African malaria patients after she attended college in Washington, DC, inspired her to pursue reform advocacy when she moved back to the United States. Reynolds is a New York City-based model who started her career just recently. The identity of the models is an essential component of the meaning of the work.

Wiley's work responds to the gender power dynamics of Manet's painting with its absurd contrast of the nude female figure and fully clothed male characters. In Wiley's painting, Inettia, Lucemy, and Soukenya are fully clothed and styled in contemporary fashion, brands and logos included. The photo shoot for the painting was in fact styled by Dee and Ricky. By representing Inettia, Lucemy, and Soukenya with equal power and assertiveness, Wiley's work recenters the conversation around identity and gender in the contemporary.

—Jeffrey Deitch

## FERNANDO BOTERO

Fernando Botero is one of the most famous contemporary Latin American artists, known for his distinct style of smooth, inflated shapes with unexpected shifts in scale. Many of his paintings and sculptures contain references to European old masters and embrace Renaissance traditions to create satirical renderings laden with social and political commentary. Born in Medellín, Colombia, in 1932, Botero died in Monaco in 2023. In recent years, the artist had lived and worked between New York, Paris, and Tuscany.

## RENEE COX

Born in 1960 in Colgate, Jamaica, Renee Cox makes photographs, collages, and installations that draw on art history, fashion photography, and popular culture. Her work invokes a critical vision of female sexuality, beauty, power, and heroism through nudity, religious imagery, and symbolism that inform her interdisciplinary process. She is most noted for her larger-than-life photographs of female bodies. She reexamines the Black female figure in the context of structures of power. Inspired by critical epochs and artistic styles, her works are often reimaginings of art history. The artist lives and works in New York.

## TACITA DEAN

Tacita Dean is a British artist born in 1965 in Canterbury. She lives and works in Berlin and Los Angeles, where she was the artist in residence at the Getty Research Institute in 2014–15. The art critic and professor Adrian Searle qualified Dean's work as carried by a sense of history, time, and place, light quality, and the essence of film itself. The focus of her subtle but ambitious work is the truth of the moment, the film as a medium, and the sensibilities of the individual.

## BEAUFORD DELANEY

Born in 1901 in Knoxville, Tennessee, Beauford Delaney is acknowledged as an essential contributor to American modernism. In 1923, Delaney moved to Boston to study art and spent considerable time at local museums such as the Museum of Fine Arts Boston and the Isabella Stewart Gardner Museum, where he became familiar with Impressionist painting. From 1929 to 1953, Delaney lived in New York City and painted portraits, still lifes, street scenes, and modernist interiors, all executed with a dense impasto, undulating lines, and bright colors. He then moved to Paris, and feeling a new sense of personal freedom, focused on creating nonobjective abstractions that consisted of elaborate, fluid swirls of paint applied in luminous hues. The artist died in 1979 in Paris. His work has consistently been shown in prominent institutional group exhibitions over the last decade.

## UMAR RASHID

Born in Chicago in 1976, Umar Rashid makes paintings, drawings, and sculptures that chronicle the grand historical fiction of the "Frenglish Empire (1648–1880)," which he has been developing for more than seventeen years. Each work represents a frozen moment from this parallel world that often recalls our own fraught histories—both canonized and marginalized—with familiar signifiers and iconographies that channel the visual lexicons of hip-hop, ancient and modern pop culture, gang and prison life, and revolutionary movements throughout time. Rashid builds upon his encyclopedic knowledge of global colonial history and conjures new fabulations that underline the roles of race, gender, class, and power in the tales of what was, what was recorded, what was negated, and what could have been.

## FAITH RINGGOLD

Born in New York in 1930, Faith Ringgold is an artist, activist, educator, and author of numerous award-winning children's books. Her artworks weave together autobiographical details, fictional accounts, and historic events into ambitious narratives that speak to universal truths of the human condition. *American People*, Ringgold's first major traveling retrospective, appeared first in New York at the New Museum in 2022, followed by the de Young Museum, San Francisco; Musée Picasso, Paris, in 2023; and Museum of Contemporary Art Chicago in 2024.

⁂

I

Dear Aunt Melissa,

Today I was invited to paint in the garden of the celebrated painter Claude Monet at Giverny. There, in an area of the garden composed of water-lily ponds, with weeping willow trees and beautiful flowers everywhere, was a group of American women artists and writers having a picnic and discussing the role of women in art.

2

I strolled through the beautiful *jardins*, taking in the fantastic, beautiful flower beds and trees, passing over the matrix of Japanese bridges that connect the wildly wooded areas of the *jardins* with the fields of flowers near Monet's house. Then I settled on the same area near the water-lily ponds flanked by weeping willow trees near the American women who were picnicking.

3

I kept seeing Manet's *Le Déjeuner sur l'herbe*, the painting that caused such a scandal in Paris. It was not allowed at the salon because it showed Manet's brother-in-law and a male friend having a picnic with two nude women, all of whom were recognizable. I kept thinking: why not replace the traditional nude woman at the picnic with Picasso in the nude, and the 10 American women fully clothed?

4

That would be crossing Monet's beautiful *Nymphéas* with Manet's scandal, and a reaction to the conversation about the role of women artists to show powerful images of women. They were discussing female nudes in the company of fully clothed men in paintings like Manet's *The Picnic*. Seeing it and wondering what to paint, this seemed a good idea to begin *ma nouvelle conscience*.

5

What to paint has always been my greatest problem as an artist. And then how to paint it? These were the questions I looked hard for answers to. Now there is the role of women artists? Some special niche we can occupy, like a power station? A woman artist can assume the rights of men in art? And be seen? I am very excited to meet these women. This may be the very first day of my life.

6

They are speaking of *la libération et la liberté* for women. Sometimes we think we are free, until we spread our wings and are cut down in mid air. But who can know a slave by the mere look in her eye? Ordinarily I would just paint the *jardin* and include in it some of these women at a picnic. That was before the question of freedom came up. Is it just the beauty of nature I am after?

7

Monet painted his most wonderful masterpiece, *Décorations des Nymphéas*, of the garden and the water-lily ponds. Those paintings hang in the circular galleries of the Musée de l'Orangerie in the Tuileries Gardens in Paris. That must be wonderful, to have your work so approved and revered by people to have them hanging in a space specially made for it. What does that amount of respect feel like?

8

Can a woman of color ever achieve that amount of eminence in art in America? Here or anywhere in the world? Is it just raw talent alone that makes an artist's work appreciated to the fullest? Or it is a combination of things, *la magie par une exemple, le sexe pare une autre, et la couleur est encore une autre*, magic, sex, and color.

9

One has to get the attention one needs to feed the magic. There is no magic in the dark. It is only when we get it that we know a transformation has taken place, a wonderful idea has been created into art. If we never see it we never know, and it didn't happen. Isn't that why I and so many other negro artists have come to Paris—to get a chance to make magic, and find an audience for our art?

10

Should I paint some of the great and tragic issues of our world? A black man toting a heavy load that has pinned him to the ground? Or a black woman nursing the world's population of children? Or the two of them together as slave, building a beautiful world for other to live free? *Non!* I want to paint something that will inspire—liberate. I want to so [sic.] some this WOMEN ART. *Magnifique!*

11

What will people think of my work? Will they just ignore it or will they give it some consideration? Maybe tear it apart and say that it is the worst ever and this artist should have her brushes burned and her hands, too. And isolate me as a woman artist because I am no longer trying to paint like, or to be like a man. Paris is full of these women artists who have no first names, wear men's trousers and deny they are married or have children.

12

I paint like a woman. I always paint wearing a white dress. Now I have a subject that speaks out for women. I can no more hide the fact that I am a woman than that I am a Negro. It is a waste of time to entertain such subterfuge any longer.

13

There are enough beautiful paintings of nude women in the world. I now want to see nude men painted by women, or nude men in the company of fully clothed women. *C'est de la fantaisie pure.* The men are expressing their power over women. But I am not interested in having power over anyone. I just want to see nude men in the company of fully clothed women for a change.

14

I am deeply inspired by these American women and their conversations about art and women in America. It makes me homesick for my country. And for their women's movement. I have created this painting *Picnic at Giverny par la tribut*. They have given me something new to ponder, a challenge to confront in my art, a new direction. And pride is being a negro woman.

—Faith Ringgold, 1991

As inscribed on *The French Collection Part I, #3: The Picnic at Giverny*

## JACOLBY SATTERWHITE

Born in 1986 in Columbia, South Carolina, Jacolby Satterwhite is celebrated for a conceptual practice addressing crucial themes of labor, consumption, carnality, and fantasy through immersive installation, virtual reality, and digital media. He uses a range of software to produce intricately detailed animations and live-action film of real and imagined worlds populated by the avatars of artists and friends. These animations serve as the stage on which the artist synthesizes the multiple disciplines that encompass his practice, namely, illustration, performance, painting, sculpture, photography, and writing. Satterwhite draws from an extensive set of real and fantastical references, guided by mythology, modernism, contemporary visual culture, and video-game language to challenge conventions of Western art through a personal and political lens. An equally significant influence is that of his late mother, Patricia Satterwhite, whose ethereal vocals and diagrams for visionary household products serve as the source material within a decidedly complex structure of memory and mythology. He lives and works in Brooklyn, New York.

## RAQIB SHAW

Raqib Shaw's transgressive vision is explored through highly personal imagery that is both opulent and fantastical. Combining iconography from both East and West, Shaw draws on a wide range of sources including art history, mythology, poetry, theater, religion, science, and natural history. Highly detailed, his paintings are executed with pools of enamel and metallic industrial paints meticulously applied and manipulated to the desired effect with a porcupine quill. Every motif is outlined in embossed gold, a technique similar to cloisonné found in early Asian pottery, which is one of many sources of inspiration to him. Shaw was born in 1974 in Calcutta (now Kolkata), India, and currently lives and works in London.

## KYUNGMI SHIN

Born in 1963 in Busan, South Korea, Kyungmi Shin is a visual artist living in Los Angeles, working with painting, sculpture, and photography. Using her own family archive and painting historical and cultural narratives in juxtaposition, she places the marginalized bodies at the center of the work—creating artworks that shift the gaze from dominant narratives to immigrant, creolized, and complex stories.

## BOB THOMPSON

Born in 1937 in Louisville, Kentucky, Bob Thompson relocated in 1958 to New York City's Lower East Side, where he embraced the vibrant bohemian culture of the downtown avant-garde scene. He quickly arrived at his mature style by reworking the compositions of European old masters into simplified, abstracted forms rendered in palettes alternately hot and violent or cool and dark. The pantheon of figures that populate his landscapes often feature specific people, monstrous creatures, mythically oversize animals, and silhouetted men in hats—the latter frequently a symbol of Thompson's own spiritual and physical existence. Thompson passed away in Rome in 1966 and has since been the subject of numerous solo exhibitions, with his work also regularly exhibited in group shows worldwide.

## KARA WALKER

Born in 1969 in Stockton, California, Kara Walker was raised in Atlanta from the age of thirteen. She studied at the Atlanta College of Art (BFA, 1991) and the Rhode Island School of Design (MFA, 1994), and she is the recipient of numerous awards, notably the John D. and Catherine T. MacArthur Foundation Achievement Award in 1997. Walker is best known for her candid investigation of race, gender, sexuality, and violence through silhouetted figures that have appeared in a myriad of exhibitions worldwide.

## PLATES I

Nina Chanel Abney
*Outdoor Dining #1*, 2022
Spray paint on canvas
60 × 60 in. (152.4 × 152.4 cm)
Private collection
© Nina Chanel Abney
Photo by Joshua White
Courtesy of the artist
p. 47

Diane Arbus
*A family one evening in a nudist camp, Pa. 1965*
Printed by Diane Arbus 1966–69
Gelatin silver print
Sheet: 20 × 16 in. (50.8 cm × 40.5 cm)
© Estate of Diane Arbus
p. 49

Vanessa Beecroft
Jeffrey Deitch and Deitch Projects artists posing in a set inspired by Paul McCarthy's *The Garden* (1991–92) for *Harper's Bazaar* in 2000
Photo by Jason Schmidt
Courtesy of the artist and Jeffrey Deitch
p. 51

Cecily Brown
*Le Déjeuner sur l'herbe*, 2021–22
Oil on linen
Diptych, overall: 105 ½ × 211 in. (268 × 535.9 cm)
Collection of the artist
Photo by Genevieve Hanson
Courtesy of the artist
pp. 52–53

Cecily Brown
*Luncheon on the Grass*, 2021–22
Oil on linen
73 × 83 in. (185.4 × 210.8 cm)
Private collection
Photo by Genevieve Hanson
Courtesy of the artist
p. 55

Cecily Brown
*Go Wild in the Country*, 2021–22
Oil on linen
73 × 83 in. (185.4 × 210.8 cm)
Private collection
Photo by Genevieve Hanson
Courtesy of the artist
p. 57

Caitlin Cherry
*Mixed Clout Relationships (Feast of the Ass)*, 2022
Oil on canvas
59 × 102 in. (149.9 × 259 cm)
Private collection
Photo by Joshua White
Courtesy of the artist
p. 59

Joe Coleman
*Le Déjeuner sur l'herbe avec la Dieu Fée Mère de l'Avant-garde (Luncheon on the Grass with the Fairy Godmother of the Avant-garde)*, 2020
Acrylic on panel
14 × 11 in. (35.6 × 27.9 cm)
Collection of KAWS
Photo by Joshua White
Courtesy of the artist
p. 61

Robert Colescott
*Sunday Afternoon with Joaquin Murietta*, 1979
Acrylic on canvas
Framed: 73 × 85 in. (185.4 × 215.9 cm)
Collection of the Jordan Schnitzer Family Foundation, from the Arlene and Harold Schnitzer Collection
© 2024 The Robert H. Colescott Separate Property Trust/Artists Rights Society (ARS), New York
p. 63

Somaya Critchlow
*Mr. Peanut! (The Picnic)*, 2020–21
Oil on linen
35 ½ × 27 ¾ × 1 ⅜ in. (90 × 70.4 × 3.5 cm)
Collection of Jeffrey Deitch
© Somaya Critchlow
Image courtesy of the artist and Maximillian William, London
p. 65

Celeste Dupuy-Spencer
*Ode to Enjoyments*, 2022
Oil on linen
70 × 60 in. (177.8 × 152.4 cm)
Craig Robins Collection, Miami
Photo by Joshua White
Courtesy of the artist and Nino Mier Gallery, Los Angeles
p. 67

Dominique Fung
*Sans Les Mains*, 2022
Oil on canvas
81 ⅞ × 104 ⅛ in. (208 × 264.5 cm)
The Huntington Library, Art Museum, and Botanical Gardens
Purchased with funds from Dominic and Ellen Ng
Photo by Joshua White
p. 69

Alain Jacquet
*Le Déjeuner sur l'herbe*, 1964
Silkscreen on canvas
68 ⅞ × 76 ¾ in. (175 × 195 cm)
Unique variant (in a series estimated at 100)
Private collection
© 2024 Artists Rights Society (ARS), New York/ADAGP, Paris
Photo by Joshua White
Courtesy of Perrotin
p. 71

Sophie Matisse
*Be Right Back*, 2003
Gouache on paper
Framed: 14 × 16 in. (35.6 × 40.6 cm)
Private collection, Los Angeles
Photo by Joshua White
Courtesy of the artist
p. 73

Kurt Kauper
*Men in the Park*, 2022
Oil on dibond
36 × 48 in. (91.4 × 121.9 cm)
Private collection
Photo by Joshua White
Courtesy of the artist, Ortuzar Projects, New York and Marc Selwyn Fine Art, Los Angeles
p. 75

Karen Kilimnik
*La Fôret*, 2021
Water-soluble oil color on canvas
14 × 18 in. (35.5 × 45.5 cm)
Courtesy of the artist, Galerie Eva Presenhuber, Zurich/Vienna, and Sprüth Magers
p. 77

Cindy Ji Hye Kim
*Luncheon on the Grass, after Manet*, 2022
Graphite and acrylic paint on wall
82 × 104 in. (208.3 × 264.2 cm)
Photo by Joshua White
Courtesy of the artist and Francois Ghebaly, Los Angeles
p. 79

Jeff Koons
*Gazing Ball (Manet Luncheon on the Grass)*, 2014–15
Oil on canvas, glass, and aluminum
63 × 81 ¼ × 14 ¾ in. (160 × 206.4 × 37.5 cm)
Collection of the artist
© Jeff Koons
Photo by Tom Powel Imaging
p. 81

Ella Kruglyanskaya
*The Rug and the Blinds (Red)*, 2022
Oil on linen
82 × 64 in. (208.3 × 162.6 cm)
Private collection
Photo by Joshua White
Courtesy of the artist
p. 83

Liu Xiaodong
*Newcomers in the Village—Response to Manet*, 2021
Oil on canvas
98 ⅜ × 118 in. (250 × 300 cm)
© Liu Xiaodong
Photo by Joshua White
Courtesy of Lisson Gallery
p. 85

Liu Xiaodong
*Coming across a scene like this one cannot but think of Manet's Le Déjeuner sur l'herbe 2020.06.12*, 2020
Watercolor on paper
10 ¼ × 14 ⅛ in. (26 × 36 cm)
© Liu Xiaodong
Courtesy of Lisson Gallery
p. 87

Tala Madani
*Pickled*, 2022
Oil on linen
15 × 12 in. (38.1 × 30.5 cm)
Collection of Lauren Taschen
Photo by Joshua White
Courtesy of the artist and David Kordansky, Los Angeles
p. 89

Paul McCarthy
*CSSC, Luncheon on the Grass, Mary, Ronald, Adam, and Eve*, 2019
Lightjet print
40 × 60 in. (101.6 × 152.4 cm)
Edition of 3, 2AP
© Paul McCarthy
Photo by Ryan Chin
Courtesy of the artist and Hauser & Wirth
p. 91

Paul McCarthy
*CSSC Luncheon on the Grass*, 2018
5 lightjet prints
Print 1: 27 × 21 ⅝ in. (68.5 × 54.9 cm)
Prints 2, 3, 4: 21 ⅝ × 27 in. (54.9 × 68.5 cm)
Print 5: 27 × 18 in. (68.5 × 45.7 cm)
Edition of 3, 2AP
© Paul McCarthy
Photo by Fredrik Nilsen
Courtesy of the artist and Hauser & Wirth
p. 93

Paul McCarthy
*Mary and Adam, Study for CSSC Luncheon on the Grass*, 2013
Clay, paint, artificial foliage, wood, and light
37 × 30 × 27 in. (94 × 76.2 × 68.6 cm)
© Paul McCarthy
Photo by Joshua White
Courtesy of the artist and Hauser & Wirth
p. 95

Sam McKinniss
*Picnic (Cecile and Kathryn)*, 2021
Oil and acrylic on linen
42 × 77 in. (106.7 × 195.6 cm)
Collection of Joel Lubin, Los Angeles
Photo by Genevieve Hanson
Courtesy of the artist and JTT
p. 97

Sam McKinniss
*Bather (Sebastian)*, 2021
Oil on linen
54 × 99 in. (137.2 × 251.5 cm)
Private collection
Photo by Genevieve Hanson
Courtesy of the artist and JTT
p. 99

Jill Mulleady
*Suddenly, Last Summer*, 2022
Oil on linen
66 × 58 in. (168 × 147 cm)
Andrew and Rachel Marks Collection
Photo by Joshua White
Courtesy of the artist and Gladstone Gallery
p. 101

Ariana Papademetropoulos
*It Becomes Blurry in That Moment*, 2022
Oil on canvas
92 × 79 in. (233.7 × 200.7 cm)
Private collection
Photo by Joshua White
Courtesy of the artist and Jeffrey Deitch, Los Angeles
p. 103

Naudline Pierre
*In Our Midst*, 2022
Oil on canvas
60 × 36 in. (152.4 × 91.4 cm)
Collection of Michael Sherman
© Naudline Pierre
Photo by Phoebe D'Heurle
Courtesy of the artist and James Cohan, New York
p. 105

Christina Quarles
*Yer Apart of Everything*, 2022
Acrylic on canvas
60 × 72 × 2 in. (152.4 × 182.9 × 5.1 cm)
© Christina Quarles
Photo by Joshua White
Courtesy of the artist, Hauser & Wirth, and Pilar Corrias, London
p. 107

Walter Robinson
*Affronter sur l'herbe*, 2021
Acrylic on canvas
80 × 60 in. (203.2 × 152.4 cm)
Private collection
Photo by Joshua White
Courtesy of the artist
p. 109

Giangiacomo Rossetti
*New Year*, 2023
Oil on panel
19 11/16 × 27 ½ in. (50 × 70 cm)
Photo by Zeshan Ahmed
Courtesy of the artist and Greene Naftali, New York
p. 111

David Salle
*Tree of Life (After Manet)*, 2021–22
Oil and acrylic on linen
96 × 72 in. (243.8 × 182.9 cm)
Photo by Joshua White
Courtesy of the artist and Skarstedt
p. 113

Katja Seib
*A Picnic Inside*, 2021
Oil on canvas
96 × 66 in. (243.8 × 167.6 cm)
Collection of Aishti Foundation, Beirut, Lebanon
© Katja Seib
Photo by Joshua White
Courtesy of the artist and Sadie Coles HQ, London
p. 115

Tschabalala Self
*12pm on 145th*, 2019–21
Jean fabric, digital printed T-shirt, velvet, lace, tulle, painted canvas, dyed canvas, acrylic, and Flashe on canvas; three parts
Overall: 96 ⅛ × 228 in. (244 × 579 cm)
Photo by Pierre Le Hors
Courtesy of the artist and Galerie Eva Presenhuber
pp. 116–17

Vaughn Spann
*Juneteenth on the grass (after lunch)*, 2022
Oil on canvas
78 × 130 × 1 ½ in. (198.1 × 330.2 × 3.8 cm)
Photo by Joshua White
Courtesy of the artist and Almine Rech
p. 119

Mickalene Thomas
*Le Déjeuner sur l'herbe les Trois Femme Noires d'aprés Picasso*, 2022
Rhinestones and acrylic paint on canvas mounted on wood panel
96 × 120 in. (243.8 × 304.8 cm)
Collection of The Broad Art Foundation
© Mickalene Thomas
Courtesy of the artist
p. 121

Salman Toor
*The Garden*, 2020
Oil on panel
30 × 24 in. (76.2 × 61 cm)
© Salman Toor
Photo by Farzad Owrang
Courtesy of the artist and Luhring Augustine, New York
p. 123

John Wesley
*Chocolate Major*, 2002
Acrylic on canvas
63 × 53 × 2 in. (160 × 134.6 × 5 cm)
© John Wesley
Courtesy of The John Wesley Foundation
p. 125

Kehinde Wiley
*Lunch with Inettia, Lucemy and Soukenya*, 2022
Oil on paper
Unframed: 48 × 72 in. (121.9 × 182.9 cm)
Private collection
Courtesy of the artist
p. 127

Fernando Botero
*Le Déjeuner sur l'herbe*, 1969
Oil on canvas
70 7/8 × 74 7/8 in. (180 × 190.3 cm)
Photo courtesy of Sotheby's Inc. © 2024
p. 131

Renee Cox
*Cousins at Pussy Pond*, 2001
Archival digital chromogenic print mounted on aluminum panel
48 × 60 in. (121.9 × 152.4 cm)
Courtesy of the artist
p. 133

Tacita Dean
*The Story of Beard*, 1992–93
Billboard sited in Manchester, Belfast (destroyed), and London
Courtesy the artist; Marian Goodman Gallery, New York/Paris/Los Angeles and Frith Street Gallery, London
p. 135

Beauford Delaney
*The Picnic*, 1940
Oil on canvas
25 × 30 in. (63.5 × 76.2 cm)
© Estate of Beauford Delaney by permission of Derek L. Spratley, Esquire, Court Appointed Administrator
Courtesy of Michael Rosenfeld Gallery LLC, New York
p. 137

Umar Rashid
*Le dejeuner sur l'herbe a été interrompu par des chefs de guerre (After Manet). [The luncheon on the grass was interrupted by warlords]. Or, the historical origin of Kolonial Fried Chicken.*, 2022
Acrylic and ink on canvas
72 × 84 × 1 1/2 in. (182.9 × 213.4 × 3.8 cm)
© Umar Rashid
Photo by Josh Scaedel
Courtesy of the artist and Blum & Poe, Los Angeles/New York/Tokyo
p. 139

Faith Ringgold
*The French Collection Part I, #3: The Picnic at Giverny*, 1991
Acrylic on canvas with pieced fabric border
73 1/2 × 90 1/2 in. (186.7 × 229.9 cm)
Collection of Barbara and Eric Dobkin
© 2024 Faith Ringgold/Artists Rights Society (ARS), New York
Courtesy ACA Galleries, New York
p. 141

Jacolby Satterwhite
*Black Luncheon*, 2020
Animated neon and hand-painted enamel on 3D-printed resin
84 × 88 × 12 in. (213.4 × 223.5 × 30.5 cm)
© Jacolby Satterwhite
Courtesy of the artist and Mitchell-Innes & Nash, New York
p. 143

Raqib Shaw
*From Narcissus to Icarus after Déjeuner sur l'herbe*, 2017–18
Acrylic liner and enamel on birchwood
60 5/8 × 71 11/16 in. (154 × 182 cm)
© Raqib Shaw
Photo © Prudence Cuming Associates Ltd.
p. 145

Kyungmi Shin
*and the sweet upside-down cake (Lunch on the grass)*, 2022
Acrylic on archival pigment print and UV laminate
56 1/8 × 71 7/8 in. (142.6 × 182.6 cm)
Photo by Shin Gray Studio
Courtesy of the artist and Various Small Fires, Los Angeles/Dallas/Seoul
p. 147

Bob Thompson
*Untitled (After Manet)*, 1961
Oil on board
3 7/8 × 5 7/8 in. (9.8 × 14.9 cm)
© Michael Rosenfeld Gallery LLC, New York
Photo courtesy of Christie's Images Limited, 2024
p. 149

Kara Walker
*Picknicky*, 2022
Ink and cut paper on paper
76 3/4 × 74 1/4 in. (194.9 × 188.6 cm)
Artwork © Kara Walker
Courtesy of Sikkema Jenkins & Co. and Sprüth Magers
p. 151

FIGURES

Fig. 1: © RMN-Grand Palais (Musée d'Orsay)/ Benoît Touchard/Mathieu Rabeau, Donation Etienne Moreau-Nélaton, 1906

Fig. 2: © 2023 RMN-Grand Palais (Musée Picasso)/Estate of Pablo Picasso/Artists Rights Society (ARS), New York

Fig. 3: The Metropolitan Museum of Art, New York, Rogers Fund, 1919

Fig. 4: Courtesy of the Custodia Foundation, Paris

Fig. 5: The Metropolitan Museum of Art, New York, H. O. Havemeyer Collection, Bequest of Mrs. H. O. Havemeyer, 1929

Fig. 6: The Metropolitan Museum of Art, New York, H. O. Havemeyer Collection, Bequest of Mrs. H. O. Havemeyer, 1929

Fig. 7: The Metropolitan Museum of Art, New York, Gift of William Church Osborn, 1949

Fig. 8: Sir Hugh Lane Bequest, 1917, The National Gallery, London. In partnership with Hugh Lane Gallery, Dublin

Fig. 9: Photo courtesy of Ny Carlsberg Glypothek, Copenhagen

Fig. 10: © 2016 RMN-Grand Palais (Musée du Louvre)/Michel Urtado

Fig. 11: © RMN-Grand Palais (Musée d'Orsay)/ Art Resource, NY, Photo by Patrice Schmidt

Fig. 12: The Metropolitan Museum of Art, New York, Purchase, Mr. and Mrs. Richard J. Bernhard Gift, 1957

Fig. 13: Collection of the Museo Nacional de Bellas Artes, Buenos Aires, Argentina

Fig. 14: The Metropolitan Museum of Art, New York, Rogers Fund, 1919

Fig. 15: The Metropolitan Museum of Art, New York, Gift of John Wolfe, 1893

Fig. 16: Petit Palais, Musée des Beaux-Arts de la Ville de Paris

Fig. 17: Acquisto dal principe Giovannelli, 1932. Gallerie dell'Accademia di Venezia, Sala VIII. © G.A.VE Archivio fotografico. Courtesy of Ministero della Cultura

## CONTRIBUTORS

### JEFFREY DEITCH

Jeffrey Deitch has been involved with modern and contemporary art for fifty years as an artist, writer, curator, dealer, and advisor. Deitch coauthored a monograph on Keith Haring (Rizzoli, 2008) and edited and wrote the introduction to *Jean-Michel Basquiat, 1981: The Studio of the Street* (Charta, 2007). He has written many other books, including *Unrealism: New Figurative Painting* (Rizzoli, 2019) and *City as Studio* (2021), a compact history of street art. In 2022, he organized *Luncheon on the Grass: Contemporary Responses to Édouard Manet's "Le Déjeuner sur l'herbe"* at his eponymous Los Angeles gallery.

### VIOLA ANGIOLINI

Viola Angiolini is an art professional and writer based in New York. She is director of research and curatorial projects at Jeffrey Deitch's gallery, where she co-organized *Luncheon on the Grass: Contemporary Responses to Édouard Manet's "Le Déjeuner sur l'herbe"* in 2022.

### THOMAS E. CROW

Thomas E. Crow teaches the history of art at the Institute of Fine Arts, New York University. He is the author of *Restoration: The Fall of Napoleon in the Course of European Art, 1812–1820* (2018), among other books on French painting of the eighteenth and nineteenth centuries.

### ARUNA D'SOUZA

Aruna D'Souza writes about modern and contemporary art, intersectional feminisms and other forms of politics, and how museums shape our views of one another and the world. Her work appears regularly in 4Columns.org, where she is a member of the editorial advisory board, and she is a contributor to the *New York Times*. Her book *Whitewalling: Art, Race & Protest in 3 Acts* (Badlands Unlimited), was named one of the best art books of 2018 by the *New York Times*.

### MARINA MOLARSKY-BECK

Marina Molarsky-Beck is an art historian, writer, curator, and current PhD candidate at Yale University. Her dissertation explores the representation of queer subjectivity in European modernism.

### LOWERY STOKES SIMS

Lowery Stokes Sims is an independent curator and art historian who served on the education and curatorial staff of the Metropolitan Museum of Art (1972–99), was executive director and president of the Studio Museum in Harlem (2000–2007), and retired as curator emerita from the Museum of Art and Design (2007–15). She has written about Robert Colescott since the late 1970s and was co-curator of the retrospective of his career organized in 2019 by the Contemporary Arts Center in Cincinnati. Sims was a visiting professor at the Institute of Fine Arts, New York University (2018–20), and the 2021–22 Kress-Beinecke Professor at the Center for Advanced Study in the Visual Arts at the National Gallery of Art, Washington, DC.

### ALEXANDRA M. THOMAS

Alexandra M. Thomas is a Black queer feminist writer and curator based in Hartford, Connecticut. She is completing her PhD in African American studies and history of art, with a certificate in women's, gender, and sexuality studies at Yale University, and is an incoming assistant professor at Fordham University in 2024.

This publication is based on the exhibition *Luncheon on the Grass: Contemporary Responses to Édouard Manet's "Le Déjeuner sur l'herbe"* at Jeffrey Deitch, Los Angeles, February 19–April 23, 2022.

First published in the United States of America in 2024 by

Rizzoli Electa
A Division of Rizzoli International Publications, Inc.
300 Park Avenue South
New York, NY 10010
www.rizzoliusa.com

Facebook.com/RizzoliNewYork
Twitter @Rizzoli_Books
Instagram.com/RizzoliBooks
Pinterest.com/RizzoliBooks
Youtube.com/user/RizzoliNY
Issuu.com/Rizzoli

On behalf of Jeffrey Deitch
Editor: Viola Angiolini
Editorial Coordinator: Sabeena Khosla
Research Assistant: Simon Brewer

On behalf of Rizzoli
Publisher: Charles Miers
Associate Publisher: Margaret Chace
Editor: Loren Olson
Copy Editor: Richard Slovak
Production Manager: Alyn Evans

Design: Folder Studio



2024 2025 2026 2027 / 10 9 8 7 6 5 4 3 2 1
Printed in Hong Kong
ISBN-13: 978-0-8478-9987-6
Library of Congress Control Number: 2023947034

On the front cover: Robert Colescott, *Sunday Afternoon with Joaquin Murietta*, 1979, Acrylic on canvas, framed: 73 × 85 in. (185.4 × 215.9 cm). Collection of the Jordan Schnitzer Family Foundation, from the Arlene and Harold Schnitzer Collection. © 2024 The Robert H. Colescott Separate Property Trust/Artists Rights Society (ARS), New York

Front endpapers: Cecily Brown, *Le Déjeuner sur l'herbe*, 2021–22, Oil on linen, diptych, overall: 105 ½ × 211 in. (268 × 535.9 cm). Collection of the artist. Photo by Genevieve Hanson. Courtesy of the artist

Alain Jacquet, *Le Déjeuner sur l'herbe*, 1964, Silkscreen on canvas, 68 ⅞ × 76 ¾ in. (175 × 195 cm). Unique variant (in a series estimated at 100). Private collection. © 2023 Artists Rights Society (ARS), New York/ADAGP, Paris. Photo by Joshua White. Courtesy of Perrotin

Back endpapers: Cindy Ji Hye Kim, *Luncheon on the Grass, after Manet*, 2022, Graphite and acrylic paint on wall, 82 × 104 in. (208.3 × 264.2 cm). Photo by Joshua White. Courtesy of the artist and Francois Ghebaly, Los Angeles

Tschabalala Self, *12pm on 145th*, 2019–21, Jean fabric, digital printed T-shirt, velvet, lace, tulle, painted canvas, dyed canvas, acrylic, and Flashe on canvas, three parts, overall: 96 ⅛ × 228 in. (244 × 579 cm). Photo by Pierre Le Hors. Courtesy of the artist and Galerie Eva Presenhuber

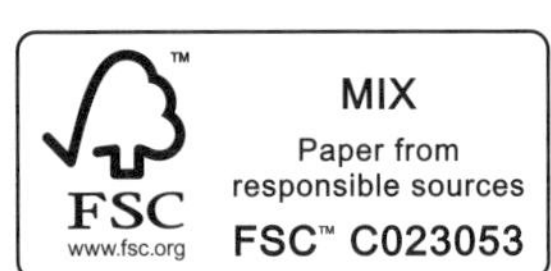

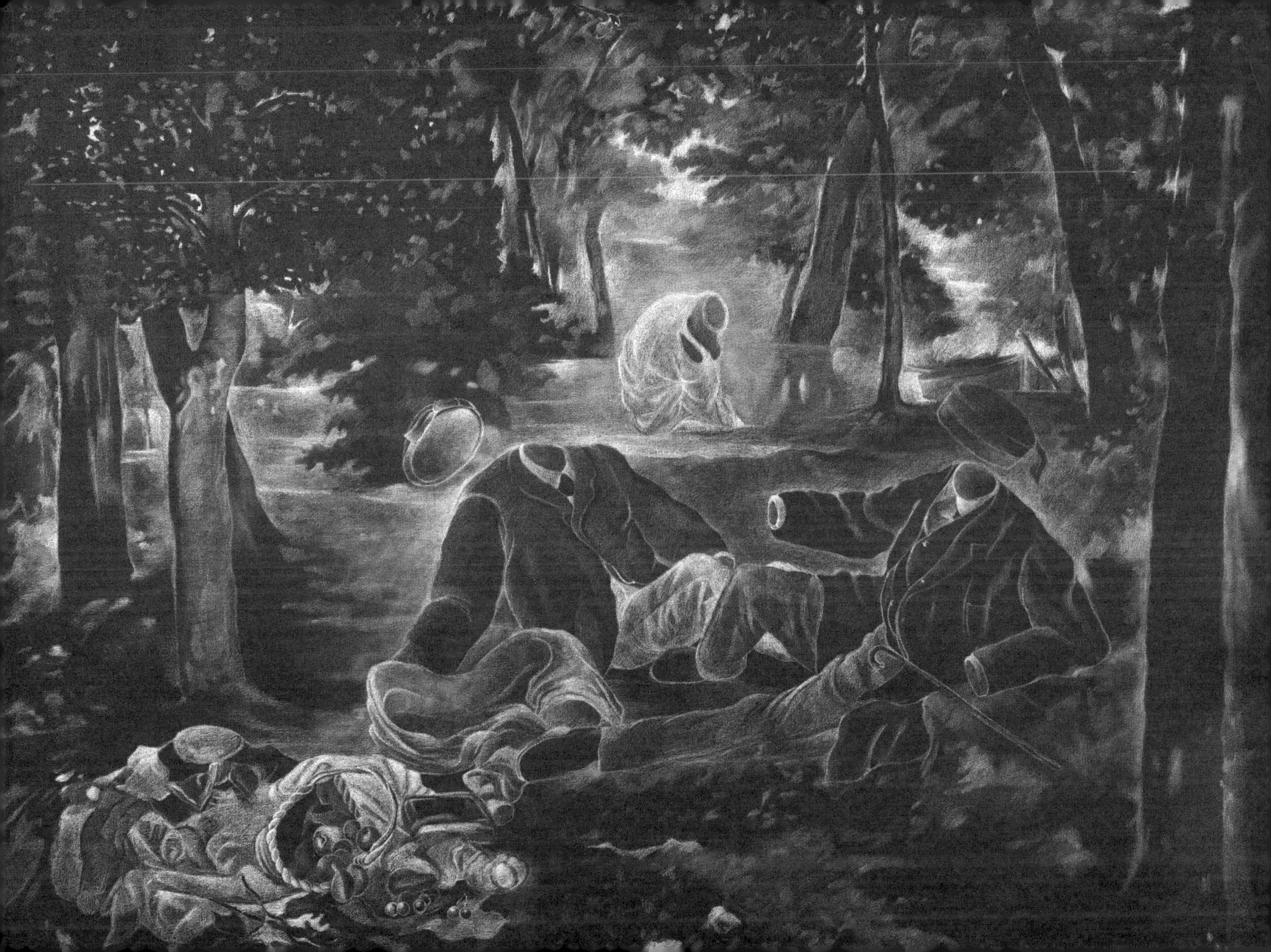

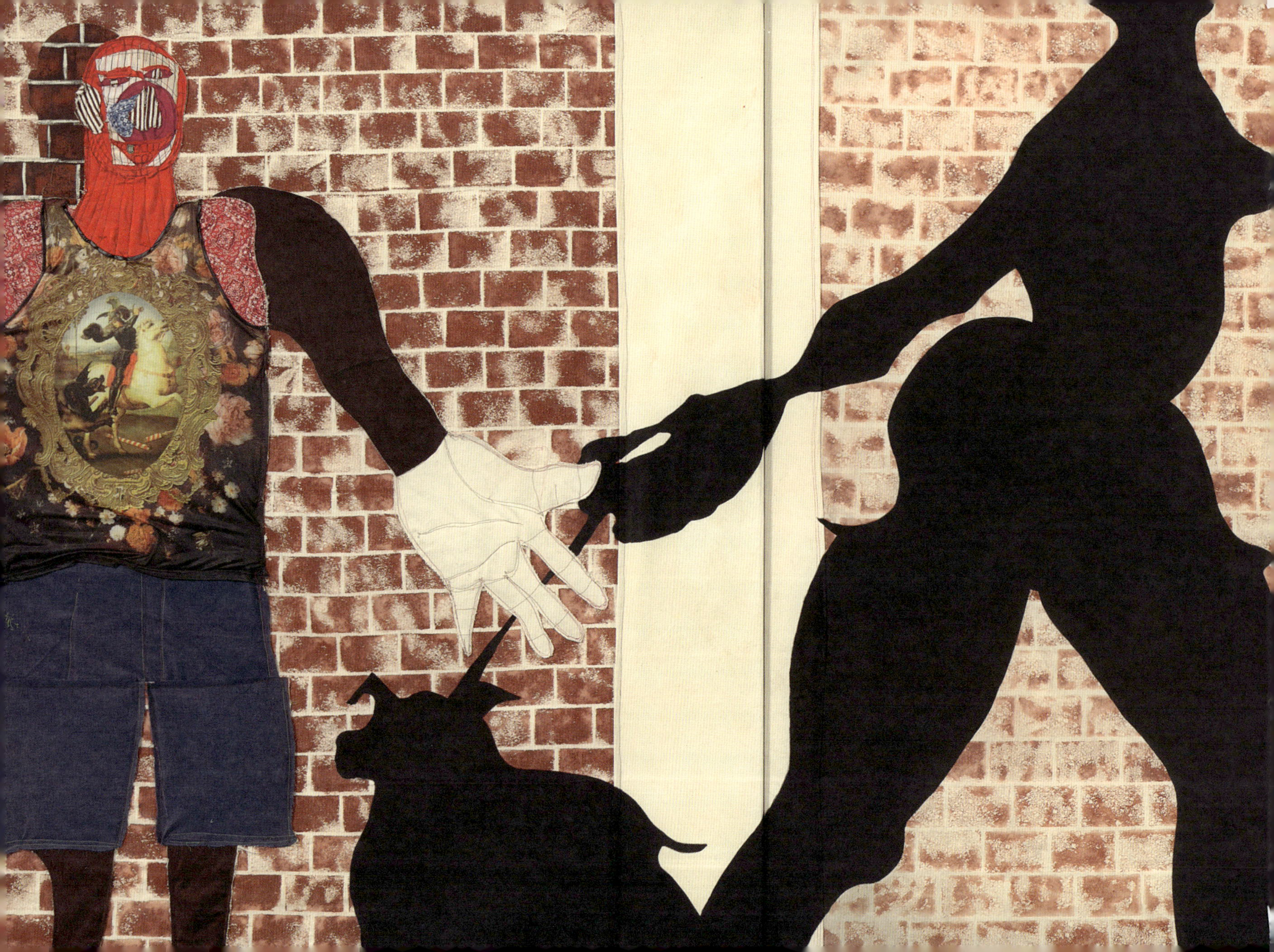